PRAISE
THE POWER OF

"*The Power of Saying No* is an exceptional guide to setting boundaries and prioritizing your time. With practical insights and advice, this book is a must-read for anyone looking to create balance and fulfillment in their personal and professional lives. Highly recommended!"

—Dr. Marshall Goldsmith, *Thinkers50* #1 executive coach and *New York Times* bestselling author of *The Earned Life*, *Triggers*, and *What Got You Here Won't Get You There*

"If you're tired of agreeing to annoying asks and thankless tasks, read this book. *The Power of Saying No* offers the smartest advice I've ever encountered for declining requests without risking your reputation or your relationships. This essential guide will sharpen your mind and steel your spine to live life on your own terms."

—Daniel H. Pink, #1 New York Times bestselling author of *The Power of Regret, Drive and To Sell Is Human*

"*The Power of Saying No* will stay within arm's reach for me. It offers the explanations and the inspirations I need to take charge of my life and career, with concrete tools to make it happen. I was able to put Vanessa Patrick's lessons to work the day I started reading the book and have continued every day since. Read this book. Twice."

—Dolly Chugh, author of *The Person You Mean to Be* and *A More Just Future*, Jacob B. Melnick Term Professor at the NYU Stern School of Business

"Saying 'no' can be empowering, but you should say 'yes' to this book! Vanessa shares wise, practical tips for setting boundaries and living life with conviction, so you can spend more time on what matters and spend less time on what doesn't."

—Laura Vanderkam, author of *Tranquility by Tuesday* and *168 Hours*

"Saying no is a superpower, and it can be yours when you read Vanessa Patrick's paradigm-shifting book. If you want to learn how to say no so you can say yes to your life, pick up this book and read it."

—Whitney Johnson, *Wall Street Journal* and *USA Today* bestselling author of *Smart Growth*

"*The Power of Saying No* is an absolute game changer. Dr. Patrick illuminates the reasons saying no is so darn hard, provides a framework for deciding when to say yes versus no, and most importantly, teaches readers how to say an empowered no they can feel confident about and that won't invite pushback. I highly recommend this book for anyone who struggles to say no—so basically everyone!"

—Jill Stoddard, PhD, author of *Imposter No More* and co-host of the *Psychologists Off the Clock* podcast

"If you've ever struggled to say no, then this is the book for you. Which, let's be honest, is all of us at some time or other. Highly readable, the book its filled with practical tips that are backed by scientific research. What's more, it explains why saying no isn't just a case of getting your way but the key to being more authentic, more human and more fulfilled. Packed with insights and engaging stories, *The Power of Saying No* is an absolute pleasure to read."

—Christian Hunt, author of *Humanizing Rules*
and founder of Human Risk Limited

"This book saved me $1,000 within 24 hours of finishing it—best immediate ROI of any book I've ever read! It's full of practical science and great ideas, and I'll be referring back to it again and again."

—Zoe Chance, PhD, author of *Influence Is Your Superpower: How to Get What You What Without Compromising Who You Are*

"Let's be honest, who doesn't struggle with saying no? This book offers tips not only for saying no when you want to, but for being more mindful about deciding what you really want to say no—or yes—to.

—Vanessa Bohns, PhD, author of *You Have More Influence Than You Think: How We Underestimate Our Powers of Persuasion, and Why It Matters*

"*The Power of Saying No* is a life-changing book. You can set boundaries without damaging your relationships, and Vanessa Patrick shows you how to do it."

—Jonah Berger, bestselling author of
Contagious and *The Catalyst*

THE POWER OF SAYING NO

THE NEW SCIENCE OF HOW TO SAY NO THAT PUTS YOU IN CHARGE OF YOUR LIFE

Vanessa Patrick, PhD

Cover design by Lauren Harms
Internal design by Tara Jaggers/Sourcebooks

Published by Sourcebooks
P.O. Box 4410, Naperville, Illinois 60567–4410
(630) 961-3900
sourcebooks.com

Cataloging-in-Publication Data is on file with the Library of Congress

Originally published in 2023 in the United States of America by Sourcebooks.

Printed and bound in the United States of America.
SB 10 9 8 7 6 5 4 3 2 1

For my daughter

CONTENTS

INTRODUCTION

I spent my twenty-fourth birthday in an empty office, staring at a fax machine.

The office, if you can picture it, was a large, rectangular open space designed in white and gray with accents of red. Rookies like me shared tiny cubicles in the bottom left corner. Away from the hustle and bustle, the more senior folks had cubicles of their own that occupied the center. The fax machine also had its own glass enclosure, a place of pride at the top right corner. This was the mid-1990s, and India's economy had only recently opened for business to the world. It was a time when the fax machine was the beating heart of the advertising agency, pumping information with rhythmic regularity to and from our multinational clients.

On that afternoon, our account team had a routine conference call with a client. As the most junior person on the team, it was my responsibility to type out a summary of the meeting—"the minutes"—and fax it to the client, who would send a fax back when they received the minutes. Both the agency and the client lived in a "cover-your-ass" world where everything had to be documented in writing. I wasted no time completing this familiar task—type the minutes, show them to the boss, fax the minutes, done! After all, I had a birthday party planned for that evening, and my friends and family were invited for the celebration.

I watched the clock eagerly, waiting for 5:00 p.m., ready to dash out to avoid being stuck in Mumbai's notorious rush-hour traffic. I picked up my bag and was about to leave when I sensed the tall, angular frame of my boss leaning over the top of my cubicle as she was apt to do. She was leaving the office herself and had swung by to ask (in a casual voice) whether we had received the faxed receipt of the minutes from the client. I responded that we hadn't yet. She glided away toward the elevator, but then she turned back. I smiled amiably, thinking she was going to say, "Enjoy your evening" or, "Have a great party," but instead she instructed me, "Do not leave until you receive the fax confirming that the client has received the minutes."

I stood there shell-shocked. Tongue-tied. Too powerless to respond.

The hours of the evening slipped away as I waited for the incoming fax. I positioned myself outside the glass room, staring through its walls, watching for the white paper to spew out of the fax machine. Occasionally I walked in to look around just in case I had blinked and missed it. The office began emptying around 7:00 p.m. I will admit that I did consider leaving the office and just going home, but I was terrified about the consequences... Would my boss find out? Could I get fired? What would my friends and family say if I lost my first real job?

I called home a few times that evening. My parents, or one of my sisters who happened to pick up the phone, informed me which of my guests had arrived, and as the evening drew on, updated me on which guests had eaten dinner, said goodnight, and left with their birthday wishes and apologies (it was a Tuesday). At around 9:30

p.m., the fax finally arrived. I picked it up from the fax machine, placed it on my boss's table, and went home.

Well, that was my turning twenty-four...captured in its entirety with three little words: "Received, with thanks."

My disappointment has since faded, but that day opened my eyes to the (sometimes) harsh reality of working life, and especially to the (often pointless) personal sacrifices one sometimes has to make to get bumped up from a shared cubicle to a solo one. The incident also triggered in me a curiosity about, and a deep desire to understand, the complex and intricate ways in which people think, feel, and act.

As you have likely surmised, in time I moved from that job to another, and then to another, before I finally decided to pursue a PhD at the University of Southern California. I took to academia like a fish takes to water, and now I fully embrace the intellectual life of being a professor at the University of Houston. It's a job I love and firmly believe I was born to do!

My life today is centered around knowledge: I *create* knowledge with my research, I *share* knowledge via my teaching and writing, and I *acquire* knowledge from reading extensively and investing in learning from the experiences of others. My research over the years reflects an unwavering focus on empowerment and personal agency that goes back to the fateful day when—let's face it—*I was caught completely off guard, stripped of power by a person who forced me to skip my own birthday celebration to do what I will later describe in the book as nothing short of a "bullshit job."*

I am mortified just writing this and reliving that moment. But I resolved on that day to never again let something like that happen to me or to anyone else if I could help it.

It has been a little over a decade since I first coined the term "empowered refusal," together with my then doctoral student and now long-time research collaborator, Henrik Hagtvedt. We used this term in our research articles to represent the superskill of saying no in a way that is persuasive and does not elicit pushback from others. Empowered refusal is a way of saying no that begins with you and reflects your unique identity. In this book, we will delve in great depth into understanding empowered refusal, what makes it an effective way of saying no, and the toolkit of three competencies you will need to develop to communicate an empowered no response. But for now, let me just say that empowered refusal overcomes the inherent difficulty of saying no because it does three things:

→ It reflects your identity and gives voice to your values, priorities, and preferences (your no is about you, not the other person).
→ It conveys conviction and determination (comes across as empowered and confident).
→ It is persuasive and does not invite pushback (so your relationship with the asker is secure and your reputation untarnished).

After those initial research articles were published, I used my

"Professor + Educator" platform to share my ideas and research insights about empowered refusal in numerous media outlets, in lunch-and-learn workshops, and at conferences. Intriguingly, something interesting started to happen. Participants in my classes and workshops began asking for more. When I considered these requests from the perspective of a marketer (marketing is, after all, the process of designing and delivering marketplace offerings—products, services, experiences, even books—that create value and meet the needs of the most diverse customer base), I realized in dismay that when people expressed a need for additional resources, I had nothing of value to offer. All I could give them were my research articles (whose results I had just explained) or copies of my PowerPoint deck (pathetic!). Committed to making a difference in the world of people and ideas, and as an avid reader myself, I decided that I had to share more deeply my knowledge of, and passion for, empowered refusal, in the form of a book. This book.

A common thread in the advice that many successful people give to others is to say no to the things that do not matter. Apple's Steve Jobs believed that "focusing is about saying 'no' to things". Oprah has emphasized that "no is a complete sentence." Former UK Prime Minister Tony Blair opined that "the art of leadership is saying no." And Berkshire Hathaway's Warren Buffett has said, "We need to learn the slow 'yes' and the quick 'no.'" Similarly, best-selling authors from Marshall Goldsmith (make a list of things to stop doing) to Greg McKeown (say yes only to the things that matter) to Ryan Holiday (be ruthless to the things that don't matter) to Matt

Haig (learn to say no to things that get in the way of life) and Seth Godin (just saying yes because you can't bear the short-term pain of saying no is not going to help you do the work) underscore the importance of saying no.

Despite this plethora of advice about the need to say no, there is no systematic and proven way that demonstrates *how* to say no in a way that maintains your relationships, secures your reputation, and does not invite pushback from the asker. This is where this book comes in. In this book, I will draw on research (my own and that conducted by others) to provide you with the toolkit of competencies you will need to say no in a way that works. You will be equipped with the ability to decide *what* to say no to and with the superskill of *how* to communicate that no from a place of empowerment.

Let me provide you with a road map of how I have organized this book and what you can expect to take away from each of its three parts.

In Part 1: Saying No Is a Superskill, we will understand why the simple two-letter word *no* is so daunting to so many. We will uncover the reasons why we say yes, even when we want to say no. We will learn that we are socialized to believe that saying no to others is a surefire way to bust the harmony out of any situation. For some, saying no can be fraught with conflict and anxiety, yet we need to prepare for and navigate the uncomfortable moments immediately following a request. This initial groundwork will lead us to the solution I propose: empowered refusal. You will learn about the science of saying no in a way that does not invite pushback. As the term implies, empowered refusal is a new and proven way of saying no that puts you in control of your own life. Instead of being frazzled and frustrated, you become calm and choosy; the latter is clearly the wiser choice and does wonders for your reputation and relationships.

In Part 2: The A.R.T. of Empowered Refusal, we will delve into the three competencies you will need to master the A.R.T. of empowered refusal. The handy acronym A.R.T. stands for these three competencies:

Awareness
Rules, not Decisions
Totality of Self

In the chapters in Part 2, I will introduce you to the empowered refusal toolkit. Because of the you-centeredness of empowered refusal, a key competency to invest in is increased self-awareness. You will learn strategies to enhance both internal self-awareness (an understanding of your own values, preferences, and beliefs and a vision of what success and happiness looks like to you) and external self-awareness (an understanding of what other people think about you). You will also learn how to rely on this self-awareness to expertly categorize the requests that come your way to determine how best to respond.

A fundamental building block of empowered refusal is establishing rules for yourself to respond to "asks" that come your way. I call these rules "personal policies." I will show you how to establish personal policies (simple rules we set for ourselves based on our principles, values, and priorities) that reflect our identity. We will find that personal policies highlight the "why" behind our desire to say no and empower us to say no with greater conviction and determination.

Finally, I will make a (hopefully) compelling case that effective empowered refusal is a whole-body activity, and that becoming mindful of the power of our nonverbal cues is a crucial aspect of empowered refusal. One of the insights you will take away is the two-pronged benefits of nonverbal cues in empowered refusal: they can be used to convey empowerment as well as to secure your relationship with the asker.

In Part 3: The Practicalities of Empowered Refusal, we will translate theory to practice. Rather than merely thinking about empowered refusal as a superskill that you would like to develop, we will get down to how empowered refusal works when you practice it in your daily life. We know that practice makes proficient. We are better off also knowing what could come in the way of our success. Occasionally, we will get pushback to our empowered refusal. This is inevitable. However, if we learn to identify the types of pushback we might receive and have strategies in place about how to respond, we are more likely to effectively manage the pushback.

Throughout the book, you will learn that empowered refusal is not only about saying no to others, but also about saying no to yourself. Taking an empowered stance can have pervasive effects for the whole of your life. You will learn the importance of developing self-talk that guides you to personal and professional mastery. The catchy phrase "it goes the way you say" will be evident in the number of practical situations that come up in daily life that require you to say no to your impulses and yes to your purpose. There are many daily issues we face that we need to conquer in our path to personal and professional mastery—whether to skip the gym (or not), how to develop the confidence to embrace new (and perhaps daunting) opportunities, and how to stop worrying and silence the annoying voice in your head telling you things you don't want to hear. We will conclude with some perspective of how empowered refusal promotes human agency and gives us permission to wholeheartedly pursue what is important and meaningful to us.

Like design principles in art and architecture, the tenets of empowered refusal I will share in this book will not tell you precisely what to do, what to say, or when to say what. Instead, my goal is to provide you with the insight and understanding you need to master the superskill of empowered refusal. With this raw material, you can craft an empowered refusal response that is tailor-made for you to work for the situations that you have to navigate and the people that you will likely encounter in your unique circumstances.

What has been consistently gratifying for me in doing the research that forms the heart of this book, as well as in writing the book itself, is the significant practical importance of empowered refusal for people in all walks of life. There is nearly universal agreement in virtually every group I have spoken to over the past eight years—executives, professors, young professionals, government officials, university administrators—that whatever path you are on—first job, full professor, CEO, university president—the way to get there is not by saying yes to every request, but through the ability to effectively say no to the things that are not aligned with your aspirations. These folks all agree that daily happiness would soar, stress would dissipate, and there would be more time and energy if they knew how to address the common, perplexing, and global problem of saying no. And now, I am happy to share the solution: empowered refusal.

With this book, I hope to offer you a unique, positive, and meaning-filled approach to saying no by providing a framework for empowered refusal, a new purpose-driven mindset, and the toolkit of competencies you will need to convey an effective, authentic, and empowered no. Together, we will develop a plan of action that will empower you to go from wherever you are right now to a place filled with possibility, self-appreciation, and purpose.

PART 1

SAYING NO IS A SUPERSKILL

CHAPTER 1

Why We Say Yes When We Want to Say No

When he opened his eyes that morning, he had no way of knowing that this would be a day he would remember for a long, long time. As the early morning sunlight poured through the bare window of his quarters, he closed his eyes and indulged himself in the fantasy that he was back in England with no other prospect before him that day than reading the newspaper while eating breakfast in a cozy, wood-paneled dining room.

The loud ringing of his telephone jarred him into reality. Here he was, a subdivisional police officer in the remote outpost of Moulmein in lower Burma. A mere cog in the mighty gears of the British Empire. He picked up the receiver, wondering what could possibly be wrong *now*. The grainy voice of a sub-inspector at a cross-town police station was telling him about a runaway elephant creating havoc in the bazaar.

He knew he was not popular in the village. With him as a tangible target, the villagers expressed their anti-British sentiment in subtle ways. They delighted in tripping him during a soccer game or running over his foot with their bicycle in the crowded bazaar. He understood their resentment and empathized with their predicament. Secretly, he was not feeling too pro-Empire himself, especially after he saw how poorly the local people were treated—stripped of wealth and dignity. He could not bear to see the squalor in which they lived and the poverty they had no choice but to endure. He often longed for the Empire to be toppled, so that he, George Orwell,[1] could return home.

He dressed quickly, recalling with mild familiarity that "musth" was the crazed state—something like heat, for females—that male elephants could get into when their hormones went haywire. He rode a pony to the bazaar where he was met with a large group of villagers who told him that the elephant had disappeared. He soon found out that the elephant had killed a man and damaged a house. On learning this, Orwell decided to send an orderly to fetch an elephant rifle in case he needed to defend himself. He was sure that he would not use it, but if he was in charge, he did need to be prepared. As soon as the villagers saw the elephant rifle, they started loud murmurs that he was going to shoot the elephant. The villagers followed him in droves as he led the way in search of the elephant.

Finally, he spotted it. There was the beast, alone in a field, calmly tearing up bunches of grass with his trunk, beating them against his forelegs to remove the dirt, and shoving them into his mouth. The "musth" seemed to have passed, as the elephant looked serene. In fact, Orwell recalls the animal's actions in the gentlest terms, as the "preoccupied grandmotherly air that elephants have."

But here he was holding the gun with the villagers expectantly watching his every move. Caught between the placid-looking elephant and the increasingly loud and impatient murmurings of the crowd, Orwell sensed that the villagers wanted the show they had been waiting for. When was he going to ready his rifle and shoot?

Should he say yes and give the villagers what they wanted, or should he say no and let the local *mahout* (the title given to a person who trains and looks after elephants) come and guide the elephant back home?

He feared that any hesitation or uncertainty on his part could lead his already shaky authority to take a dive. He knew that it was not a trivial matter to shoot a working elephant. Elephants were valuable laborers and shooting the creature would be like destroying a prized piece of machinery.

The pressure mounted. It was hard to think clearly about what to do with hundreds of villagers' expectant eyes watching. He lifted his rifle and took aim, justifying to himself what felt like the only choice he had. In his essay he wrote: "A sahib has got to act like a sahib; he has got to appear resolute, to know his own mind and do definite things. To come all that way, rifle in hand, with two thousand people marching at my heels, and then to trail feebly away, having done nothing—no, that was impossible."

When the first shot rang out, it was drowned by the cheering of the crowd. Another two shots followed in quick succession. Orwell had succumbed to the demands of the crowd and said yes when he wanted to say no, for his own sake and for what he had convinced himself was the sake of the British Empire. In that moment, he felt hopeful that the villagers would finally bury the hatchet.

However, years after the incident, he recalled with lingering regret, that neither his reputation nor his relationship with the villagers improved in the time he spent in Moulmein after the elephant incident. The villagers still "accidentally" knocked him over during a soccer game in the muddy temple courtyard or "inadvertently" ran over his foot with a bicycle in the crowded bazaar. Orwell had betrayed his principles and instincts in saying yes to shooting the elephant—and in doing so made a terribly wrong decision, one that plagued him for the remainder of his life.

We All Sometimes Say Yes When We Want to Say No

Contemporary philosopher Michael E. Bratman observed that "We are not frictionless deliberators." Although today, more than a century after George Orwell shot the elephant in colonial Burma, we are so far removed from the circumstances of Orwell's story and will not be faced with the same decision he had to make, it can sometimes feel like our choices are as momentous as that one. Yes, times have changed, yet the social pressure we experience to abide by the expectations of others can leave us feeling trapped and conflicted in much the same way as Orwell did.

All of us have likely said yes to things we wanted to say no to and succumbed to the expectations of others, simply because we did not know how to refuse. Social psychologists call the tremendous power that others wield over our decisions *social influence*. It shapes how we respond to situations when we are under social pressure or feel under the scrutiny of others. The simplest evidence of social influence's power is our willingness to conform to what other people want of us. This often means that when we feel on the spot we will agree or say yes even when it makes complete sense to say no. In Orwell's case, even years later, when he recalled the incident, the familiar pit-of-the-stomach sensation was accompanied by an uncomfortable feeling of shame and reproach for his younger self.

To begin, we will unpack the forces that cause us to say yes even when we want to say no. We will recognize that because we are social creatures with a need to belong, our decisions and choices are not frictionless. Indeed, to be human is to bear a heavy evolutionary burden of instinctively valuing cooperation and compliance over individual achievement and volition. Simply put, saying no involves the unpleasant task of downthumbing[2] a request to put yourself and what you want first. This simple two-letter answer can be a source of anxiety and angst. You debate your response because the wrong response could lead you to risk your relationships (*Will they still like me?*) and damage your reputation (*What will they think of me?*).

We Think in People Terms

Anthropologists have found that human societies are founded on the notions of trust and cooperation. In all cultures, human beings naturally formed groups in which individuals cooperated with each other for survival. It makes sense that our ancestors would live in groups because, simply put, there is immense strength in numbers. It was just easier and safer to protect yourself from dangerous wild animals, hunt for and gather food, rear children, and raise domesticated animals, if you lived together with other human beings who shared the same goals of safety and survival. In fact, in many societies today, the extended family still exists because of the conveniences that family structure affords.

Regardless of where societies evolved across the world, members of the same tribe developed social norms that governed cooperative behavior. Social norms of cooperation, kindness, and politeness continue to undergird modern society.[3] Early in life, children are taught that to be viewed as valuable members of society, they need to get along with others by being accommodating and helpful. To prepare children for a successful life, parents and teachers impart important lessons of kindness, caring, compassion, consideration for others, and thoughtfulness.

Unsurprisingly, society shapes us to belong. Fables and stories from various cultures, both ancient and modern, are used to tell stories of great self-sacrifice and the rewards that befall people who give up their own desires for the sake of others. From the Bible to the *Ramayana*, from *Aesop's Fables* to *Grimm's Fairy Tales*, we learn that valuable members of society sometimes take on unpleasant tasks for the greater good and this confers on them immeasurable rewards.

One of my favorite stories and pertinent to the topic of saying no was narrated by Nelson Mandela in his autobiography, *Long Walk to Freedom*. Mandela writes: "Whereas my father once told stories of historic battles and heroic Xhosa warriors, my mother would enchant us with Xhosa legends and fables that had come down from numberless generations. These tales stimulated my childish imagination and usually contained some moral lesson. I recall one story my mother told us about a traveler who was approached by an old woman with terrible cataracts on her eyes. The woman asked the traveler for help, and the man averted his eyes. Then another man came along and was approached by the old woman. She asked him to clean her eyes, and even though he found the task unpleasant, he did as she asked. Miraculously, the scales fell from the old woman's eyes and she became young and beautiful. The man married her and became wealthy and prosperous. It is a simple tale, but its message is an enduring one: virtue and generosity will be rewarded in ways that one cannot know."

Storytelling is an ancient art that persuades, informs, and entertains. Although variations of this narrative exist in a variety of cultures, the particular story that Mandela recounts leaves us with the belief that the first traveler who said no by averting his eyes lost out. He lost out on good fortune, a beautiful wife, and a happy life. The second traveler, on the other hand, was bestowed with all these bounties by doing what appeared to be an unpleasant task.

Researchers find that the need to belong is a fundamental human motivation.[4] This need often results in us making decisions in other-people terms as opposed to on our own terms. Psychologist Mark Leary and his colleagues designed a need-to-belong scale that measures how far a person would be willing to go to feel included.[5] When people have a high need to belong, they become more other-centric. They are more likely to set their own needs aside and comply with what others want. They are more likely to take other people's feelings into consideration because they are concerned about the disappointment, frustration, and inconvenience that their decisions might cause others. They might do things to avoid rejection and negative evaluation by members of their group.

This Māori proverb beautifully captures this idea of what it means to be human and think "in people terms":

He aha te mea nui o te ao
What is the most important thing in the world?
He tangata, he tangata, he tangata
It is the people, it is the people, it is the people

"No": The Harmony Buster

One might imagine that saying no to things we do not want to do, or think we shouldn't do, ought to be easy. After all, it seems logical that if we know what we don't want, we should be able to say, "Sorry, not interested" or "No thank you" or simply "Nope, not for me." However, for most people, saying no is awkward and difficult, mostly because it involves sometimes having to put aside other people's expectations or reject what they want or wish for.

But why is it so painful to say no? Because saying no is a socially dispreferred response. Let's unpack this idea, because it forms the central premise of why we often say yes when we want to say no. Consider the last time someone made a request of you, invited you to go somewhere, made you an offer, or gave you a suggestion. Most likely they did so fully expecting your agreement and cooperation. They would not have been unreasonable in this expectation, given that there is a fairly robust social norm that suggests that we should adjust our own plans to accommodate others when they ask for it.[6] Often this translates to agreeing to even the most frivolous requests. Hardwired to help and conditioned to be cooperative, we are psychologically poised to say yes even when we want to say no. We intuitively recognize that saying no involves violating a social norm and can result in dire consequences, both in terms of the negative emotions and actions of others and in the bad feelings we have about ourselves.[7] Research finds that rejecting another person causes anxiety[8] and results in the refuser feeling depleted and de-energized.[9] Sometimes saying no can hurt the refuser as much, or perhaps more, than it hurts the refused.

While saying yes is socially approved, saying no is almost always a harmony buster. In fact, refusing someone by saying no has been described by one linguistic researcher as a "face-threatening act that tends to disrupt harmony in relationships."[10] *Whether we like it or not,* we are motivated to maintain long-lasting positive relationships with other human beings. We work hard to maintain social ties and resist their dissolution. We feel anxious at the thought of losing an important relationship and distressed if we caused another person harm. *It is this basic human instinct that sets us up to say yes more readily than to say no to a request.*

If we are honest with ourselves, we would see that our yeses come faster than our noes more often than we would like. Linguist Nick Enfield finds that this literally occurs in everyday speech: no matter which language is spoken, a no answer to a request will come slower than a yes response.[11] Most of us can think of at least one request in the past month that we did not know how to get out of and at least one thing on our calendar today that we wished we did not have to do.

Society Favors the Asker

So characteristically human is the notion of compliance that an entire subfield of social psychology is dedicated to the study of "influence"—when and how one person gets another person to do their bidding. Even though human beings are wired to be cooperative, the irony is that if you can get others to do what you want them to do, you gain social status, power, and a more advantageous position in the hierarchy of society.[12]

Consequently, researchers have spent decades understanding the effectiveness of different factors of persuasion, such as the power or status of the asker relative to the asked (your boss, for instance) or reciprocity norms (returning a favor), to produce automatic compliance: a willingness to say yes without thinking first.[13] Numerous books have been written about persuasion tactics that get people to do what you want, the assumption being that gaining compliance from others is a hallmark of your own success. Bestselling author Robert Cialdini has popularized influence tactics with catchy names like "foot in the door" and "door in the face" that are tools to get people to do your bidding.

But it turns out you don't have to work too hard to get people to comply with your request, as Cornell social psychologist Vanessa Bohns, who investigates people's response to everyday requests, finds. A key takeaway from her work is that people should ask for what they want, even if they themselves deem the ask outrageous, because the person you ask will likely comply. In her research studies, she has participants ask strangers to do things that were personally intrusive (Can I use your cell phone?), time consuming (Will you fill out a questionnaire?), and sometimes just wrong (Will you deface this library book?), and in all cases she found that a majority of people asked will comply.

A different rendition of Bohns's insight, but from a real-life experience perspective, comes from entrepreneur and speaker Jia Jiang, who after a spate of soul-crushing disappointments set out to conquer his fear of rejection by seeking out rejection every day for 100 days. In his book, *Rejection Proof*, Jiang provides hilarious anecdotes about the ways in which he strove to be rejected. He spent a year going out of his way "boldly seeking out rejection." He knocked on a stranger's door and asked, "Can I use your backyard to kick around a ball?" The answer he got: "Sure!" He asked a flight attendant whether he could make an announcement on the loudspeaker during a flight, and he was handed the microphone.

One of my favorite examples is Jiang's experiment in which he walked into a doughnut shop and asked the cashier, Jackie, to make him a set of doughnuts in the shape of the Olympic symbol. Jackie took this project on with sincerity and zeal. She discussed the different ways in which it would be possible to create the doughnuts, going as far as to look up the precise design and colors of the Olympic logo to give him what he asked for.[14] Furthermore, she did not even charge him for this extreme request!

What Jia Jiang and Vanessa Bohns both found is that even when people ask for completely crazy things that they would never even expect others to say yes to, they often receive a yes rather than the no the request clearly warranted.

It is apparent that we are already poised to be more compliant than unyielding. Recall that acceptance is always the preferred response, while refusal is dispreferred. This is pretty powerful stuff if you are the person on the asking side of the equation—but not so great if you are on the other side, where a lot of us find ourselves at one point or another. On this side, we are very often stumped. We feel trapped and stuck, and we react accordingly.

The Dual Drivers of Yes: Relationships and Reputation

People relate to each other with both their heart and their head. These correspond to the *feelings* one might have about the other person and *thoughts* that come to mind when we think of the other person. These feelings and thoughts can be either positive or negative. Think about a family member (a parent or a close relative) and examine the feelings this person evokes in you and the thoughts that come to mind when you think of them. Think about someone at work, a colleague or your boss. What thoughts and feelings come to mind about them? What do you think you evoke in people when they think of you?

We all want to be thought of as kind, cheerful, and lovely to be around. Most human beings want people to have positive thoughts about them. Researchers label these feeling-based associations we have about people a *warmth stereotype*. We also want people to think that we are capable, intelligent, and valuable to have on one's team; researchers label these capability-based associations a *competence stereotype*. Research finds that when we evaluate other people, we see them as either warm or as competent, usually not both. In perceiving others, the warmth and competence stereotypes do not always go hand in hand.[15] But, when it comes to other people evaluating us, *we* want them to see us as both warm and competent. It should come as no surprise that maintaining positive social bonds (relationships) and holding a positive image of the self (reputation) are two central goals of human beings.[16]

After evaluating hundreds of survey responses and discussing this with numerous leaders, I find that these two motivations map onto the two overarching reasons for why we say yes when we want to say no.

We say yes when we want to say no because we value our *relationship with the asker* and saying yes maintains this relationship. We also do this because we are concerned about our *reputation* and want people to see us in a good light. When we say yes when we want to say no, we are motivated by either the drive to maintain our relationship with the other person by striving to come across as nice, obliging, and accommodating (the warmth stereotype), or to secure our reputation in the other person's eyes by coming across as competent, capable, and hardworking (the competence stereotype).

I get it; to say no and still maintain a positive relationship with the asker while simultaneously securing your reputation can feel like an impossible task. But I hope that it is something you will learn to achieve through this book by mastering the art of empowered refusal.

Together we'll look at why our concern for securing our relationships and our desire to maintain a good reputation can lead us to saying yes when we want to say no. And in doing so, you can ask yourself a few simple questions to determine which one might be a stronger driver for you in your life.

Concern for Relationships

Imagine Mark, your colleague at work, asks you to take on a new project, and you agree, even though you already have a ton of prior commitments. Is this a familiar scenario for you? Or suppose your friend Jenny asks you out on Sunday afternoon for a glass of wine and a heart-to-heart and you say yes, knowing full well that the last time you went out with her you felt emotionally drained afterwards. Or perhaps your cousin Kay suggests it would be fun to organize a family get-together so that all the kids in the family can bond, and you feel responsible to do it even though this is not a great time for you to add another commitment to your calendar.

In an ideal world, you would like to agree to all these asks and emerge from each obligation unscathed and energized. However, everything is a trade-off. Taking on more at work would certainly please Mark, but it might mean missing out on your child's next piano recital. Hanging out with Jenny to help her feel better might leave you needing a few days to get back to feeling good yourself. If organizing events is not as energizing for you as it might be for Kay, it might leave you feeling angry and resentful.

When we know that we don't want to do something and we do it anyway, chances are that we are driven by fear of putting a strain on a good relationship, which might outweigh the time and energy we will have to commit to doing what was asked. It might also be motivated by the desire to strengthen a weak relationship: we rationalize that saying yes is a show of support, and as a result the asker is likely to see us as a friend and ally. It might also be the golden "do unto others" rule of reciprocity operating: either the asker has done something for you in the past and you feel the need to reciprocate, or you can envision a time in the future where you might need help from the asker, and if you decide to say no now you might not get the help you could need later. The bottom line is that we are socialized to believe, for a variety of reasons, that saying no could make us unlikeable, unpopular, turn our friends into enemies, or at the very least weaken our social ties.

Labels That Disable

It is quite common in my research studies for people to describe themselves as "people pleasers." They feel terribly guilty if they do not help, because their concern for their relationship with others far exceeds meeting their own needs and desires. If you are a parent, you have probably heard the parenting advice to not give your kids labels like "slowpoke" or "bossy" or "stubborn" or "lazy." In this exact same way, we need to free ourselves from the labels that disable us. For the so-called people pleasers out there, I have a simple request: *please don't give yourself a label.* All labels do is carry messages or prompt self-talk that confine us to a particular role or behavior. In the same way a child called "a troublemaker" will begin to perceive herself as such and live down to these labels, labeling yourself a people pleaser will result in you taking the easiest way out in the short run by saying yes in the moment, only to pay the price later.

Each time you define your identity as a people pleaser, you generate a deeper and deeper pathway in your belief system that dictates who you are and what you need to do and say to be accepted by others. Labeling yourself a people pleaser makes you a victim in a situation. It is an excuse to not make any change and permission to be resentful of people you say yes to.

When I think of chronic people pleaser, I think of Maggie Carpenter, the character Julia Roberts played in the movie *The Runaway Bride.* It was an important revelation for her to learn that she did not actually have a favorite way she liked her eggs. She simply chose whatever her boyfriend at the time liked. Maggie later reflected, "I would rarely say no because I believed love was conditional, and that I had to be a specific way to be worthy of love. I thought I had to want to eat at the same restaurant they liked, have the same taste in music, or validate every opinion they had (even if I didn't like it) because if I did, it would please my partner, and they would love me."

In his book *Give and Take,* psychologist Adam Grant argues that the workplace is divided into givers and takers. It is likely that the givers are not always the ones who *want* to be givers, but more likely perhaps the ones unable to say no when asked to give. Grant writes, "I learned that there's a big difference between pleasing people and helping them. Being a giver is not about saying yes to all of the people all of the time to all of the requests. It's about saying yes to some of the people (generous givers, and 'matchers' who aim for quid pro quo, but not necessarily the selfish takers) some of the time (when it won't compromise your own goals and ambitions), [and] to some of the requests (when you have resources or skills that are uniquely relevant)."[17]

What we need to do when an ask comes our way is to honor our true and authentic selves and say yes only to things that don't push us over the edge of our current capacity. We need to do our best for others while keeping in mind what is right for us. When we do not, we fall into a victim (*Others made me do this.*) or martyr (*I always have to do this because no one else will.*) mode. The dark side of being a victim or a martyr is that we are not living our best life, which can easily lead to feelings of being overwhelmed or constantly busy, feelings of guilt, anxiety, frustration, anger, and blame. In fact, people pleasing is much more than just being nice to people. When we engage in a pattern of behavior in which we put other people's needs before our own, often to the detriment of our health and well-being, we feel resentful and taken advantage of. Pulitzer Prize-winning journalist Herbert Bayard Swope once said, "I can't give you a surefire formula for success, but I can give you a formula for failure: try to please everybody all the time."

In the leadership classes I teach and the workshops I conduct, I request participants to complete a short survey so they have a sense of where they stand on their concern for relationships. To assess where your own concern for relationships lies, consider rating the truthfulness of each of the following statements.

Below are some statements that may or may not apply to you. For each item, please indicate how well the statement describes you. When finished, add up your responses to obtain your total score.

Scale Items: Concern for Relationships	Not true	Slightly true	Moderately true	True	Very true
I avoid conflict and disagreements at all costs.	1	2	3	4	5
I accommodate others even when it is inconvenient to me.	1	2	3	4	5
I have noticed that I have a strong need to please others.	1	2	3	4	5
I am what you would call a "people pleaser."	1	2	3	4	5
I have a hard time ending a meeting or conversation when I want.	1	2	3	4	5
I'd rather lie than face disapproval or rejection of certain people.	1	2	3	4	5

Give yourself the points associated with your response. For instance, for every "Very true" give yourself five points, for every "True" give yourself four points, and so on.

If you scored:

- **20 or higher:** You have a strong tendency to be a people pleaser and strive to avoid conflict, disagreements, and any negativity in your relationships. What will be valuable for you is the opportunity to learn to say an empowered no, while still maintaining close relationships with others. *Hint*: Learn to look inward and use *your* values, priorities, preferences, and beliefs as a lens to respond to other people's requests. More on this to come.
- **10–19:** You will benefit from reflecting on the situations and people who might elicit a stronger "need to please" in you. Remember to pay attention to how you can maintain relationships and still say no by developing your empowered refusal competencies.
- **9 or lower:** You have healthy and reciprocal relationships with others and do not feel the pressure to conform to other people's expectations. Remember that *how* you say no to others matters, and empowered refusal can help you forge stronger and more long-lasting relationships.

The Acquaintance Trap

Given that our yeses are often motivated by our need to belong, it is no wonder that the strength of our social ties plays a role in who we say yes to and why. As one might expect, our desire to maintain good relationships with people varies based on the relationship we have with the asker. There are individuals with whom we interact every day, like those we live with or those who are part of our work team, with whom we enjoy a secure relationship, and then there are strangers with whom we have no relationship at all.

It is both functional and adaptive for human beings to distinguish between relationships that are transactional, ad-hoc, and pertain to exchange versus those that are communal and grounded in cooperation and interdependence.[18]

The phenomenon I call the *acquaintance trap* is characterized by the inability to say no to the many people who fall in between—they're in your life, but you hold loose ties and a tentative or even fragile relationship with them. My research finds that it is easier to say no to the people who are very close to you (such as family and close friends) and those who are complete strangers, whom you are unlikely to ever see again. In the first case, you are secure in the relationship, and so your refusal will not break the bond you have. In the case of strangers, there is no relationship to break!

Consider the story of Raveena Tandon, an Indian actress who watched herself play a role she had played over and over again in dozens of movies—the glamourous heroine in a predictable love story that her fans loved and that had made her a popular movie star. Yet she did not recognize any part of herself that resembled or resonated with the person she played on screen. She knew in her heart, despite her success, that she often agreed to make films for the wrong reasons.

Success in Bollywood is about who you are and who you know. Raveena Tandon, daughter of Bollywood director Ravi Tandon, was born into the industry. It has been her extended family in the best and worst sense of the word. It is a family that gives you a chance to succeed in a cutthroat environment, but it is also a family that decides your screen identity based on your looks and what the audience wants before you have a chance to mold it yourself. You are cast, it appears, in stone. You get offers for a particular type of role and you get to play it again and again. Indeed, that is what success looks like. So, you say yes to those roles for fear of losing your fan base or not running with the in-group. You operate out of fear and insecurity. In an interview, Raveena Tandon mused, "The problem with us girls is that we are not taught to be assertive enough. We don't know how to say no without being apologetic. I too couldn't say no, I landed *(sic)* up doing some crazy films because of that. 'It's a friend's film. How can I refuse it?' But it did me no good, and eventually I learnt that being assertive is a good quality. One needn't feel apologetic about saying what one feels."[19]

Again, it is easier to say no to the demands of our family as well as to complete strangers, but as Raveena experienced, the biggest challenge is to meet the demands of a whole group of people in our lives who fall in the "acquaintance" bucket. We can put off demands and disappoint our parents, siblings, and partners because they will understand and love us anyway. But we are deeply concerned about our reputation (*What will they think of me?*) and our relationships (*Will they no longer regard me as a friend?*) with the people we work with or with whom we are casually acquainted, and we fall into the abyss of the acquaintance trap quite frequently.

Let's think about this issue. Most of the people we know fall into the category of acquaintances. Chances are we would not invite them to our wedding or add them to our guest list for a casual barbeque. We certainly would not know specific details of their lives, like where they grew up, what food they like, or even where they live. We might not even know their last name. Right?

But, when they make a request of us, why do we feel obliged say yes?

Concern for Reputation

It is our reputation that we are concerned about when we imagine that people are thinking about us or talking about us. Since reputation is an important factor in assessing the worth of an organization, a product, or an individual, it is natural to strive for a good reputation.[20] To enjoy a good reputation means to feel the esteem of others. Our reputations are at least in part under our own control. To build a good reputation, we have to manage ourselves so that people see that we are acting properly and that our behavior meets society's expectations and social norms.[21]

A particularly dark *Black Mirror* episode titled "Nosedive" is set in a society where people can rate their interactions with others on a scale of one to five stars, which ultimately determines their socioeconomic status. The episode begins with Lacie Pound, a nice, smiley woman with a regular office job, jogging around her neighborhood. What we don't know yet is how consumed she is with being rated at five stars. She is frustrated that despite how pleasant and outgoing she is, her reputation score has plateaued. She needs to up it by 0.3 points to obtain a discount on a luxury apartment. However, the more desperate Lacie becomes to increase her score, the more mishaps come her way, until she drops to below one star and is imprisoned. Ironically, in this society, prison is the one zone of personal freedom where one can be one's worst self. After all, when you have no reputation at all, there is nothing to damage.

The House of Cards Trap

The question we need to ask ourselves is: Can saying yes to everything that comes our way truly enhance our reputation? Indeed, we might say yes to maintain our reputation in the moment, but when we are overwhelmed with commitments and have signed up for more than we can possibly handle, our performance on each task will suffer. I like the metaphor of the house of cards. Each new responsibility you add to your plate is another card you have to use. There comes a breaking point, and a new card will cause your whole structure to collapse. You are not doing your reputation any favors by biting off more than you can chew.

It turns out that employees who are stressed at work, feeling overburdened, or burned out are more likely to miss deadlines, make mistakes, put less effort into what needs to be done, and perform poorly.[22] Is it better to say no to additional tasks and do well with what you have committed to, or should you take on more tasks and allow your whole house of cards to collapse? I suspect that dropping the ball on a regular basis is more damaging to your reputation than saying no in the first place.

Vanessa Van Edwards, author of the book *Captivate*, experienced first-hand the consequences of saying yes to everything—common advice given to many novice entrepreneurs seeking success. She describes this as "the worst advice I was ever given: Say Yes to everything, say Yes to networking events, coffees with strangers, and random conferences, because you never know what opportunity might come your way." She goes on to describe this popular recommendation as "a big smelly sack of baloney." After three years of spending every weeknight trudging the professional circuit and networking with everyone she could, she ended up with loads of business cards but no business.[23]

Personal reputation is about delivering results; handling situations; and your attitude and behavior toward work, life, and play. Your reputation is the trace you leave behind every time you leave a room. If you are a yes person who cannot say no to any request, you will gain a reputation as a pushover, not a professional.

A successful businesswoman and consultant, let's call her Linda, shared with me that her tendency to be "nice" led to her reputation as a pushover. Her colleagues would often point people in her direction saying, "Ask Linda. She will definitely say yes."[24] This is not the reputation you want for yourself!

Instead, you need to build your personal reputation by saying no to the things that are not aligned with your strengths or to which you are unable to devote the necessary time or energy. In that way you can maintain and deliver excellent results and be seen as reliable, responsible, and someone who has their work and life in balance and under control. Research finds that a strong personal reputation is an intangible asset of "brand you"—it is linked to a position of power, the freedom and autonomy to do things your way, and it ultimately leads to career advancement and professional and personal success.

Now assess for yourself your own concern for reputation. Below are some statements that may or may not apply to you. For each item, please indicate how well the statement describes you. When finished, add up your responses to obtain your total score.

Scale Items: Concern for Reputation	Not true	Slightly true	Moderately true	True	Very true
My reputation matters a great deal to me.	1	2	3	4	5
I want people to think and say good things about me.	1	2	3	4	5
It is important to me that people see me in a good light.	1	2	3	4	5
I like to get praise and appreciation from others.	1	2	3	4	5
I want people to see how much I do.	1	2	3	4	5
I am concerned about what people think of me.	1	2	3	4	5

Remember, give yourself the points associated with your response. For instance, for every "Very true" give yourself five points, for every "True" give yourself four points, and so on.

If you scored:

→ **20 or higher:** Your score indicates that you could fall prey to the house of cards trap. You value your reputation highly and might say yes out of fear that your reputation will drop in the eyes of the asker or that news will spread that you are uncooperative, unhelpful, and unobliging. Remember that when you learn the competencies of empowered refusal, your no response will come across with conviction and determination, thus leaving your reputation intact.

→ **10–19:** You care about your reputation, but not in a way that would sabotage your own preferences and desires. Remember to use the tools in this book to practice empowered refusal in a way that secures your relationship with the asker while maintaining your reputation.

→ **9 or lower:** You appear not to be very concerned with what other people think of you. This might result in you disregarding a request or responding with a lack of concern. This could negatively affect your relationships with others.

A Reluctant Yes or a Resounding Yes: What's the Difference?

Singer-songwriter Alicia Keys was exhausted and overwhelmed. Her career had taken off, but she felt like she was on a constant merry-go-round that just would not stop. In her book, *More Myself: A Journey,* Keys confesses that she found herself saying yes to every opportunity her team proposed. She writes, "I would be so overwhelmed or overworked—I was just saying yes to everything, and then I'd be exhausted. And there's no joy—it steals your joy." She goes on to say, "I didn't understand that you could say no. It took me so long to know on tour I could say, 'Oh, this is someone special to me's birthday, let's make sure that I'm not working on that day.' I didn't even know how to do that. I didn't even realize that I could."

Keys credits Oprah Winfrey for teaching her the importance of recognizing what a "resounding yes" feels like. Winfrey has been thinking for a long time about the importance of saying no to things that do not resonate with her. In fact, it was on April 10, 1994, when Oprah wrote the words that she keeps on her desk as a daily reminder: "Never again will I do anything for anyone that I do not feel directly from my heart. I will not attend a meeting, make a phone call, write a letter, sponsor or participate in any activity in which every fiber of my being does not resound *yes*. I will act with the intent to be true to myself."[25]

Numerous guests on *The Oprah Winfrey Show* report that they have walked away with a permission slip to say no to anything that steers them away from their purpose. Tara Westover, the author of the memoir *Educated*, was asked in an interview after she had been on the show, "First things first: Tell me all the advice Oprah gave you off stage." Her response: "We talked about how to protect yourself and how to say no. So yeah, it was a lot of practical advice. I'm trying to figure out how to be useful and do things that are good to do but still have something that resembles a life. It doesn't have to be a full-on life, just a resemblance of a life. And she was saying to me, 'No is a complete sentence.'"[26]

I imagine that being on *The Oprah Winfrey Show* is amazing! But it is especially valuable if you as a guest get to leave feeling empowered to create your own success in a way that is meaningful to you. It appears that Oprah gives many of her guests the gift of "no" and the permission to reject the things that distract them from their purpose. I surmise that Oprah gives this gift because she recognizes the difference between a reluctant yes, in which you comply for all the wrong reasons, and a resounding yes, where you agree because it feels like absolutely the right thing to do.

"Today, that sounds so obvious, and so, like, 'Yeah, duh,'" said Keys. "But at that moment, no one had ever explained it so simply to me. It means that, if someone presents you with a question, you know right away when it's like, 'Hell yeah, I'm dropping everything and I'm doing that.' And you know right away when you're like, 'I don't know about that.' And if you don't know about that? You don't have a resounding yes."

This is the same Oprah-inspired question we need to ask

ourselves: *Am I listening and hearing the difference between my resounding yes versus my reluctant yes and then making a concerted effort to convert my reluctant yeses to noes?* A resounding yes is a true yes that gives voice to your values and priorities and reflects your preferences and best interests. As spiritualist writer Paulo Coelho wrote, "When you say yes to others, make sure you are not saying no to yourself."[27]

There Is No Upside to the Reluctant Yes

I conducted a study to compare how people feel after saying a reluctant yes, one in which we say yes when we want to say no, compared to one in which we say no to something we did not want to do, and it worked.

Two hundred and twenty-eight people participated in this study. I divided participants (using random assignment) into two groups. All participants first read this brief introduction to the study: "'No' is often the hardest word to say. In our daily lives we are often faced with temptations that we have to say no to. Or we get requests from friends, family or work colleagues that we need to decline. Sometimes we say yes when we want to say no, but sometimes we are able to say no effectively. We are interested in your story."

Then half the participants were told, "Please tell us about a time when you were able to effectively say no. Someone asked you something you didn't want to do or you were tempted by something, but you found the courage to say no. Please describe in as much detail as possible the entire incident. Please tell us the thoughts and feelings you experienced and currently experience in writing about this incident. You can change the names of people and places to maintain anonymity." These participants became the "Said No Effectively" group.

The other half of the participants were told, "Please tell us about a time when you wanted to say no but did not. Someone asked you something you didn't want to do or you were tempted by something, but you did not have the courage to say no. Please describe in as much detail as possible the entire incident. Please tell us the thoughts and feelings you experienced and currently experience in writing about this incident. You can change the names of people and places to maintain anonymity." These participants became the "Said Yes When Wanted to Say No" group. After they had written out their stories, they reported on scales of 1 (not at all) and 7 (very much) how they had felt in terms of a range of specific positive and negative emotions. Here are the results.

Let's look at the *positive emotions* first (Figure 1.1). Saying no feels significantly better than saying yes when it is something you don't want to do. Across the board, the people who said no to things they did not want to do felt more happy, powerful, content, proud, and in control than did those who said yes when they wanted to say no.

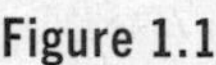

Figure 1.1

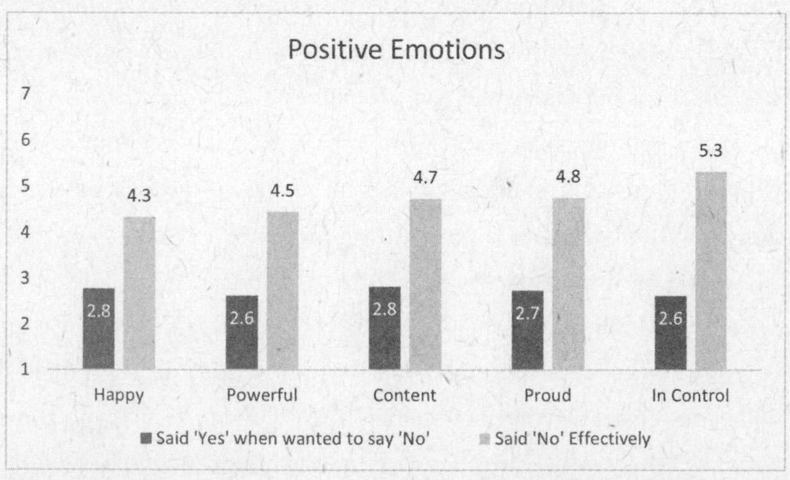

A big reason we say yes when we want to say no is because we think we will feel bad about saying no. Here is where we are wrong.

Let's look at the *negative emotions* next depicted in Figure 1.2. What the data shows is that when we say yes when we'd prefer not to, we feel significantly more regretful, more frustrated, more stressed, more guilty, and more helpless. It appears, contrary to what we'd expect, that we feel much worse when we say yes to something that we don't want to do than if we had just said no.

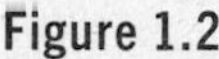

Figure 1.2

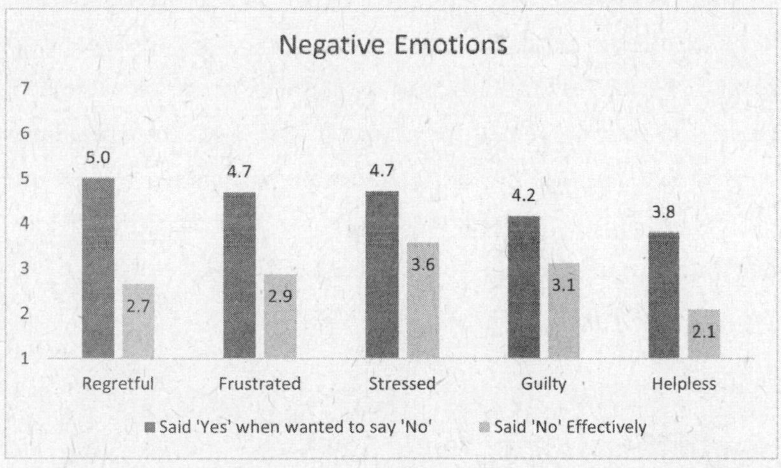

There is little upside to saying yes when we want to say no. We feel fewer positive emotions and more negative emotions. Saying no might feel a bit uncomfortable in the moment. But when we're saying yes to something that we don't want to do, we reexperience the negative feelings each time we pick up the dreaded task that we did not want to do in the first place. Learning to say no is the better route for us overall.

This is exactly what dancer and choreographer Twyla Tharp discovered the hard way. Like most professionals at the top of their field, Tharp places an immense value on time and does not like to waste a minute. She writes in her book *The Creative Habit* of a time, however, when she agreed to choreograph "a bad piece of music" purely out of a sense of obligation to the asker.

After six torturous weeks, intense practice with sixteen dancers, and hours of studio time, Twyla Tharp was forced to admit that "Hollywood Kiss" was simply not working out. She writes, "Whatever your reasons for starting with a project—whether crass or noble—they have to be clear and unencumbered. Obligation is a flimsy base for creativity, way down the list behind passion, courage, instinct, and the desire to do something great." She ruefully recalls the advice that she was once given and wished that she had heeded at the time she agreed to take the project on, "You only need one good reason to commit to an idea, not four hundred. But if you have four hundred reasons to say yes and one reason to say no, the answer is probably no."

How Difficult Is It for You to Say No?

How difficult is it for you to say no? To assess this (and to identify how you will best make use of this book), please answer the following questions.

Below are some statements that may or may not apply to you. For each item, please indicate how well the statement describes you.

Scale Items: Difficulty Saying No	Not true	Slightly true	Moderately true	True	Very true
I often say yes when I want to say no.	1	2	3	4	5
I don't know how to say no when a request is asked of me.	1	2	3	4	5
I can't find the right words to say no even when I should.	1	2	3	4	5
I can't say no to things even when they don't benefit me.	1	2	3	4	5

When finished, add up your responses to obtain your total score. If you scored:

- → **14 or higher:** You are in the right place. With this book, you will learn the invaluable superskill of empowered refusal to feel more in control about how you live your life. You will have to set aside your natural tendency to please others and focus on your values and priorities. Following the insights in this book will undoubtedly help you say no more easily to the things that do not matter.
- → **7–13:** You will benefit a great deal from becoming more effective at saying no. Remember to pay attention to the empowered refusal competencies you will learn in this book to master the art of empowered refusal.

→ **6 or lower:** You do not seem to have difficulty saying no. This is a good first step. However, remember that *how* you say no matters. You will benefit from paying attention to how your noes are affecting your relationships and your reputation. An empowered no, conveyed with conviction and determination using both verbal and nonverbal cues, will keep your relationships secure and your reputation intact.

Now that we understand that the best of us can succumb to social influence and we have a better understanding of where we stand in terms of our concerns for relationships, our reputation, and our ability to say no, let us now examine how these factors come into play at the moment an ask is made of us. How do we feel? What do we think? How do we (versus how should we) respond?

CHAPTER 2

The Spotlight Effect

At first blush, stadium proposals seem romantic. Because of this, they are big business and quite an expensive way to start an engagement. It can cost as much as $2,500 to propose at Dodger Stadium in Los Angeles. Some venues offer a stadium proposal package with tickets, champagne, roses, and a commemorative DVD thrown in. But stadium proposals make me cringe—not because they involve the marketing of romance, but because of what the stadium proposal represents: the quintessential set-up for perfect compliance.

Consider for a moment how a typical stadium proposal works. The jumbotron puts the couple in the spotlight at a prespecified time. The proposal is featured live on a video board in the presence of tens of thousands of onlookers (to say nothing of the TV audience). Most often it is a man asking a woman to marry him. Ideally, she knew this was coming and wants to say yes. But with an entire stadium watching and cheering her on, can she choose to say no?

While most of us have not been proposed to in a stadium, we experience mini versions of the stadium proposal in many spheres of our daily lives. When a stranger, a friend, or even a family member makes a request of us that we want to refuse, we feel like we are the center of attention—on the jumbotron in our own mind—and it often feels impossible to say no.

Consider the following examples of stadium proposal moments that might feel familiar.

You are on a flight in an aisle seat. You have taken care to reserve this seat months in advance because it is your preference. Just as you are nicely settled into your seat with your headset on and your book in hand, a flight attendant shakes you out of your reverie. She asks if you will move to a middle seat to accommodate a family traveling together. You obviously want to say no, but the hopeful family and the folks in the seats next to you are all watching and waiting for your response. You feel in the spotlight. What choice do you have?

Imagine you are attending the regular Monday morning meeting at work. You have your week planned out and your to-do list in order. As the meeting is about to close, your boss mentions the holiday office party in a couple of weeks. He asks for a volunteer to organize the event. He says that while everyone will help out, he needs someone to take the lead. He glances at you at the very moment a colleague volunteers you for the task, praising the great job you did last year. You already have a lot on your plate and do not need another time-consuming task to add to it. But with a spotlight shining on you, what can you do?

In my research I have come across hundreds of everyday examples of similar "stadium proposal moments" that people can readily recall and regularly find themselves in. You might agree that having the Burmese villagers' eyes on George Orwell, expectantly waiting for him to shoot the newly apprehended elephant, likely made him feel he was in the spotlight. Can you think of an instance when this has happened to you? Can you relive that moment and recall what you thought and how you felt?

Clearly in these situations, the answer you want to give is a vehement no, but it is not easy to do so. We have discussed that no is an undesirable social response—a harmony buster. Admittedly, *no* is a hard word to say: we want to protect our reputations, and we want to maintain our relationships. Let's now take a look at what happens when someone requests us to do something. Why do we experience the stadium proposal moment—the feeling that we are the focus of attention, flooded with negative feelings of conflict and anxiety? By learning to recognize stadium proposal moments when they occur (or when they are about to occur), we can minimize the glare of the spotlight and make it easier for us to say no to the things we do not want to do.

When Someone Makes a Request

I recently taught an executive class on leadership for women in which I explained the stadium proposal moment. During the class, we did a little role-playing. I said to a participant, "Imagine that someone—perhaps your boss—has asked you to do something you want to say no to." I gave her a moment to think about an instance and then continued. "Your reasons for wanting to say no—whether personal or professional—are legitimate." I gestured with my hands so that an imaginary spotlight would be shining on her and said, "You feel the spotlight on you. Tell us what you are feeling. What are the thoughts and feelings that are going through your mind?"

She said, "I would be thinking, *If I say no, I would be disappointing this person. This person will think I am unprofessional and not committed to my work.* And *Yikes, I really don't know how to say no to this person.*" I nodded and smiled at her reassuringly. What she was experiencing was completely normal. I proceeded to do my "stinking pile of garbage" act to demonstrate how these uncomfortable and difficult situations often play out.

Here's how it goes: I ask the group to imagine that I am carrying around a stinking pile of garbage. I first go to one woman and ask her, "Can I put my stinking pile of garbage on your desk?" She might say an emphatic, "No." I walk away and turn to another woman. The second woman might shake her head vigorously before I even ask her. Her hands up, protecting herself and her entire body, she might say, "No way!" But then I go to a third woman and implore her for her help. She hesitates and gives a tiny nod. I quickly dump my imaginary pile of stinking garbage on her desk. I dramatically shake all the last bits of imaginary dirt off myself and say, "Now it is your stinking pile of garbage."

At this point, the group usually laughs nervously, recognizing three important things with my little one-act performance. First, that the feeling of being in the spotlight is real and it can make you agree to things you don't want to do. Second, that my imaginary pile of stinking garbage is an apt metaphor for all the things you don't want to do but that you take on simply because you have no idea how to say no. Whether it is because you care about your reputation or because you want to maintain a good relationship with other people—or because you simply don't know how to say no—you are the one who now has the garbage on her desk. I make it a point to home in on the realization that the more garbage that piles up, the less you can see your own path, and your control over how you spend your time decreases. It's a recipe for unhappiness and being overwhelmed. Third, and perhaps most counterintuitively, if you say no to a request that you don't want to do, as the first two women did, the asker simply turns to the next person available.

Now let's look at what the research says about all of this, and what insights we can glean from social scientists that can help us understand the stadium proposal phenomenon better.

Standing Out in Our Own Minds

To make sense of what happens when a person makes a request of you, we need to understand the interplay between the social environment and the influence it has, and we need to understand our own psychological makeup—in other words, our own thoughts and feelings and how both these factors come together to shape how we respond. The uncomfortable feeling that emerges when we have to say no to a request is a characteristically human feeling that has more to do with how we appear to others and the consequences of our response than it has to do with the actual request. The focus we place on ourselves at the time of a request is grounded in some fundamental ideas from social psychology that deal with group influence and self-attentional or egocentric biases.

Group Influence: The Sway of the Swarm

Bees, ants, wasps, and termites are social insects that live in organized societies and operate based on group norms and social influence that dictate the division of labor within the group, the cooperative care of offspring, and the systematic living and working arrangements in the colony. This high level of group cohesion and cooperation is called *eusociality* from the Greek word *eu* meaning good and the Latin word *socii* meaning allies. Most situations are harmonious when each individual group member allies with and collaborates with the other members of the group.

Our human societies are not much different. There is a reason why human beings and our primate relatives are often referred to as "group-living species"[1] or "social animals."[2] It is because the groups we belong to establish the rules and norms that guide our behavior. Social norms are the "rules or standards that are understood by members of a group, that guide and/or constrain behavior without the force of laws."[3] When we are part of a group, we have to balance our own selfish desires with the needs of the group for collective survival. Since cooperation and group belonging are valued goals for most people, being helpful is a social norm. And successful social norms promote survival-related actions—acquiring status, affiliating with others, and acquiring food or shelter.

Deviating from social norms can have dire consequences. I am reminded of the Disney movie *Antz* in which worker ant Z Marion-4195—Z for short—yearns to express his own individuality. The twists and turns in the plot consistently reveal the ways in which the other ants try to get Z to conform to the goals of the colony. Although (spoiler alert) Z does get to marry his true love, Princess Bala, it is not without risking the wrath of the colony's leaders.

Researchers Robert Cialdini and Melanie Trost in their review of social influence write, "Those who wish to understand fully the process of personal change must understand just as fully the process of interpersonal influence." [4]

Returning to our context of requests and refusals, since we are socialized to help other people, when someone makes a request of us, it is normative (read: good and expected) for us to respond positively as a sign of cooperation and to ensure belonging to the social group. By saying no, we put ourselves at risk of social isolation and abandonment by our group. Cooperation is a rewarded behavior, but refusal is not. This idea is at the heart of Cialdini's widely read book *Influence,* which is described as "an examination of the psychology of compliance (i.e., uncovering which factors cause a person to say yes to another's request)."

The vast body of research on group influence reveals that making the social consequences of noncompliance salient is an effective way to gain compliance. While the opposite of compliance is noncompliance, the word *noncompliance* is tinged with negative meaning and suggests rebelliousness and disregard for rules. Although refusing a request is by its very nature a noncompliant behavior, I prefer not to think of it in this negative way. By all means, you do need to manage your reputation and care about your relationships with others, but not at the cost of your own happiness and well-being. I encourage you to consider the big picture and think beyond the simplistic idea of social norm violation to consider the consequences of spending your time doing things that you don't want to do simply because someone asked. You might be familiar with Dale Carnegie's bestselling book *How to Win Friends and Influence People,* in which he provides tips on how to gain popularity and influence, largely by getting people to like you. But I contend that in the context of responding to a request, one can go too far in trying to be liked. The question you have to ask is: *Do I want to win friends by being overly influenced BY people?*

Egocentric Bias: The Jumbotron in Our Head

While our desire to conform to social norms can make saying no to a request uncomfortable and distressing, our own thoughts and feelings play an important role in how we think about refusals. The spotlight effect phenomenon is an egocentric bias in which people tend to believe that they are being noticed more than they really are.[5] We tend to overestimate the extent to which others notice and evaluate our appearance, our performance, and our blunders—as if a spotlight is shining on us. To demonstrate this effect, researchers asked some participants to wear a bright yellow T-shirt with a big picture of Barry Manilow's face on it and then walk briefly into a classroom filled with students. Other participants were asked to wear a regular white shirt and walk into a similar room. Under the guise of being a memory test, participants were asked to estimate how many people in the room would remember their T-shirt. When it was an unusual, somewhat embarrassing, Barry Manilow tee, participants dramatically overestimated how many people would remember that shirt compared with when it was a regular white shirt. People's own judgments of how embarrassing or attention-grabbing the T-shirt was colored their estimates of how others would perceive them.

There are numerous other studies that document egocentric biases. When we work on a project, we often believe that we have contributed more to its success than others have.[6] When we see a group of colleagues giggling together in the break room, we feel certain they are gossiping about us.[7] When we are not prepared for a meeting or a class, we are convinced that we will be called on that day.[8] This latter bias is called the *self-as-target bias* and might well explain the sudden onset of stomach pains or headaches when we want to avoid a class or a meeting for which we are not prepared.

These egocentric biases can cause social anxiety. When we exaggerate the attention that we feel, we experience negative emotions like embarrassment, anxiety, and fear. As we will later see, the attentional focus we experience simply from someone asking us to do something we do not want to do can make us feel at the center of attention as well as evoke feelings of discomfort, the anticipation of conflict, the fear of embarrassment, and the worry of disappointing the other person. I particularly like the way the author Martha Beck described the consequences of these feelings of social anxiety in *O, The Oprah Magazine*.[9] She wrote: "In the beam of imaginary spotlights, many of us suffer untold shame and create smaller, weaker, less zestful lives than we deserve. Terrified that the neighbors might gossip, the critics might sneer, the love letter might fall into the hands of evil bloggers, we never even allow our minds to explore what our hearts may be calling us to do. These efforts to avoid embarrassment often keep us from imagining, let alone fulfilling, the measure of our destiny."

When It's a Request That You Want to Refuse

To understand what it feels like to experience a stadium proposal moment, I conducted some experiments. In one study, I randomly assigned undergraduate student participants to groups and asked them to imagine it had been a very busy spring semester and a particularly busy week at school with projects and deadlines. This is a scenario most undergraduate students relate to. They were then told they were looking forward to a much-needed spring break. On Friday night, they went out with friends. At that time a friend, Sarah, mentioned that she was looking for volunteers to call potential donors and sponsors for a charity she was passionate about and asked them if they could make twenty to twenty-five phone calls on her behalf during the next couple of weeks. It was clear to all participants in the study that this was not how they wanted to spend their free time during spring break. In other words, it was clear that this was a request for which their response should be a no.

Now, I varied some information in these scenarios. In this study, I changed how the social situation they were in was described. One group of participants (the Social Ask group) read that when Sarah asked them to volunteer to make the calls, she did so in front of the whole group of friends and that all their friends had agreed to help. The other group (the Solo Ask group) read that Sarah was the only one at the table when they arrived at the restaurant and she asked them for help.

Drawing from the social psychology research I described, I had a straightforward hypothesis that the interplay between the social situation (Social Ask vs. Solo Ask) coupled with the individual's owns thoughts and feelings about the situation would determine the feeling of being in the spotlight and the intensity of negative emotions they would experience. After the participants read the scenarios, I asked them to report their experiences on a number of survey-type questions.[10] First I wanted to compare the extent to which participants felt that they were the focus of attention (see Figure 2.1). I did this by asking three questions: To what extent do you feel that everyone is paying attention to you? To what extent do you feel that everyone's eyes are on you waiting for your response? To what extent do you feel that you are expected to say yes to help Sarah out? These were assessed on a scale of 1 to 7 where 1= not at all and 7 = very much, so higher numbers implied feeling more in the focus of attention while lower numbers implied feeling less in the focus of attention. The figure shows that people reported that they did feel that they were the focus of attention (since this was a request that came out of the blue, and everyone wanted to say no, we would expect this), but to varying degrees.

Further, when the request was a social ask, both men and women felt in the focus of attention, possibly because everyone in the group had agreed and they felt compelled to take the group's expectation into account. Regardless of gender, if there are other people expecting a certain response or egging you on in a particular direction, it is hard to refuse. You do not want to risk your relationship with others, especially if they are acquaintances and you worry about your reputation.

However, when you look at the data for the solo ask, you find that women felt a stronger attentional focus compared with males. Let's look at the accompanying emotions before we interpret this curious finding.

Figure 2.1

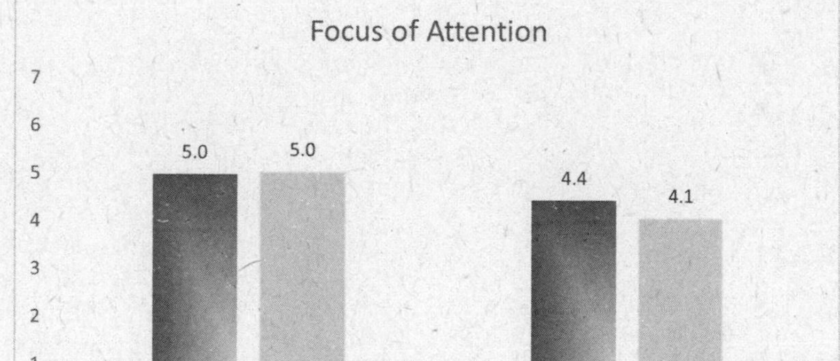

I asked participants to report how uncomfortable, conflicted, and trapped they felt. When we examine the intensity of these negative emotions (combined into a single scale, 1 = not at all; 7 = a great deal; see Figure 2.2), we find that saying no is fraught with negativity. All participants reported feeling uncomfortable, conflicted, and trapped, but again to varying degrees. Women tend to feel more intense negative emotions (higher numbers on the scale) regardless of whether the ask is social or solo. Men feel more intense negative emotions when they are in a social situation but less when they are asked in private.

Overall, the feeling of being in the spotlight is characterized by being the focus of attention, and experiencing negative emotions shines brighter and is more intense when a person is in a group and wants to say no compared with when a person is asked privately. However, women tend to feel that they are the focus of attention and experience equally intense negative emotions regardless of whether the ask is a social or a solo one.

Figure 2.2

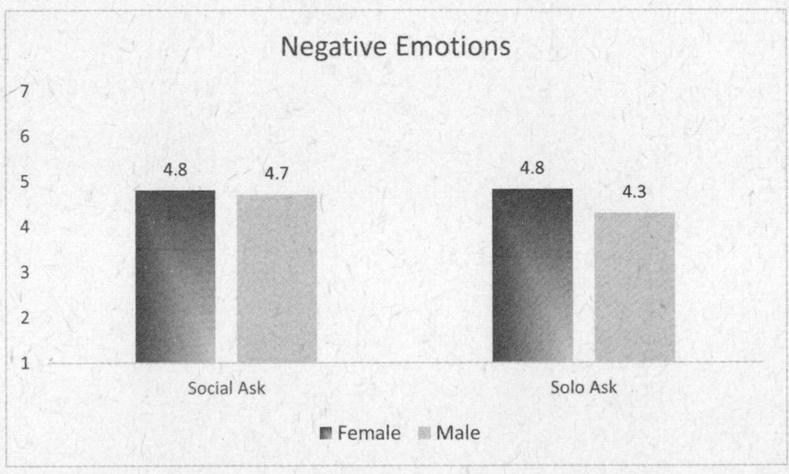

The next thing I wanted to assess was how this feeling of being in the spotlight orients a participant's response toward the actual request.

I asked people how obligated (Figure 2.3) they would feel to help Sarah out and how guilty (Figure 2.4) they would feel if they did not. When a request was made in a group, both men and women felt equally obligated to help Sarah and equally guilty if they did not. The differences between how the men and women felt depended on the context—whether it was a social ask vs. a solo ask. Women felt as obligated and guilty when asked individually as when asked in a group. In contrast, men felt much less obligated and much less guilty when it was a solo ask.

The data seems to suggest that women are at a much greater risk of saying yes when they want to say no. They feel a stronger attentional focus, more intense negative emotions, and greater feelings of obligation to help and guilt for not helping. In fact, the spotlight that women manufacture is equally intense whether it is a social or a solo ask. It is as if women not only imagine a spotlight, but also conjure up an imaginary group of onlookers, making the situation much more stressful and making it more likely that they say yes to the request.

Figure 2.3

Figure 2.4

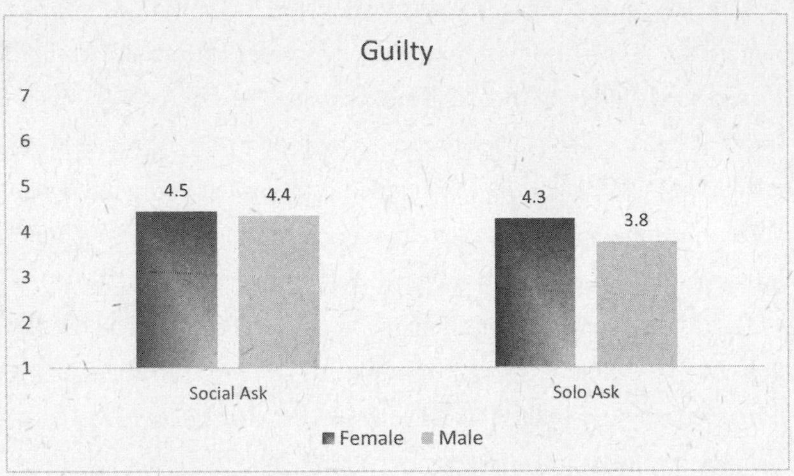

This finding is consistent with research in organizational behavior that finds that women are more likely to say yes to workplace requests than men are.[11] Perhaps more troubling is related research that shows that women are more likely to be asked to volunteer for, and also take on, thankless tasks that are low in promotability potential.[12] In other words, women are more likely to take on the workplace housekeeping tasks that no one wants to do, like cleaning out the break room refrigerator or organizing an office party that can take hours of time with no recognition or reward. As an aside, in my classes, sharing this fact results in knowing nods and disappointed shakes of the head from the female students.

Now let's look at how the participants in the study responded to the request. I asked participants to "write down the exact words you would use to respond to Sarah's request." After they had recorded their response, I asked them to describe their "thoughts and feelings about this situation in as much detail as possible." There were three categories of responses:

1. The unambiguous refusal
2. Saying yes when you want to say no
3. The different shades of no

Analyzing their written responses was an eye-opening exercise. Let's look at what happened within each group.

THE UNAMBIGUOUS REFUSAL

One group of people just said no. They used words that conveyed a clear and unambiguous no response, although they were not the majority. A clear no sounded something like, "Sorry, that's not really my thing and I'd rather not. I hope the best for you, though!" "I would really like to help out, but I do have other plans." "Nah, I think I'm good. I'd rather not." Their thoughts and feelings supported their words.

The other two groups were much more nuanced, and there is much to learn from both these groups.

SAYING YES WHEN YOU WANT TO SAY NO

Despite the task being described as one that they did not want to spend spring break doing, there was a group who said yes when they wanted to say no. What's interesting about these people is that while they were obliging and compliant in their response, what was going on in their minds and how they justified their response was quite revealing.

While people were responding with a typical yes response,

saying, "Sure thing! I would love to help you out on your project," or "Yes, definitely count me in," they were also feeling resentment toward the other person or trying to find ways to feel better by justifying their decision. As established earlier, there is a great deal of evidence in the data that people were saying yes to protect their own reputation ("I don't want people to think I am a bad person.") and to manage their relationship with Sarah in the way they felt was most cooperative and amicable ("I think about how much whatever it is they are asking means to them.").

In 1974, researchers Chris Argyris and Donald Schön developed a tool to uncover the inner dialogue we have with ourselves while we are engaging with other people.[13] During an interpersonal interaction, there might be two conversations taking place. One uses words and is an explicit conversation between two or more people. The other conversation consists of the thoughts and feelings going through the heads and hearts of the speakers. Argyris and Schön asked participants to divide a page into two columns where the right side of the page is the conversation or words being said, and the left side of the page is what the person is thinking and feeling. Using this tool to analyze the data in this study, I found that although the words people say convey a yes response, their minds are swirling with negative emotions, worry about their reputation, concerns about their relationships, and a desperate search to justify their yes so that they can live with themselves. For instance, a person might say "Sure, happy to help" to the other person while thinking to themselves: "I don't like feeling pressured to say yes."; "This situation is stressful to say the least. I don't like to be put on the spot."; "I feel like I'm obligated to help or say yes."; or "I'm not good at talking on the phone, I'm more of a face-to-face person."

One treacherous and yet extremely common thing that occurs is that we try to justify our response to feel better about it. Later in the book we will delve into the operation of the psychological immune system that helps us cope with and bounce back from negative experiences. Suffice it to say that this is a system that is great for building resilience and coping with the bad things that might happen in life, but it is also a system that prevents us from learning from our mistakes. One of the prevalent thoughts that runs through our mind is self-justification. We say something like this to ourselves: *After all, it's only twenty calls, and if I split it up over five days, I can organize things to help a friend out.* Sadly, self-justification does not make us learn; it only makes us more likely to repeat the mistake again in the future.

THE DIFFERENT SHADES OF NO

The majority of respondents did not say no directly but tried to buffer the harshness of the unambiguous no response. Let's look at the different shades of no.

Some people buffer the harshness of a no response with flattery and affection. Clearly this is easier to rely on for people you know well and can be familiar with. For instance, you might take a few seconds to smile at Sarah, compliment her on her initiative, and tell her you appreciate how she has chosen to spend her time. After this infusion of positive energy into the conversation, it is easier to say no. By lightening the mood, you also deflect the spotlight while securing your relationship with the other person.

A number of people say no by deferring the request to a later time. They often say, "I can't help now, but I will help you the next time." This serves as a no in the present but leaves the door open for the same request to be made in the future.

Other people use excuses for why they cannot help out right now. In fact, my analysis shows that using excuses seems to be the default way to say no. We often say we can't do something because of some fill-in-the-blank excuse. It is quite likely that we are taught to give excuses because explaining why you cannot help out seems more polite. Excuses are like a bandage: they are temporary fixes that work in the moment, but they do not stop a person from coming back with the same request a short time later. I will expand on this a bit later in the book.

It appears from the data that people often do not convey a clear no response. Their response lies somewhere in the gray zone between a yes and a no. The compromise offer is meeting someone halfway while the wishy-washy no is simply a yes disguised as a no. A compromise sounds like this: "Hmm...I'm not sure if I have time to do twenty calls, but I can do maybe ten for you. Is that OK with you?" While a wishy-washy no might sound like this: "I am probably not the best person to be doing calls to sponsors for you, but if you want me to I would help out." Clearly, both these refusal responses are ineffective, because they will probably result in you doing at least a little bit of what you did not want to do. This half-way position does not help you or the requester, even though it feels like the nice thing to do.

What we will discuss next are the different ways to recognize the spotlight, manage its glare, and deal with the self-manufactured social pressure. The goal of the exercise—and the promise of this book—is not to feel pressured, helpless, and out of control but to be in the driver's seat of your own life. Learning to say an empowered no stems from your identity by reflecting your values and priorities and maintains both your reputation and relationships.

The Stadium Proposal Moment Demands Triage

Triage is a problem-solving approach that originated to help medical professionals categorize the injured after a battle. Injured soldiers were divided into three groups: those who will survive without immediate medical assistance, those who would likely die even if they received medical attention, and those for whom medical care could mean the difference between life and death. Now an established emergency room procedure, triage focuses attention on the last group, where medical attention would have the greatest impact. When resources are scarce, as they are in an emergency room, you have to make tough choices. For example, even if there is a crying teenager and a frightened infant who witnessed a car crash and are in shock, the focus of attention needs to be on the badly injured patient who was in the crash and could survive with timely medical help.

So how can you triage a situation to manage the spotlight more effectively? There are three strategies: 1) be prepared; 2) diffuse the spotlight; and 3) endure the spotlight. Within each of these strategies are a variety of ways the strategy can be implemented. I invite you to try them, to adapt them to suit you, and to develop your own ways of managing the spotlight.

BE PREPARED

The feeling of being in the spotlight is exacerbated in situations that are unfamiliar, unexpected, or atypical. If you anticipate that an unwanted request is coming your way (even if you don't know what it is), you might be in a better position to diminish the spotlight or even make it go away.

If you are lucky, you will get a heads-up from a friend or colleague about an upcoming request. In a study similar to the spring break study, some people read that a friend gave them advance warning that Sarah was going to make a request. It turns out when they were prepared for the ask, the glare of the attentional spotlight dimmed a bit. Having a network of people who will keep you in the loop can help a great deal. If you know someone is going to ask you to do something, prepare your response. Rehearse the words or practice talking to a friend or family member about whether your response sounds empowered. By the end of the book, I will help you ensure that your refusal is empowered through the words you use and with your body language.

Being prepared can sometimes simply be the result of knowing your own preferences. If you are clear about your values and priorities and a request comes in that does not align with those values and priorities, you are better prepared to refuse. One of the things you will learn in this book is that one of the competencies of empowered refusals entails developing personal policies—simple rules for yourself that stem from your identity and reflect your values and priorities. When your refusal is grounded in a personal policy that gives voice to your values and priorities, you are better equipped to say no.

In an ideal world of complete transparency, you can imagine that no one asks you to do anything you don't want to do, because they have the advance knowledge that you will say no. The closest thing I have found to this is a form letter that social and literary critic Edmund Wilson sent out in response to the increasing amount of mail he was receiving. Wilson was clear about his commitment to his own writing and editing for *Vanity Fair*, the *New Yorker*, and the *New Republic* and recognized that the requests he often received took away from these writing and editing priorities. His form letter listed eighteen things in two groups of lists that (regretfully) were impossible for him to do. The first list included things he would not do without compensation "read manuscripts," "judge literary contests," or "address meetings". The second list right below it categorically stated the things he would not do under any circumstances like "autograph books for strangers," "supply personal information about himself" or "receive unknown persons who have no apparent business with him".

Suffice it to say that his laser focus and clear set of priorities allowed him to do work that led to him to receiving both the Presidential Medal of Freedom and the National Medal for Literature. When we learn about personal policies, we will draw inspiration from Edmund Wilson to create our own set of rules rooted in our values and priorities, that will provide us the means by which to decide which requests we agree to and which requests we don't.

DIFFUSE THE SPOTLIGHT

The word *decide* has similar Latin roots to words like *suicide* and *homicide* Decide comes from the Latin word *decidere*, which is a combination of two words: *de* = "off"+ *caedere* = "cut." To decide literally means to cut off everything except the things that matter most. So, to decide entails "killing the alternatives" and sometimes time is what we need to do that. Take the time you need to think through your decision, because making good decisions is an essential key to productivity.

In my office, I have a little red book that is in my line of sight. It is Elizabeth Cogswell Baskin's *Hell, Yes!: Two Little Words for a*

Simpler, Happier Life. The takeaway from the book is simple: if it is not a Hell, Yes, it is a Hell, No. For me, the book serves as a visual reminder to be very clear that the decision about what to say yes to is mine and that I might need, and should take, the time to think about a request before responding. Most of the time, if someone walks into my office with a request, they will not get a definite response from me at the time of the ask, unless I am sure that it is a "Hell, Yes."

You might even consider making an Edmund Wilson–type list of your own on your desk or desktop. Visuals that are endowed with meaning can serve as useful devices to help ground us in our values and priorities and remind us what is important and what is not.

Another way to diffuse the spotlight is to use scenario thinking. Ask yourself: *What happens if I say no?* And perhaps more important, *What happens if I say yes?* When you are in the spotlight, it feels impossible to say no. We will later discuss the notion of opportunity costs and the use of pros and cons lists that constitute scenarios thinking. But consider this: If you said yes, could it be that you have just accepted a whole bunch of stinking garbage? And what is likely to happen if you simply said no? It is more than likely that the spotlight will move from you to someone else.

Another useful tactic to diffuse the spotlight is to imagine giving advice to a friend. What would you counsel a friend to do in this same situation? When you emotionally distance yourself from a difficult situation, you can see more clearly. You might remind a friend, for instance, that if they said yes to something they do not want to do, they might be depriving someone of an opportunity that is a Hell, Yes for them. You might even help a friend redirect the spotlight on someone for whom the task is a Hell, Yes.

Remember that pile of garbage? You might remind a friend that if they simply said no, I would look for someone else to take it on. And perhaps, what looks like a stinking pile of garbage to one person might be a bunch of sweet-smelling roses for someone else.

ENDURE THE SPOTLIGHT

In some situations, you have to endure the spotlight and stand your ground. If the issue is important to you, you can summon up the courage and refuse to budge even though the spotlight is shining on you and getting brighter with every passing moment. I have observed in my research that people who could say no more readily were those who recognized the similarity of the situation they found themselves in to other situations in the past. When you reflect on the times you say yes when you want to say no and learn from those instances, you are better able to endure the spotlight and resist the pressure.

I am reminded by what writer Audre Lorde observed about facing challenges: "Sometimes we are blessed with being able to choose the time, and the arena, and the manner of our revolution, but more usually we must do battle where we are standing."[14]

One notable and famous empowered refusal is the story of Rosa Parks. Rosa Parks was the brave woman who refused to give up her seat to a white man on a Montgomery, Alabama, city bus on December 1, 1955. This single action is galvanized the Civil Rights Movement. The details of what actually happened on the bus are worth contemplating.

After Rosa Parks got off work, she went to catch her usual bus home. As she paid her fare, she recognized the driver as the man who had put her off the bus more than a decade before, in

1943. She took a vacant seat and sighed, wishing she had not taken this particular bus or that she had noticed the driver before getting on. When the driver told her and some other passengers to vacate their seats, others got up, but she remained sitting. The driver asked her again to move, refusing to drive on until she did. Imagine the glare of the spotlight Rosa Parks had to endure. After a long day at work, everyone just wanted to get home, so the exasperated stares of the other passengers—both Black and White—were probably unavoidable.

Rosa Parks had a choice: to comply with the driver's command as she had all those years before or to hold her ground and refuse. As she described in her autobiography, *My Story*, she was anxious, worried, and conflicted, unaware of what was going to transpire. She wrote: "As I sat there, I tried not to think about what might happen. I knew that anything was possible. I could be manhandled or beaten. I could be arrested. People have asked me if it occurred to me then that I could be the test case the NAACP had been looking for. I did not think about that at all. In fact, if I had let myself think too deeply about what might happen to me, I might have gotten off the bus. But I chose to remain."

If you analyze Rosa Parks's empowered refusal from the lens of the stadium proposal moment, you will see that she had a lot going against her and very little going for her. She was a Black woman disobeying the instructions of a White driver in the Deep South in the 1950s. Others, men included, simply got up and vacated their seats, but she did not. It was late, probably getting dark and close to dinnertime, and it was she who was holding up the bus. Exasperated people started getting off the bus and asking for transfers so they could continue their journeys home. She was likely aware that she was inconveniencing a bunch of people and probably felt the social pressure to comply.

What made her stick to her position? Perhaps recognizing the driver and reliving the incident from 1943 made her realize that she had to stand her ground. She later wrote that the situation called to mind her grandfather and all the fears they had lived with for years. She did not let some angry stares and a darkening sky stop her from standing up for what she believed in. She needed to focus on the big picture. In her autobiography she wrote, "I was not tired physically, or no more tired than I usually was at the end of a working day. I was not old, although some people have an image of me as being old then. I was forty-two. No, the only tired I was, was tired of giving in." Her strength came from overcoming her fears. She also wrote, "You must never be fearful about what you are when it is right."

Now that you recognize the situations that make the glare of the spotlight and the negative emotions that accompany it feel more intense, you can begin to manage your response to the stadium proposal moments in your own life with three broad strategies:

→ **Be prepared:** Invest in a network, prepare your responses based on your values and priorities, and share them.
→ **Diffuse the spotlight:** Implement strategic postponement and scenario thinking, and imagine advising a friend in the same circumstances.
→ **Stand your ground and resist the pressure.**

Remember, the idea here is to focus your talent and energy on the few situations in which you can make a real difference for yourself. Develop the skill to walk away from all the other situations that make claims on your time and energy—as deserving as they might be. If you think this is hard for you, remember author Robin Sharma's wise observation: "All change is hard at first, messy in the middle, and so gorgeous at the end."

By now, I hope you agree that there is a preponderance of evidence that refusing a request is hard, and the feeling of being in the spotlight is real. Now let's delve into the art (and science) of empowered refusal.

CHAPTER 3

The Art (and Science) of Empowered Refusal

American ballet was in its infancy in the early 1900s. In fact, at that time the words *American* and *ballet* did not go together. American ballet productions struggled to compete with their counterparts in Paris or Moscow. In fact, to garner any audience interest, a ballet performance had to originate, or at the very least *appear* to originate, in Europe. Nothing else would do. Most ballet dancers, particularly those who rose to prima ballerina status, were of French or Russian origin.

In ballet, as in a lot of things in life, origins matter. The provenance of things helps us deem them authentic. We want our whisky to be Scottish, our watches Swiss-made, our leather goods Italian, and our celebratory sparkling wine from Champagne.

But fate does not know geography. Ballerinas can be born anywhere. Elizabeth Marie Tall Chief,[1] future prima ballerina of the New York City Ballet, was born in Fairfax, Oklahoma, on an Osage tribal reservation, to an Osage Indian father, Alexander Joseph Tall Chief, and a Scottish Irish mother, Ruth Porter. When they were young girls, Betty Marie, as she was then called, and her sister Marjorie sang songs and performed Indian dances at county fairs and community gatherings to celebrate their heritage.

Betty Marie had started taking ballet lessons when she was just three years old in the basement of a local hotel. Before long, she had outdone her contemporaries and was showing extraordinary promise. Recognizing the talent of both her daughters, Ruth moved the family to Los Angeles so that her girls could have better opportunities to learn from professional instructors. After graduating from Beverly Hills High, Betty Marie moved to New York and joined the Ballet Russe de Monte Carlo, a predominantly Russian ballet group where she began her professional dance career.

Things seemed to be going reasonably well for Betty Marie, despite the not-so-infrequent scraps and petty resentments between the American and Russian dancers. The hostility took a whole new form when Betty Marie was selected for a key role in a ballet. Despite her exquisite performances, her fellow dancers could not get past her heritage and made her life very difficult to endure.

Still, through most of the 1940s, she became one of the Ballet Russe's star ballerinas and eventually went on to become the first prima ballerina of the New York City Ballet. But this transition was not exactly a smooth one. The biggest barrier she faced was something she could not change—who she was. She had the talent needed to be successful, but as far as the professional ballet world was concerned she had the wrong name, an atypical look, and an uncommon identity.

In fact, the Ballet Russe's director advised her early on to change her last name to the more Russian sounding Tallchieva. In a ballet culture dominated by Europeans, it is not surprising that Maria Tallchief was asked to "fit in."

"Never," Maria Tallchief proudly said in response to this attempt at "covering" her identity.

In his book *Covering,* Harvard law professor Kenji Yoshino says that "everyone covers." When our social identities are looked at with disfavor, we tone down those identities. For instance, one might avoid wearing a traditional headdress, conceal a physical deformity, or change a name to hide one's heritage. Covering typically involves concealing an aspect of who you are in order to gain the approval of others.[2]

In showbiz, it is not uncommon to choose a stage name. After all, Marilyn Monroe was born Norma Jeane Mortenson. Kirk Douglas used the name Issur Danielovitch Demsky to sign up for auditions. Tallchief did eventually agree to change her first name from Betty Marie to Maria, but she insisted on keeping her Osage heritage intact. No one would have blinked if she'd also adopted Tallchieva, but nearly fifty years later, at a Kennedy Center event to celebrate her illustrious dance career, Maria Tallchief vividly recalled how much honoring her heritage mattered to her. As she narrated her story she told the audience that the ballet company had not anticipated that she would refuse the name change and had, in fact, gone ahead and printed the name "Tallchieva" inside all her outfits.

One's name is intricately linked to one's identity. Maria had confidence in her ability to perform with excellence and captivate her audiences with her artistry. She also had the experience of being put down because of her background, which most likely had strengthened her resolve to stand up for who she was. By proudly showcasing her heritage and openly promoting the need for diversity in the world of ballet, Maria Tallchief broke down the longstanding ethnic barriers to pave the way for great performers like Debra Austin, the first African American to be promoted to principal dancer at the Philadelphia Ballet; Lauren Anderson, the first African American to be promoted to principal dancer at the Houston Ballet; and, most recently, Misty Copeland, who made history as the first African American female principal dancer with the American Ballet Theatre. Imagine where American ballet would be if Maria Tallchief had chosen cover instead of courage.

Who we are is to be acknowledged and embraced, not covered up. We need to have the courage to say no to attempts by others to gloss over essential aspects of who we are, what we care about and what we find meaning in. Occasionally, we even have to push back again and again because people choose not to hear.

Puerto Rican–born Major League right fielder Roberto Clemente's eighteen-year baseball career was nothing short of legendary. Despite his humble beginnings as the son of a sugarcane farmer, Clemente became a two-time World Series champion, a fifteen-time All-Star, twelve-time Gold Glove winner, and the first Latin American player inducted into the National Baseball Hall of Fame. But this rise was not without its challenges. One notable slight that Roberto frequently experienced was the media's efforts to discount his Hispanic heritage. A story on the official website for the National Baseball Hall of Fame describes this attempt at covering[3]: "A number of writers and broadcasters insisted on calling Clemente Bob or Bobby instead of his given name of Roberto. Even Clemente's baseball cards listed him as "Bob Clemente," a practice that persisted through the 1969 Topps set. Clemente did not approve of the effort to Americanize him. He felt that it was disrespectful to his Puerto Rican and Latino heritage. When members of the media interviewed him and called him Bob or Bobby directly, he would correct them. "My name is Roberto Clemente," he said repeatedly.

There are similarities between the stories of Maria Tallchief, Roberto Clemente, and scores of other individuals whose empowered no stems from deep-rooted values that originate in their identity. As we will learn, the secret sauce behind empowered refusal—saying no effectively and persuasively from a place of personal power—is to ground your refusal in who you are, what you value, and what you find meaningful. We will learn that a no that reflects your identity is an authentic and empowered response to an ask, and one that gains compliance, not pushback, from the asker.

Empowered Refusal

Saying no is what some might call a "wicked" problem.[4] Compared to easily managed tame problems, wicked problems are hard to manage and have an inbuilt complexity that defies easy resolution. As we have discussed, saying no can be a harmony-busting response that requires us to balance the expectations of others with our own needs. We have pinpointed that we worry that our noes might alienate our colleagues and friends and damage our reputation. It is this dynamic and interconnected nature of the power of social influence, our desire to fit in, the complex interpersonal concerns for maintaining good relationships, and securing a good reputation for ourselves, that makes saying no so hard.

This is where empowered refusal comes in. Even wicked problems can have solutions. When faced with a request that we want to refuse, our natural tendency is to look outward and consider the demands of the other person. We might feel guilty for saying no, worry about the pushback we might receive or the backlash that might ensue. Empowered refusal requires you to turn that natural response on its head and do quite the opposite. Empowered refusal begins with you. With empowered refusal, you need to turn inward and put yourself—your identity, who you are—at the center of your decision to say yes or no. Empowered refusal is a way of saying no that effectively conveys your stance based on your values, preferences, and priorities.

An empowered no comes from allowing your true and authentic self to shine through. No one can bestow power on you; you must find the power within yourself. Keep in mind that these feelings of power are not positional—they do not come from having a powerful place in a hierarchy or getting elected to a prominent position. When your actions reflect your authentic self and you act on your true values, you implicitly tell yourself that *you* are worthy. This self-affirmation of your worth as an individual is empowering and fuels you with personal power to refuse the things that come your way that you do not want to do.

Because empowered refusal comes from a place of personal power, it puts you in the driver's seat of your own life and is less likely to invite pushback, to strain or damage your relationship with the asker, or to hurt your own reputation.[5]

EMPOWERMENT COMES FROM LOOKING WITHIN AND AFFIRMING YOURSELF

Researchers often use the "ultimatum game" to look at how people make social decisions (i.e., decisions in which more than one person is involved and where the individuals are concerned with their self-interest as well as the interests of others). In the ultimatum game, there is a proposer and a responder who are given an amount of money that they get to split. The proposer decides how to split the money, and the responder has to decide whether to accept the offer (the money is split based on the proposer's offer) or to reject it (both players walk away with nothing). Based on a reward maximization theory, if you are the responder, you should accept any offer, because walking away with some money is better than walking away with nothing.

But as human beings, we are programmed to want fairness in our interactions, and we can immediately detect when we are being taken advantage of. Feeling taken advantage of or being used by others is the worst kind of feeling. This is why in an ultimatum game, when responders get less than 30 percent of the total sum to be split, they sometimes reject the offer. If the amount to be split was $10 and the responder offered $2, it is likely that you would forego that $2 (and have the responder forego $8) and walk away with nothing instead of being treated unfairly.

In research designed to demonstrate how self-affirmation might boost the rejection of unfair offers, Ruolei Gu and colleagues set up an ultimatum game scenario to test their hypothesis.[6] They divided their participants into two groups—one given a self-affirmation task and the other given no task (the experimental control). Members of the self-affirmation group were asked to choose one value from a set of four domains (knowledge, wealth, creativity, and social network) that they and their family cherished. They then had to write about why that value was important to them and relate an incident in their life that reflected that value. Reflecting on our values and how they play out in our daily lives is a method researchers use to remind people of who they are.[7]

Each participant received twenty Chinese Yuan as payment for participating in the study but could earn more by accepting the terms of the offer presented to them. Each offer was for ten Yuan (approximately $1.50 USD). What the researchers found is that, as expected, fair offers (twenty rounds of equitable offers were made where the splits were 50:50 or 40:60) were accepted in both the self-affirmed and control group, but the self-affirmed group were more likely than the control group to reject an unfair offer (twenty rounds of inequitable offers were made where the splits were 10:90 or 20:80). When we reflect on what we value, we give voice to those values in how we make decisions.

What I have not mentioned yet is that these participants were also hooked up to an EEG machine (electroencephalogram) during this study, and their brain activity was being recorded as they made their decision to accept or reject the offer. The brain data showed that the pattern of brain activity of self-affirmed participants was different from that of control participants. The authors conclude that self-affirmation boosts people's psychological resources to allow them to reject unfair offers. When we look within and affirm our own values and give voice to them, it empowers us to refuse an offer that does not align with what we value.

EMPOWERMENT FUELS US TO ACT IN OUR OWN BEST INTEREST

Feeling empowered keeps us open to possibilities and gives us the permission to act in accordance with the values we hold dear and the strength to withstand the pressure from others to conform.[8]

This feeling of personal power comes from being liberated from social pressure and free from feeling dominated or controlled by others. It comes from within by sweeping the depths of who we are and gaining access to our inner resources.

One of the crucial benefits of feeling empowered is the sense of feeling free from the influence of other people and external forces.[9] In a simple demonstration of what it feels to be empowered, Adam Galinsky and his colleagues showed that when participants in their study were faced with an annoyance (in their case a fan blowing in the participant's face), whether they took the initiative to remove it or did not depended on their feelings of empowerment. Sixty-nine percent of the empowered participants turned the fan away or turned it off, compared with 42 percent of the disempowered participants. When we are empowered, we are more likely to act in our own best interest and deal with an annoyance instead of simply enduring it.

Numerous studies show that empowered individuals are more likely to make the first offer in a negotiation, debate a contentious issue, and haggle over the price of a car.[10] Feeling powerful liberates us from the confines of a situation and gives us the freedom to act in accordance with our own interests. Feeling empowered also makes us feel that we have access to the resources we need to handle a situation. It allows us to think more abstractly about an issue and see relationships and patterns. When you feel empowered you not only might be able to say no, but also, you might find novel solutions to help the other person.

When we are empowered, we feel confident, unafraid, and free from the expectations and demands of others.

It is no wonder that the German sociologist, thinker, and

foremost management theorist Max Weber provided one of the first definitions of power in an individual: to have the ability to carry out one's own will.[11] Weber famously railed against bureaucratic organizations and was deeply concerned about the importance of humanity and individual freedom that could be silenced by the "iron cage" of bureaucracy.

EMPOWERMENT HELPS US RELATE TO AND ADVOCATE FOR OTHER PEOPLE

Feeling empowered does not mean that we act selfishly. In fact, research finds that empowered people display greater interpersonal sensitivity. When we feel empowered, we can read other people and relate to them better.[12] To demonstrate this, researchers activated feelings that made people feel more or less powerful. The typical way to do this in the lab is to have people write about a time they had power over another person (powerful) or a time when another person had power over them (powerless). Then they were shown images of faces that displayed different emotional states from anger to sadness to joy and pride. It turned out that feeling powerful made people more accurate in judging the emotional expression in the image. Feeling powerful allows you to relate to and empathize with other people more readily than when you feel powerless. Owning your power boosts your emotional intelligence and provides greater awareness of how you can assist yourself and others in making good decisions and achieve meaningful goals. Research finds that when you feel empowered, you are better able to handle any pushback you might get from others when you say no.

In a similar vein, feeling powerful also makes you more likely to forgive others' transgressions. Empowerment can give you the ability to empathize with the asker's need, to think on your feet, and come up with a solution, without having to say yes to the request yourself. Personal power can help us lean into our vulnerability and compassion without losing ourselves in the process.

I used the term "empowered refusal," in my research to introduce the idea that there was an effective way to say no that stemmed from the speaker's identity to convey personal power and the feeling of being in control. The initial work that I published together with Henrik Hagtvedt was based on the insight that most people know that they need to say no more, and even what they need to say no to, but they do not know *how* to effectively communicate that no. Specifically, our research identified a novel way to say no that puts you in the driver's seat of your own life. And all it took was two words.

"Standing up" Words

Empowered refusal boils down to being an act of communication. Effective communication involves considering *what* information is conveyed (content) but also on *how* that information is conveyed (manner and style).

I regularly ask the participants in my executive leadership classes, to please say these sentences with me:

"I don't work on weekends."
"I never take the elevator when I can take the stairs."
"I will not take a red-eye flight."
"I always start my day with meditation."
"I don't take phone calls between 6:00 and 9:00 p.m."

I then ask, "How do you feel when you say these words?" The common responses are that these words feel "powerful," "firm," "determined," "strong," and "decisive." My favorite response came from a participant who said, "When you say these words, you stand up tall."

The words we use matter. When we say, "I don't..." "I never..." "I always..." they reflect conviction and determination. These "standing up" words are empowered—they convey your stance on a matter and do not invite pushback. This is exactly what my research shows: the empowered "standing up" phrase "*I don't*" is more persuasive than it's helpless and disempowered "*I can't*" counterpart.

My empowered refusal research is grounded in the idea that the words we use to frame our refusal matters. When we say "I don't," we come across as empowered and in control. In contrast, when we say "I can't," we come across as disempowered, helpless, and weak—a victim of our circumstances.

When refusing an invitation to go out to a bar on a Tuesday night, you might say, "I don't go out on weekdays." If you are being pulled into a meeting at 8:00 a.m. when you have scheduled that time to get your day on track, you might say, "I don't do early morning meetings." When saying no to someone who is offering you a slice of chocolate cake you might say, "I don't eat chocolate cake." This even works when we talk to ourselves. Sometimes we have to talk ourselves out of succumbing to temptation. You might have to occasionally tell yourself, "I don't skip the gym," or "I don't take phone calls during dinner." Saying "I don't" conveys that you are your own boss and your words communicate your stance on a matter. You leave no room for negotiation. There is enormous power in saying no to the things that you do not want to do, but also enormous power in recognizing and practicing the most effective way to do it. In our research article, we write "using the word 'don't' serves as a self-affirmation of one's personal willpower and control in the relevant self-regulatory goal pursuit, leading to a favorable influence on feelings of empowerment, as well as on actual behavior. On the other hand, saying 'I can't do X' connotes an external focus on impediments."[13]

Try replacing each of these examples above with "I can't" and see the power seep away from your words. When you say "I can't come to an early morning meeting," "I can't eat chocolate cake," or "I can't take phone calls during dinner," your words convey your helplessness and your lack of control, and worst of all, invite pushback from others. When you say "I can't..." your words may be interpreted as "I'd really like to, but...." In fact, as soon as you utter the words I can't, it begs the question, "Why not?" Or even, "Who says?" This invites debate, counteroffers, and small compromises by the asker. If you are clear that this is not something you want to do, then I can't should be banished from your vocabulary, because it suggests that in another set of circumstances you would gladly take it on.

William Dean Howell quoted Mark Twain in *My Mark Twain,* saying, "A powerful agent is the right word. Whenever we come upon one of those intensely right words...the resulting effect is physical as well as spiritual, and electrically prompt." Replacing I can't with the "intensely right" I don't makes your refusal sound final, nonarguable, and empowered.[14]

The Science behind Empowered Refusal

Henrik and I designed a set of research studies to show that when you use language that implicates your identity, you convey conviction and determination and are less likely to receive pushback from the asker.[15]

In one study, we created mock sales scenarios. Students who were part of the University of Houston's Sales Excellence program participated in this study. They were tasked with cold-calling people door-to-door to sell magazine subscriptions. They were partnered with a potential client. What they did not know was that the "client" was trained by us to refuse the salesperson by using either "empowered" language or "disempowered" language. One half of the clients were given empowered refusal training using scripts like, "I don't make decisions to buy without advance planning," "I never buy a subscription without consulting my family," or "I won't be purchasing any magazines today." The other half were given disempowering scripts that used powerless language like, "I can't make decisions to buy without advance planning," "I shouldn't buy a subscription without consulting my family," or "I am not able to purchase any magazines today." After the sales interaction, each salesperson was asked to report on the interaction and how successful they felt they were in persuading the client. Specifically, they reported on how determined, committed, and convincing the client was (on a scale of 1 = not at all; 9 = very much) and also rated how persuasive the client's refusal was (on a scale of 1 = not at all; 9 = very much).

As you might already suspect, when the client used disempowered language, the salesperson saw them as easy targets (see Figure 3.1). They did not come across as committed in their refusal and were more likely to get pushback from the salesperson. They were also seen as less persuasive in their refusal. In contrast, when the client used empowered language, the salesperson was more convinced that they were committed and determined not to buy the magazine subscription and also came across as more persuasive in their refusal.

Figure 3.1

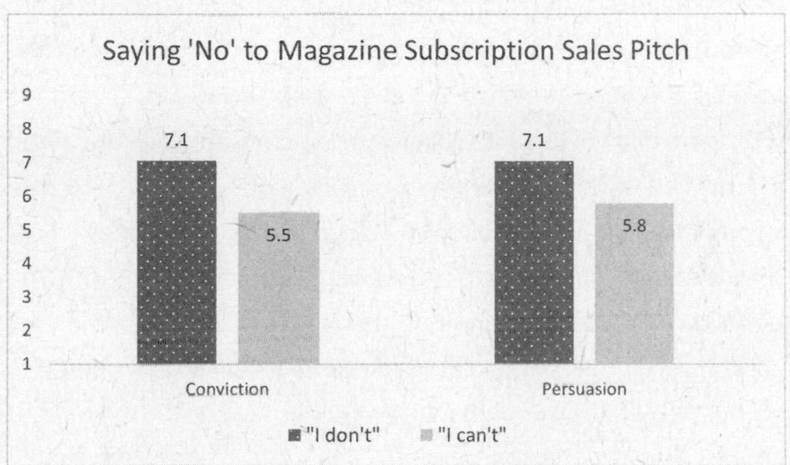

Grounding your language in your identity has powerful implications because people tend to respond, and respond positively, to YOU.

In a second study, we asked people to imagine that they were hosting a party and had chosen a rich chocolate cake to serve for dessert. They were told that one of their guests refused the offer of dessert either saying, "I don't eat chocolate cake," or, "I can't eat chocolate cake." They were then asked to report the extent to which the guest's refusal conveyed conviction and how persuasive their guest's response was (in a similar manner as the magazine subscription study, scored on a scale of 1–9 where 1 = to a low degree and 9 = to a high degree). They were also asked their impressions of whether their guest's refusal was identity-based (i.e., conveyed his/her identity and stance as an individual). With this question, we were attempting to demonstrate that identity-based refusals convey greater conviction and are more persuasive. Figure 3.2 shows that in the experimental condition in which the guest used the words "I don't" to refuse the offer of dessert, the refusal was perceived to be more grounded in the identity of the guest, conveyed greater conviction, and was more persuasive when compared with the experimental condition in which the guest used the words "I can't" to refuse the offer of dessert. This result supports the idea that when you say "I don't," you are firmly closing the door on an issue by conveying conviction and a decisive stance that does not allow room for debate and pushback. Your choice of the words "I don't" are persuasive because they indicate that your decision is based on a hard-and-fast rule that you have set for yourself.

Figure 3.2

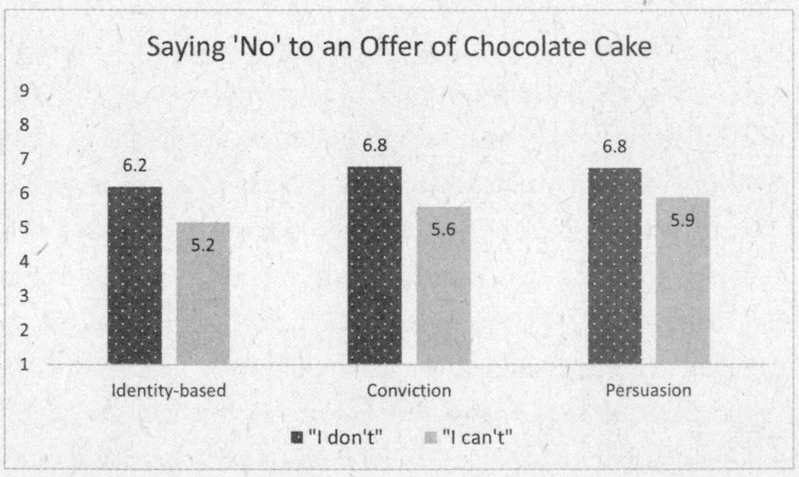

According to communications expert Holly Weeks, people usually argue their no backwards.[16] They might open with an anecdote or provide flimsy reasons for rejecting a request, rather than getting straight to the point and conveying their no by using empowering language. A roundabout way to getting to no can be counterproductive. People value honesty, and there is nothing more honest and sincere than a refusal that stems from your identity to give voice to who you are and what you care about.

Practice using powerful "standing up" words like *don't* or *won't* to communicate your refusal and connote determination, commitment, control, and empowerment. These words convey a decisive, permanent state of being, tied to your identity and character. They do not invite negotiation from others, because they reflect a firmly entrenched attitude rather than a temporary stance on a matter. Avoid powerless words like *can't, shouldn't,* or *oughtn't* that signal deprivation, loss of control, and even helplessness. Because these words invoke an external cause, they come across as excuses and invite discussion, debate, and negotiation.[17]

"I Don't" vs. "I Can't" as Self-Talk

Our choice of words matters even when we talk to ourselves. The voice in your head saying no to you works much the same way as saying no to others. Using identity-based language to convey to yourself a decision you have made or a stance you are committed to is empowering. For instance, telling yourself, "I don't eat dessert," is likely to shape your behavior when you walk by the dessert tray. Having a personal policy like, "I don't respond to emails first thing in the morning," is likely to keep you on track with your exercise routine, your meditation practice, or your daily writing before you get sucked into your inbox. Even when speaking to yourself, the words *I don't* convey a strong, powerful stance leaving no room for debate.

In another series of studies, Henrik and I demonstrated that using a phrase like *I don't* has a powerful effect on how we respond to temptation, not only in the moment, but also over time.[18] What we wanted to show was that by saying *I don't*, you are communicating to yourself: (1) I have made a decision, (2) I am in control, and (3) I have the power in this moment over how I will respond to this temptation.

In our studies, we showed that the way a statement was framed affected how well people could stick to it. Saying "I don't eat X" when tempted by an unhealthy snack, for example, made participants feel more psychologically empowered than using can't. The same held true with a scenario about resolving to exercise each day: "I don't skip my workout" was a more powerful motivator to get to the gym than "I can't skip my workout."

In one experiment, thirty women, ages twenty-two to fifty-three, undertook a ten-day wellness challenge involving goals like exercising more and eating more healthily. The women were divided into three groups: one was asked to use the I don't strategy, another the I can't strategy, and a third (the control group) was simply told to say no to temptations. We sent out a daily email to remind the women to use the strategies they were given. What we found was that using empowering language (I don't) as self-talk kept participants on track with their goals more so than the other strategies did. On average, women in the don't group persisted on their goals for 9.2 days of the ten-day wellness challenge, while the women in the can't group persisted for only 2.9 days. The control group who were told to say no without any specific instructions persisted for an average of 5.2 days. Another way to look at these numbers is to look at the number of people who stuck with the program for the full duration: only 10 percent of the I can't group, about 33 percent of the control group, but 80 percent of the I don't group were still using the strategy successfully ten days later.

The Facets of Empowered Refusal: Authentic, Concrete, and WOO (Wins Others Over)

There are three facets of empowered refusal that work together to make it more effective than a simple no response. Remember, what I mean by an effective no is that it does not invite pushback; it maintains your relationship with the asker, and it secures your reputation.

- → Empowered refusal implicates your identity to convey **authenticity**. Empowered refusal begins by first looking within and then communicating your refusal based on your values, principles, preferences, and priorities.
- → Empowered refusal involves **clear and concrete** communication to express conviction. You clearly communicate the refusal response using your whole self, relying on both verbal and nonverbal cues.
- → Empowered refusal is persuasive and helps **win people over**. Because empowered refusal is grounded in one's identity to convey conviction, it elicits less pushback from others. In this way you have successfully managed to say no, and also keep your relationship with the asker intact and your reputation untouched.

Let's go deeper into each of these facets to establish why empowered refusal works.

EMPOWERED REFUSAL IMPLICATES YOUR IDENTITY TO CONVEY AUTHENTICITY

One way to respond to a request is to provide a reason to say no. Reasons and excuses typically fall into two basic categories: those stemming from within oneself and those stemming from outside oneself.[19] Looking within to understand *why* you want to say no and linking your response to your values, preferences, principles, and priorities reflect your authentic self. When considering a request, if you look within yourself and think about your purpose—what is meaningful for you and what truly matters—it can become clear what your response needs to be. In Chapter 5, we will discuss how to use personal policies (simple rules we set for ourselves) as valid reasons to make your refusal more compelling and your decision to say no more persuasive.

When constructing a refusal based on your identity, remember that the choice of words you use can signal your authentic identity. A practical example of this comes from research on encouraging voting behavior. This research demonstrates that invoking the self is sufficient to significantly influence whether individuals vote in presidential and gubernatorial elections.[20] In this study, the manipulation of identity relied on framing questions about voting behavior as a verb or a noun (e.g., "How important is it to you to vote [be a voter] in the upcoming election?"). Nouns were expected to invoke identity to a higher degree, and indeed, they encouraged voting to a higher degree. Specifically, when you get a sticker that says, "I am a voter," you are more likely to go vote that when you get a sticker that says, "I vote." The former implicates your identity whereas the latter implicates your behavior.

Practice identifying the nouns that describe you as a person and reflect your true identity instead of words that describe your behaviors or how you spend your time. Make a list of the things that make you the person you are. For instance, if I tell you the following information about myself using nouns:

I am a writer.
I am a mom.
I am a teacher.
I am a reader.

You are more likely to be persuaded that these aspects are a core part of me.

Compare this to your reaction if I use verbs to describe my behaviors (what I do):

I write.
I parent.
I teach.
I read.

In the latter case, the verbs represent actions that may or may not be grounded in my core identity, and they subtly convey that they are activities that I perform but are not necessarily ones I am committed to or do with passion and curiosity.

Try to use nouns to frame your refusal (and your personal policies) rather than verbs that describe your actions and behavior. You can also utilize verbs if you set up very specific information around them that indicate how those actions and behaviors take place that reflect your unique preferences. You might say, "I write between 7:00 a.m. and 8:00 a.m.," which is specifically tailored to you, or "When I teach, I am 100 percent focused on student success."

EMPOWERED REFUSAL USES CLEAR AND CONCRETE CUES TO EXPRESS CONVICTION

It seems pretty obvious that if you want to say no, your words should communicate that refusal response. Quite often, however, people struggle so much to say no that they walk away from the interaction, leaving both themselves and the other party wondering where they stand. In Chapter 2 we saw evidence for what I called a wishy-washy no.

Using the words *I don't* conveys with clarity the conviction and determination behind our refusal. Remember, our language can make us feel powerful or powerless. When we say, "I am the kind of person who..." or "I don't..." we not only sound empowered, but also, we feel empowered. Remember a time you were filled with conviction and determination. Think about how it *felt* to be determined and have strong conviction about something. This is a feeling that can take over your mind and body. It becomes central to who you are, and it suffuses you with a sense of indescribable power and energy. This feeling of conviction is the invisible force that drives the effectiveness of an empowered refusal.

You can boost your refusal by using additional words that make your "standing up" words stand even taller. Adding *absolutist words* that reflect your core beliefs and a long-term unwavering commitment to your stance can amplify your I don't response. These words include *always*, *never*, forever, and *completely*. Saying, "I always have dinner with my family," indicates that there is no room for debate. You don't allow wiggle room when you say, "I never take on a new project unless I have the bandwidth to give it my best." You're able to handle a pushy salesperson when you say, "I am completely committed to my (your preferred brand), so I am not interested in this offer." Even if you try to put disempowered words in these sentences, they don't sound right or even make sense.

Research finds that although expert witnesses are chosen by legal teams for their expertise (obviously!), in the courtroom their on-paper qualifications are not enough. One study looked at the testimonies of expert witnesses to identify specific speech markers of expert witnesses who peppered their answers with *submissive filler* words. The researchers found that adding verbal hesitations ("like," "you know," "I mean") or nonverbal hesitations (like "umm," "ehh," etc.) diminished perceptions of expertise. Ending sentences with tag questions ("That's how it happened, isn't it?") or adding hedges ("I guess," "sort of,") are the strongest indicators of low power or submissive speech.[21] In our effort to be nice, we tend to use submissive words to soften the blow of a refusal, "but umm," "you know, it is really, really hard for me to take this on." "Therefore, I guess I will have to say no this time around...." "Err, I sort of feel bad, but that how life is, isn't it?" Using submissive language does not convey that you are nice and care about the relationship, it is an invitation for pushback. We must learn to monitor our speech to avoid submissive filler words.

Sometimes when we are trying to soften the blow of a refusal, we also rely on vague or fuzzy language. Research finds that vague or abstract language can come across as hand-waving and sound insincere, less credible, and even biased and deceptive.[22] In contrast, when we use concrete language, the person we are speaking to feels seen, heard, and valued. Researchers Grant Packard and Jonah Berger examine the use of concrete vs. abstract language in sales communication.[23] These researchers found that when customer service representatives used concrete language, it boosted customer satisfaction and made customers more inclined to return and spend more in the future. Consider why this is the case. If you are a customer care representative, it's easy to say, "I'll help you with that." But in an interview, Jonah Berger explained why that phrase can seem formulaic and does not show the customer that you really listened to them. He said, "When I don't just say, 'I'll help you with that,' but, 'Sure, I'll help you get your flight rebooked from Denver to Philadelphia,' it shows you that I heard what you said, that I was listening, that I paid attention, and that I'm more likely to be able to help you in the future. Concreteness works because it makes people feel like you're listening." He adds: "But both organizations and individuals want to make people feel like we heard them. Whether we're trying to sell something or we're talking to our spouse, people like being listened to. They like feeling like others heard them. How can we communicate that we heard what others are saying? That's the reason why concrete language is more beneficial."

When the words we use are vague and abstract, especially when the information conveyed is negative, like saying no, listeners tend to think that the person has an ulterior motive or has something to hide. Let's imagine that your friend Jackie asks you to join her and a group of friends for a luxurious spa day. You decide you do not want to go because it does not fit in your budget at the moment. Embarrassed to mention money as the reason, you might resort to abstract and vague language, saying for instance, "I just don't feel like it." Instead, conveying a more concrete stance, saying for instance, "It sounds fun, but I do not have the budget for it," is more persuasive, making the listener feel that you are committed to your refusal, and it is grounded in something substantial.

Uncertain, waffling speech is a sure way to leak personal power, ultimately damaging your relationship with the asker and hurting your reputation. The insight here is that your internal feelings get reflected in your speech. If you are feeling powerless and without conviction, then your words tend to reflect that mindset. Because empowered refusal stems from your identity and who you are, it fuels your determination and so you convey that in the words you use.

In Chapter 6, we will delve deeper into how to bring your whole self—including verbal and nonverbal cues—to craft a persuasive and empowered refusal. But for now, it is important to remember that there is no *one* right way to communicate an empowered no, because each one of us has our own unique identity, our own value system and set of priorities, and consequently our own authentic basis for our empowered refusal. As long as you remember the different facets of empowered refusal, you will be able to craft one for yourself.

EMPOWERED REFUSAL IS PERSUASIVE AND WINS OTHERS OVER

How do you assess whether your refusal is effective? One of the key factors that determine whether a refusal is effective is compliance from others without pushback or reputation loss. Empowered refusal keeps things real, and keeping things real garners respect from others. When you say no by first looking within and communicate that refusal based on what you value, what your priorities, preferences, and principles are, that no is an authentic no.

In the studies on empowered refusal I described previously, the data shows that empowered refusal is persuasive and does not invite pushback. I am going to lean on one of my favorite books—the Newberry Award–winning book *The Twenty-One Balloons,* by William Pene du Bois—to illustrate how you can say no and yet garner support and encouragement to do what you believe is right.

Imagine being rescued in the middle of the Atlantic Ocean dressed to the nines in a white evening suit, hanging onto a piece of wood for dear life, surrounded by twenty balloons in various stages of deflation. This is the state in which the captain of the freighter S.S. *Cunningham* found Professor William Waterman Sherman. Naturally, everyone on the ship was curious about how the professor had got himself into such an inconvenient state—in the middle of the ocean surrounded by balloons! Unlike our tendency today to spill the beans about every little mundane aspect of our lives on every social media account from Twitter to Facebook to Instagram, the professor held his tongue. En route to New York, the captain of the freighter cajoled and pleaded with the professor to share his story. The cook laid out carefully prepared meals for the professor to help him regain his strength, and the ship doctor nursed him to health, all with the secret hope that they would be the first to hear the story. But the professor remained steadfast in his refusal.

By the time he reached New York, the president of the United States had heard about the incident and was so intrigued by the mystery of the marooned schoolmaster that he sought to meet him. Can you say no to the president? Well, Professor Sherman did.

The professor graciously declined to tell his tale even to the highest power of the nation. Why? Whether it was the ship captain, the doctor, the cook, or even the president, Professor Sherman's refusal was grounded in his loyalty to his fellow explorers at the Western American Explorer Club in San Francisco. In fact, instead of being offended at his request being rebuffed, the president proceeded to arrange for the professor to reach San Francisco at the earliest so that he could tell his story to his club members and satiate the curiosity of the rest of the world, all waiting with bated breath to find out what really happened.

Although there is much to love and laugh about in this tale, Professor Sherman's refusal illustrates the elements of empowered refusal laid out here. His refusal stemmed from his integrity and loyalty to the Explorer Club, and he remained firm in his refusal regardless of whether the ship's cook or the president tried to coax an explanation out of him. Despite the undignified state in which he was found in the ocean, he did not act in an undignified way. Furthermore, instead of being angered by his refusal, the people around him gave him the support he needed for his mission to get to San Francisco and the Explorer Club. He had won them over.

A key takeaway from this story is that you *can* say no to the person who rescues you, to the cook who sustains you, to the doctor who helps you regain your life, and even to the president of the United States, if your refusal conveys authenticity and is grounded in your identity.

I hope you, dear reader, are now ready to access the empowered refusal toolkit. Now that we understand the facets of empowered refusal and understand why and how it works, how do we become better at saying no in an empowered way? What skills do we need to learn? What competences do we need to develop to be able to enact an empowered refusal when the time comes? In the next part of the book, we will delve into three competencies that we need to develop and practice to master the A.R.T. (**A**wareness. **R**ules, not Decisions. **T**otality of Self) of empowered refusal that puts you in the driver's seat of your own life.

This is where our journey to practice the art of empowered refusal begins. Let's dive in.

PART 2

THE A.R.T. OF EMPOWERED REFUSAL: COMPETENCIES FOR CRAFTING YOUR EMPOWERED REFUSAL

CHAPTER 4

Looking Inward to Develop Self-Awareness

On the banks of the Pampa River in Kerala, a southern state in the subcontinent of India, is the tiny village of Aranmula. The families that occupy the homes and thatched workshops that dot the shores of the Pampa are the descendants of eight families who founded the village nearly five hundred years ago. As the story goes, a royal chief of the local area dreamed of building a grand temple, so he brought in expert artisans and their families from the neighboring state of Tamil Nadu to work on the mirrors of the Parthasarathy temple.

Today Aranmula looks pretty much like any small riverbank town in southern India, with a school, a medical clinic, a weekly market, and, of course, the Parthasarathy temple dominating the landscape. But this village is anything but ordinary. It is the hub of a creative industry that is famous for a flagship creation: the *Aranmula kannadi*. *Kannadi* is the word for mirror in Malayalam, the language of the people of Kerala. But the kannadi from Aranmula is quite different from the normal silvered mirrors that we all know and commonly use.

The uniqueness of the Aranmula kannadi comes from the fact that it is a first surface mirror where the reflective material, a highly polished metal alloy of tin and lead, is itself the reflective surface. This is unlike conventional mirrors whose reflective material, typically mercury or aluminum, lies below a transparent surface of glass or acrylic. Legend has it that a divine source revealed the composition of the alloy to one of the original artisans of the Parthasarathy temple in a dream. It has remained a trade secret handed down from one artisan generation to the next for the past five hundred years.

In South India, the Aranmula kannadi is considered an auspicious symbol that represents purity of the soul. It is said to bring prosperity and luck to the owner, so much so that it is one of eight auspicious items or *ashtamangalyam* that accompany a South Indian bride to her new home on her wedding day. The Aranmula kannadi symbolizes the untarnished truth, and its daily use prompts self-reflection as a path to personal growth, success, and prosperity.

Empowered Refusal Begins by Looking Within

When we gain self-awareness, we add to the store of self-knowledge that we can rely on to inform our behavior and shape our actions. By taking the time to see ourselves clearly, we come to understand our traits, motivations, and behavior. We gain insight into our values, our purpose, and what we find meaningful and engaging. We become familiar with our goals, desires, and ambitions, as well as the store of talent, skills, knowledge, and experience that we possess to make our aspirations a reality. With self-knowledge, we gain a clear understanding of what we are uniquely capable of and what we bring to the table. The wisdom we gain through introspection enables us to act authentically and in accordance with our true self.

One of the characteristics that makes us human and distinguishes us from other species in the animal kingdom is this capacity for self-awareness. Research finds that humans are uniquely able to shift their attention from the environment to look within themselves—and can do the reverse as well, to look at themselves from the perspective of others.[1] When we look inward, we can do so in two possible ways.[2] The first way is *private* or *internal self-awareness* that results when we pay attention to our own thoughts, feelings, and traits. Private self-awareness means having a deep understanding of your own needs and drives, your personal strengths and weaknesses, your preferences, values, and goals, and your emotional responses. However, there is another dimension of self-awareness that is equally valuable, and that is *public* or *external self-awareness*. This facet of self-awareness involves understanding how others see us, and it allows us to feel more empathy toward others and see their perspective. Our capacity to attend to our "looking-glass self"[3] and understand what other people really think of us helps us function more effectively in our social groups. Knowing how others see us gives us an understanding of where we stand in our relationships. Our sense of self and our identity is shaped not only by our internal self-awareness, but also by our interactions with others and the perceptions they have of us as a result of those interactions.

Perhaps one of the most crucial benefits of self-awareness is as a decision-making lens. Personal or private self-awareness provides us with a useful perspective by which to decide what is important to us and what is trivial. It helps us choose actions that have long-term benefits and nudges us to give up actions that have only short-term gains. People who are self-aware also exude self-confidence and convey personal power in the stance that they take.[4] They know what their capabilities are and they make sound decisions, communicate more effectively, and build stronger relationships—qualities that set them up for success. In fact, leaders who are self-aware are taken more seriously, have more satisfied employees, and run more profitable companies.[5]

Someone who is self-aware will be able to turn down a financially tempting job offer when it does not map onto their values or long-term priorities. In contrast, a person who lacks self-awareness might make take on a job because of the money or the prestige, but this could ultimately result in uncomfortable feelings of inauthenticity and internal strife. It is no wonder that people who are self-aware are likely to have a stronger reputation for walking the talk. Indeed one of the gifts of aging is that we have more data points on ourselves to understand and reflect on ourselves and develop self-knowledge. Pope John Paul II once mused, "The more sand that has escaped from the hourglass of our life, the clearer we should see through it."

Recall that a central aspect of empowered refusal is to ground your refusal in your identity by giving voice to your values, priorities, beliefs, and preferences. We must learn how to go about investing in self-reflection to glean valuable self-insight that can undergird our empowered refusal. For instance, if you want to say no but you cannot identify the reason behind your inclination, you must ask yourself whether you are simply procrastinating, feeling lazy, or fearful of the task. For empowered refusal to work, it must reflect your true identity, not a superficial analysis of a situation that might change from day to day. It needs to reflect what you are committed to, care about, what your goals are, and what you want to do with your life. Empowered refusal does not work for temporary fixes and short-term goals. In one study, Henrik Hagtvedt and I demonstrated that using the "standing up" words *I don't* backfired when they were used to reflect a short-term or temporary goal. From a linguistic perspective saying, "I *don't* eat dessert for two weeks till the wedding," simply makes no sense,[6] since "don't" connotes a permanent stance or personal preference.

Empowered refusal requires that we see ourselves clearly without the distractions, distortions, and aberrations that our current situation might impose on us. Think about it: If you don't take yourself seriously, or if you undermine your own values and dishonor your own intentions, how can you expect other people not to do the same? Ultimately, empowered refusal is more effective when it stems from looking within. It is grounded in the assumption that when you look within you do not come out empty.

The "R" in the A.R.T. of empowered refusal involves putting simple rules or personal policies in place to convey your refusal response. However, a crucial first step in developing a personal policy is the "A"—an awareness and understanding of the background and basis for instituting that rule in the first place. As we will see, with enhanced self-awareness we can develop a deep and more profound understanding of how we like to operate and why we like to operate that way.

Developing a Reflective Mindset

One way to gain self-awareness is through introspection and self-reflection. Executive coach Jennifer Porter observes that the hardest people to coach are those who will not invest in self-reflection to gain self-awareness.[7] So what exactly is self-reflection? Self-reflection is the careful and deep thought and analysis we engage in to learn more about ourselves—our emotions, our thoughts and beliefs, and our actions. Self-reflection provides meaning and understanding about how we operate and how we would like to operate. Conscious and constructive self-reflection can increase happiness and productivity.

Take for instance, a study of commuters in the UK who were encouraged to spend their commute thinking about and planning their day reported feeling happier, more productive, and less burned out than those who didn't.[8] This might explain the huge popularity of gratitude journals that encourage self-reflection about things that we are grateful for and that increase feelings of happiness and well-being.

Other sources of information about ourselves are the people who know us and interact with us. The reflected best-self framework is a useful tool that was devised by a group of organization behavior researchers to help us understand how we come across in the world by obtaining and using feedback from trusted others.[9] By asking the question central to this exercise, "When was I at my best?" we can get insight about strengths that we might not see and take for granted. When I conduct the reflected best-self exercise in my classes, participants are frequently encouraged by the new understanding they get of themselves. They appreciate that the people who interact with them are more likely to point out that they are "professional" or "a good listener" or "adaptable"—aspects of themselves that they would not point out themselves, perhaps because they take those central attributes about themselves for granted. For instance, for you, it might be a given to deliver *what* you say you will, *when* you say you will. But others see you as reliable. While your ability to deal with tough feedback and to persevere despite hardship is simply part of how you might operate, but others admire your resilience and fortitude. This 360-degree feedback offers us valuable insight into how we come across to other people and the impact we already have in the world.

When it comes to getting feedback from others, sometimes we have to demand the honest truth. Research shows that people who are in positions of power and those who are considered experts are less likely to get honest feedback from the people around them. Senior executives are shielded not only from organizational problems, but also from reliable information about themselves. Leaders risk becoming surrounded by a team of "yes-sayers," people who "create an echo chamber that amplifies their views rather than enriching them."[10] It is no wonder that Abraham Lincoln, known for his proclivity for deep introspection, would create a team of his own rivals (men who stood against him during the election) with differing perspectives to help him, as the newly elected president, succeed at his most pressing tasks. The wisdom he gleaned from both internal and external self-awareness prompted Lincoln to "bring his disgruntled opponents together, create the most unusual cabinet in history, and marshal their talents to the task of preserving the Union and winning the war".[11]

Self-awareness is a first step in the path to wisdom and personal mastery. It paves the way for us to lead the best possible life. As will become evident in the next few pages, self-awareness is a crucial competency to develop to be able to say no more effectively. With self-awareness, we can more clearly see what we want to do with our lives and identify our purpose and what is meaningful to us. Having a clear purpose allows us to choose to engage in "good work" and recognize what we'd have to give up in order to do things that are not aligned with our good work (trade-offs and opportunity costs).

Navigating the Landscape of Your Life

Three key and interrelated concepts can help us navigate the landscape of our life to help us identify what we value and pursue what is meaningful to us. The first concept of "purpose" helps us understand the "why" of our existence. Once you know your why, you can identify your most important personal and professional priorities and recognize what "good work" means to you. Good work, the second concept, is how our purpose shines through in what we do and the impact we make on this world. It is often tempting to take on new opportunities, but when we are driven by our purpose to engage in good work, we instantly recognize the "opportunity costs" of taking on work that is not aligned with our purpose. That's the third interrelated concept, and it means recognizing that when we say yes to one thing, we might be saying no to another, possibly more meaningful thing. As such we need to become adept at assessing the trade-offs we have to make with any decision in order to fulfill our purpose and do good and meaningful work.

KNOWING YOUR "WHY"

Purpose is defined as "a stable and generalized intention to accomplish something that is at the same time meaningful to the self and consequential for the world beyond the self."[12] Having a meaningful intention can help keep us focused on the things that are most important to us, such as family, friends, faith, work, and so on. Our purpose allows us to set priorities in our life, giving us the permission we need to say no to people or activities that don't support our goals. Perhaps, most importantly, it gives us the feeling that we are making a difference in the world.

In the business world, Simon Sinek has popularized what he calls the world's simplest idea: identifying your "why." In a popular TED talk, Sinek explains his theory of the "golden circle," saying that the way to inspire cooperation and trust is to think, act, and communicate with a purpose-driven lens.[13] He emphasizes that "people do not buy what you do, but *why* you do it." He argues that it is easy for both people and organizations to describe what they do. Try it. You might be able to describe quite easily how you spend your day doing what you do. It takes work, however, to identify *why* you do what you do. Your why is the compelling reason or motivation that drives you and your work.

Ken Burns, the award-winning documentary filmmaker, has directed and produced some of the most acclaimed documentary films ever made from the Academy Award-nominated *Brooklyn Bridge* in 1981 to *The National Parks: America's Best Idea*. For the past forty years, Burns's work has reflected his purpose: to seek an answer to the question, "Who are we as Americans?"

Clarity of purpose has the extraordinary capacity to help us choose how we approach our work and our life and helps us decide what to take on and what to let go. Aligned with his purpose, Burns chooses to exclusively make movies about American history. He does not approach his subject through political and social movements like a traditional historian would. Instead, he generally begins with personal narratives, and by sharing the story of history from the ground up, he is able to help the viewer to uncover a little bit more about who they are as Americans. Burns's overarching sense of purpose has become his signature—it shapes the projects he takes on and the way he produces the work.

Stephen Covey once observed, "If the ladder is not leaning against the right wall, every step we take just gets us to the wrong place faster." Knowing our purpose is leaning our ladder against the right wall, so that we know we are pursuing what is important and meaningful to us with every ounce of effort we invest.

WHAT DOES "GOOD WORK" MEAN TO YOU?

Since its inception in 1954, Stanford University's Center for Advanced Study in the Behavioral Sciences (CASBS) has brought together thought leaders from diverse behavioral disciplines to address some of the most poignant and puzzling issues that face human beings. It is no wonder then that forty years later, in the fall of 1994, psychologists Howard Gardner, Mihaly (Mike) Csikszentmihalyi, and Bill Damon found themselves discussing issues of creativity and morality during their year at CASBS, discussions that coalesced into their theory of "good work."

What is good work? Gardner and his colleagues propose that good work is characterized as "work that is of excellent technical quality, work that is ethically pursued and socially responsible, and work that is engaging, enjoyable, and feels good."[14] For us as individuals, doing good work involves engaging in work that brings to bear our unique skills, talents, and knowledge (excellent), work that is emotionally fulfilling and feels good to do (engaging), and work that is good also in a moral sense and feels like the right thing to do (ethical). These creative minds envisioned these three elements coming together like strands of DNA that work together to form good work.

As you might imagine, good work is very personal and varies from one individual to the next. It is personally meaningful and reflects the values you hold. It is accomplished through thoughtful reflection and constant effort and is not a box you can simply check off. Former first lady Eleanor Roosevelt pointed out the crucial importance of knowing what you value most. She said, "To be mature, you have to realize what you value most. It is extraordinary to discover that comparatively few people reach this level of maturity. They seem never to have paused to consider what has value for them. They spend great effort and sometimes make great sacrifices for values that, fundamentally, meet no real needs of their own. Perhaps they have imbibed the values of their particular profession or job, of their community or their neighbors, of their parents or family. Not to arrive at a clear understanding of one's own values is a tragic waste. You have missed the whole point of what life is for."[15]

I introduce the idea of good work here so that each of us can identify what good work means for us, in the spheres in which we operate, and to identify what work we might take on that does *not* constitute good work.

When I teach, I tend to make provocative statements. For instance, I often quote Annie Dillard, who said, "How you spend your days is how you spend your life," followed by a challenge: "If you show me what your calendar looks like, will I be able to discern your purpose? Does your calendar reveal your pursuit of good work? Most people in the class cringe, because our calendars do not always align with what we deem to be important and meaningful to us. If your calendar is filled with activities that are uninspired and do not meet your own standards of good work, it's about time to spring-clean.

The author of *168 Hours*, Laura Vanderkam, points out that "the majority of people who claim to be overworked work less than they think they do, and many of the ways people work are extraordinarily inefficient. Calling something 'work' does not make it important or necessary." She concludes from her research that we all have enough time to do the things that are important to us. Implicitly, she is making the point that before we fill our calendars, we need to know what is meaningful and important and only then pencil it in. Greg McKeown, the author of the book *Essentialism*, found to his surprise that by trimming the fat from his calendar and skipping meetings he deemed unimportant and events he thought would be empty and wasteful, he became more, not less, productive and valued by others. "Essentialism" he writes, "is not about how to get more things done; it's about how to get the right things done."[16] Essentialism is about a keen focus on doing only good work.

TRADE-OFFS AND OPPORTUNITY COSTS

Not far from where psychologist Howard Gardner worked in Cambridge is Concord, Massachusetts, the home of Henry David Thoreau. In his writings, Thoreau remarked on what economists call opportunity cost: "The price of anything is the amount of life you exchange for it." Opportunity cost is a commonly used term in economics to describe "the evaluation placed on the most highly valued of the rejected alternatives or opportunities".[17] The *Oxford English Dictionary* (2010) describes opportunity costs as "the loss of other alternatives when one alternative is chosen," and behavioral scientists tend to view it in terms of a trade-off of resources such that investing resources (time, energy, money) in one thing results in not having those resources to invest in something else that might actually be a better choice.

This seems straightforward. So you might think that it would make complete sense that people would consider the opportunity costs before making a choice, right? Wrong. There is considerable support from the behavioral economics literature that as human beings we blatantly ignore opportunity costs. Instead, we tend to only consider the attractiveness of the options on the table in deciding how to invest our resources, without thinking of whether they could be a missing option that we should hold out for. Let's consider a simple example: Marion is a consultant architect and she is offered the opportunity to choose between two office building projects that will likely occupy her for the next three years. Marion's decision process involves a comparison of the two projects at hand, but does not take into account a future school building project (her area of passion) that she would much rather spend her efforts on. This decision-making glitch is referred to as *opportunity cost neglect.*

Unsurprisingly, research finds that when people consider opportunity costs, they get more out of life than those who neglect opportunity costs.[18] Thankfully, recognizing trade-offs and developing the ability and understanding to calculate opportunity costs is a skill that can be learned. Research shows that when you encourage people to consider alternative ways in which one's resources can be utilized, they are more likely to take opportunity costs into consideration.[19]

It is no wonder that people who are planners tend to be more likely to consider opportunity costs because they are more aware of the resource constraints and trade-offs as they plan. Imagine you have set aside some time on a Sunday evening to plan the week ahead. When your calendar is open and the time slots you have available in the next week are in front of you, you very quickly realize that the time you have available to do good work is finite. During the week you can be reactive and accept calendar invitations to whatever comes your way, or you can identify productive times and assign important tasks to those times. I often advise my doctoral students (as well as faculty friends) to "pay yourself first." What I mean by that is to set aside time every day—even if it is just thirty minutes—to do your own research and writing tasks first before taking on other tasks. You have to take the time to plan, you need to be selective about what you agree to take on, and disciplined about letting go of old commitments and long-standing activities to make room for new ones. If you do not have singularity of purpose and an intentional direction for how you want to spend your time, it is very likely you won't be thrilled about where you end up.

Opportunity cost is the price you pay when you make choices that do not align with what you deem to be good work. Recognizing the opportunity costs and calculating the trade-offs we have to make can fuel your empowered refusal. Remember, people are always going to ask us for things. Because other people matter,[20] we pay attention to their asks, which come in a variety of forms—from invitations, offers, and advice, to requests, favors, and suggestions. Anything that takes up time and energy or demands your attention is an ask. Quite often we impose certain asks on ourselves. These do not look like asks, but they are demands on our time that come from the beeps and notifications from apps and devices. Blogger Niklas Göke captured this saying: "Our to-do list is a set of requests. So is your inbox. Your Facebook messages, Instagram DMs, Twitter notifications. Requests, requests, requests. And we haven't even gotten to friends asking favors. Let alone business opportunities."[21]

If we operated solely on the notion that "other people matter," we would be spending our day fluttering in the wind according to the whim and will of those around us. What remains unsaid in the phrase "other people matter" is that you matter too. When considering the asks of others, you have to weigh not only the benefits to others, but also the costs to you.

Deciphering the Ask

The Aranmula kannadi inspires us to take the time to look deeper into ourselves and become more aware of the person that we are. Deepened self-awareness is a key competency to being able to say no. Whether it is a request from a friend or colleague, a personal or professional ask, a request to engage in some activity, or an appeal for help from someone needing your talent, learning to craft your empowered refusal boils down to self-awareness.

All requests are not created equal. You need to learn to decipher the ask. You need to develop a purpose-driven lens that helps you separate the "good-for-me" from the "not-good-for-me" activities. The most important thing to remember is that a request is not a requirement—a request is an offer that you have to decide whether to take on. As we now know, there is a difference between a resounding yes and a reluctant yes. When you are veering toward a reluctant yes is when empowered refusal is most useful.

In an ideal world, when any demand comes your way, whether via email or text or in person, it is important to understand what the actual ask is. To do that you need to listen to the request without judgment. Give the request your full attention and ask follow-up questions if needed. The body language you display during the ask needs to be confident and self-assured. If you need to jot down some key points about the ask, please do so to help you make the best possible decision for both parties. Once you have understood what the request is, you need to expertly sort out the key features of the request in terms of its costs and benefits.

Develop a Napoleon-like Coup d'oeil

According to William Duggan, author of *Napoleon's Glance: The Science of Strategy*, one of the reasons why Napoleon Bonaparte won more battles than any other general in recorded history was that he spent years studying different wars to learn how military strategy played out. With this knowledge, he could make a rapid connection between a new situation at hand with the examples he had stored in his memory.[22] In his classic work *On War*, Carl von Clausewitz describes Napoleon's ability to discern at one glance the tactical advantages and disadvantages of a terrain as *coup d'oeil*, whose literal meaning is "stroke of [the] eye."

One characteristic that distinguishes experts from novices is the ability to recognize features or key dimensions of things and categorize them or sort them into buckets. Experts tend to have well-developed systems in place to quickly make sense of problems when they arise, get to the root cause of an issue, and arrive at possible solutions faster than people who are novices.

We need to develop our own *coup d'oeil* to decipher the asks that come our way.

If you want to be an expert at saying yes or no to demands and requests, you need a system in place to sift those requests—to separate the grain (the resounding yeses) from the chaff (the things you should and want to say no to). The goal is to be able to come up with a categorization scheme based on what you care about, what good work looks like for you, and how your choices reflect your values, priorities, and preferences. By separating the "good-for-me" from the "not-good-for-me" based on self-reflection and a purpose-driven lens, we make the decision to say no obvious and the reasons underlying the decision more compelling.

Let's consider one of the simplest categorization schemes, a simple cost-benefit analysis to make a reasons-based choice. This requires an assessment of what the costs of complying with the request are to you and how this is weighed against the benefits that the asker obtains if you say yes to the request. First let's examine how to spot what high and low costs and benefits look like before we get into the categorization scheme.

A *high-cost request* is one that requires you to invest a great deal of time, energy, and thought. It might even be one that you do not want to do because it goes against your values, it is not a priority for you, or something you do not enjoy. A *low-cost request* might be something that is easy for you to do or one that is aligned with your purpose.

After assessing the cost to yourself, try and look outward to determine the true *benefit to others*. With this exercise you are trying to determine whether the cost you will incur will have a meaningful benefit for someone else. A *low benefit to others request* is one that will not substantially benefit the asker or one that simply needs to be done regardless of who does it. A low benefit to others request may be one that is performed out of habit because "this is the way we do things." A *high benefit to others request* is often one that you are uniquely poised to do, is aligned only with your expertise and expands the impact you can have on the world.

When we have developed a Napoleon-like *coup d'oeil,* we will be able to rapidly identify the category of ask and train our brain to stop making yes our default response. An added advantage of a swift no response is that people seem to pick up on the cue that this is a firm stance. Waffling and debating can suggest to the asker that we are uncertain about where we stand, at which point they can swoop in and provide us with reasons why we should say yes.

There are four types of asks based on the cost to self/benefit to others framework illustrated in Figure 4.1.

SAY YES TO LOW-COST/HIGH-BENEFIT "PASS THE SALT" ASKS

Imagine you are at the dining table and someone asks you to pass the salt, and the shaker happens to be on the table by you. You instantly pick it up and pass it over. Every one of us has some low cost to us but high benefit to others set of asks that we simply do. As a professor, there are some relatively low-cost things I can do that can have exponentially high benefits to my students. Writing recommendation letters, giving feedback on student presentations, doing mock interviews with a student to prepare him or her for a job interview are "pass the salt" asks in my book. Saying yes to pass the salt requests is worthwhile because the enormous benefit to others outweighs the small cost to you. But as we will discuss later about the mickles trap, we need to manage the number of times we agree to pass the salt, since those costs can add up.

Figure 4.1: Deciphering the Ask

Cost to You	Benefit to Others: High	Benefit to Others: Low
Low	**"Pass the Salt"** *Say yes, but don't overdo it. Remember: many mickles make a muckle.*	**"Email-Tweet-Post"** *Say no, likely a bullshit job. If you can, try and eliminate completely.*
High	**"Hero's Journey"** *Say yes, but only after making sure the benefits to others are real.*	**"Bake your Famous Lasagna"** *Say no. If a non-promotable task, make sure others take their turn.*

SAY NO TO LOW-COST/LOW-BENEFIT "EMAIL-TWEET-POST" ASKS

The opposite of doing good work is performing (excuse my language) a bullshit job. David Graeber, an anthropologist, has painstakingly documented the bullshit jobs that people (sadly) engage in. A bullshit job, according to Graeber, is the type of employment that "if the position were eliminated, it would make no discernible difference in the world."[23] If this job were to disappear tomorrow, it might, in fact, make the world a better place.

Consider the following example: I met a young woman, whom we'll call Tracy, on a flight from Houston to New York. We began with polite small talk. To illustrate how small the Texas town she lived in was, she described it as having just one traffic light on the main street. As we chatted, she shared that she worked at a local business and I mentioned that I was a marketing professor. As soon as she heard that, her eyes lit up and she said, "Oh, maybe you can help me with a problem I have at work." This is how she described her dilemma: "My boss read somewhere that you have to tweet two to three times a day about your business, and she has given me that job. It is the thing that causes me the most stress at work, because I don't know what to say about our business in our little town three times every day." I felt profound empathy toward this young woman, while the thought raced through my mind (but remained unspoken): *That is a bullshit job*

It is unfortunate for Tracy, and for so many people, that other people—supervisors, bosses, family members, even parents—sometimes dole out bullshit jobs, and it is up to us to either muster up the courage to put our foot down and say no to these jobs or find a clever way out of doing them. To close out Tracy's story, I told her that she should fight fire with fire. I advised her to find articles on "message fatigue" and share them with her boss to demonstrate that tweeting a storm can sometimes backfire. Importantly, by not having to figure out three new tweets a day, Tracy might find a way to create some more engaging social media engagement that might actually be more effective and less stressful for her.

Remember that one of the benefits of empowered refusal is that feeling empowered increases your empathy for the asker. When it comes to low-benefit requests, you can engage the asker to evaluate these types of requests for themselves, by asking questions like, "Is this really needed?" or "Why now instead of later?" This can help both you and them determine the actual reason for the request and determine whether it is a priority in terms time and attention. You can have a discussion about whether there are alternatives that don't require as much effort or that can simply be delegated or outsourced.

SAY NO TO HIGH-COST/LOW-BENEFIT "BAKE YOUR FAMOUS LASAGNA" ASKS

There are some asks that are simply careless and made in an offhanded way, often in casual conversation. They are thoughtless, because they do not truly benefit the asker, but they can be highly costly to you. Consider a situation in which a friend invites you to a party that she is hosting. As you are discussing her party plan, she suddenly brightens up and says, "Can you bake your famous lasagna? It is so delicious and everyone will really love eating it!" Admittedly, you do bake a great lasagna, and yes, people do love it, but it is time-consuming and tedious to make, and this is not even your party! Should you say yes? A lot of people would say, "Sure," or, "Okay," simply because they would not know how to get out of this request.

Have you said yes to a "bake your famous lasagna" request? What have you learned? For requests that are going to be high costs to you, it is important to invest time upfront to understand the benefits that will result from your taking that on. Remember that the benefit to others is a guess or a prediction. We often overestimate the benefit that we are giving to others in response to their requests. We tend to think that we are uniquely chosen to do a particular task and that we will benefit others greatly. If we find ourselves thinking in that way, we need to do a reality check on our prediction of the importance of our doing the task, or the benefit it will confer on the asker. In the case of the lasagna request, you should be able to instantly recognize an off-the-cuff request that you should find it easy to navigate. Ask multiple questions and try to understand whether and why the asker thinks this is important and what benefits they hope to get from you making this investment. If it turns out that the actual benefit that the asker will obtain is relatively minor, it makes sense for you to say no and stop agonizing about your decision.

CAREFULLY ASSESS HIGH-COST/HIGH-BENEFIT "HERO'S JOURNEY" ASKS

Whether in ancient myths or in modern-day adventure stories, the hero's journey is a story archetype in which a hero sets out into the unknown at great personal cost in service of a greater good. The popularity of this narrative over the ages and across cultures stems from the universal appeal of living selflessly and doing something good for others.

Researchers find key differences between a happy life and a meaningful one.[24] While satisfying what you need and want for yourself leads to happiness, it does not always contribute to meaningfulness. Meaningfulness, in contrast, is associated with being a giver rather than a taker and helping those in need and doing things that benefit others. Quite notably, a meaningful life involves self-sacrifice and is often associated with stress and anxiety, but the personal cost you incur to live a life of meaning is balanced out by the impact you can have on the world. As Ralph Waldo Emerson observed, "The purpose of life is not to be happy. It is to be useful, to be honorable, to be compassionate, to have it make some difference that you have lived and lived well."

Admittedly, a hero's journey ask is one of the most tricky to determine your response to. Given that it is an ask with high cost to you, albeit a high benefit to others, you want to learn as much about it as you can before you embark on the journey. You might want to clarify what the request is really about, how much it matters, and what the options are for following through. You might ask for more details about the ask—which is entirely appropriate even when you are already inclined to say yes. The more you and the asker can be aligned up front, the better decision you'll be able to make. Often, having a ten-minute open-hearted discussion with the asker can help you decide whether you should engage in this high-cost activity. If after the discussion, you still arrive at the conclusion that this is not for you, you need to embark on an empowered refusal approach.

Some questions you might consider asking when trying to work out what your response should be:

- → Do I want to do this?
- → Do I have the resources—time, energy, and money—for this at the moment?
- → Is this aligned with my values and purpose? Is this a priority at this time?
- → Will this add value to my life? Will it be fun? Will it feel rewarding?
- → Am I saying yes only because I am scared of saying no or don't know how to get out of it?
- → What will I have to give up if I say yes to this?

Another useful thing to keep in mind is that you can always ask for more time. Making a decision in the moment—especially for a potentially high-cost/high-benefit request—might result in you doing what you don't want to do and remaining committed to it for longer than you desire.

In order to live meaningful lives, we regularly make hero's

journey decisions. But what is meaningful to you may not be similarly meaningful to someone else. Meaning can be a very personal thing. You might add a thirty-minute commute to your day for your child to attend a school better suited to her needs. You might take on the responsibility of becoming a mentor. You might volunteer your time at a local charity or take a leadership role in an organization so that you can use your talent to better the world.

You might also say no to a high-cost/high-benefit request if the time is not right or if your purpose drives you to make a different life choice. A hero's journey ask can also come from within yourself, an idea we will revisit later in the book. But the key thing to remember is to evaluate the ask with a purpose-driven lens.

Two Traps to Avoid with Deepened Self-Awareness

Despite the advantage of this categorization exercise, because both costs and benefits are perceptions, too many pass the salt requests can quickly add up to become costly to you. A bake your famous lasagna request can be framed as a hero's journey ask, if a savvy asker exaggerates the benefits through praise, ingratiation, and flattery. Let's examine two traps to be aware of because they are *so* easy to fall into.

THE MICKLES TRAP: AM I UNDERESTIMATING THE COST TO ME?

Even when the cost to us is low and the benefit to others is high, pass the salt asks can add up. Here's where a phrase attributed to President George Washington comes in handy: many mickles make a muckle. It is a phrase that is worth adopting when you find yourself saying yes to several things just because they are tiny requests that do not take a lot of time. You might tell yourself, "Oh, it's such a small thing, I should just do it," or, "It won't take much time at all." This is the trap of the mickle.

Importantly, mickles can also be small, well-meaning activities that don't amount to much in the end. If you are already operating at peak efficiency and still need to cut things from your schedule, the only things left to cut are the good things. Maybe you are on too many corporate boards or engaged in many projects at work or volunteer for a lot of events at your child's school. Sometimes you have to make the choice to cut out some of the good things, as pleasurable as they might be.

Admittedly, it is very painful to say no to good opportunities, but you have to recognize that sometimes good opportunities are not aligned with the priorities you set for yourself. Warren Buffett talks about writing a long list of things you want to do and prioritizing them. All are good things and perhaps great opportunities to pursue, but he recommends choosing a top five and relegating the rest to a "do not do" list, at least till you have completed the five you have chosen to do. A key takeaway from the many mickles make a muckle trap is not to major in minor things.

THE "ONLY YOU CAN DO IT" TRAP: AM I OVERESTIMATING THE BENEFIT TO OTHERS?

The benefit to others is a guess or a prediction, and we often overestimate the benefit that we are giving to others in response to requests. When making a request, people often persuade us with flattery and praise. They might suggest that we were uniquely chosen to do a particular task. Before saying yes to a high-cost-to-us task, we need to do a reality check on the true benefit it will confer on the asker.

One of the most insidious bake your famous lasagna asks is one that involves non-promotable tasks. Researchers Linda Babcock, Maria Recalde, and Lise Vesterlund distinguish between promotable and non-promotable tasks and define non-promotable tasks as "those that benefit the organization but likely don't contribute to someone's performance evaluation and career advancement." They describe these as " traditional office housework such as organizing a holiday party, as well as a much wider set of tasks, such as filling in for a colleague, serving on a low-ranking committee, or taking on routine work that doesn't require much skill or produce much impact."[25] What makes things even worse is that women are more likely to be asked to take on non-promotable tasks, and most often say yes to taking them on as well.[26] Now that you know this, it is up to you to see a non-promotable task for what it is. Before saying yes, evaluate an ask using your purpose and what you deem good work as a lens. Take the time to calculate the opportunity costs and the trade-offs you have to make. If you do these things, you are more likely to see office housework equitably distributed among everyone in the workplace.

To avoid the "mickles" or "only you can do it" traps, we need to get comfortable with identifying asks based on the costs to ourselves and weigh those costs against the benefits others might gain from you saying yes. If you would like, you can take a photograph or screenshot of the deciphering the ask framework and learn to spot the different types of asks that come your way.

Recognizing When to Become a Trustee of Your Own Life and When to Get Introduced to the Broom

In her book *Insight*, Tasha Eurich advises that we ask the right questions of ourselves to tap into our identity and understand who we really are rather than who we *want* to be. She has studied where people fall on the internal vs. external self-awareness dimensions. The "pleasers" spot is the one to avoid, especially in the context of saying no. Pleasers have an extreme focus on others (external self-awareness) and considerably less self-knowledge. A pleaser is so oriented to appear a certain way to others, that they might overlook what matters to them. Pleasers, Eurich writes, "tend to make choices that aren't in service of their own success and fulfillment." In contrast, "aware" individuals score high on both internal self-awareness and external self-awareness. Aware individuals tend to have a good sense of who they are and what they want to accomplish, but they also attend to opinions and advice and value others' opinions. This is the spot we need to aim for in deciding what to say no to and when.

As aware individuals, we need to adopt a big-picture view to assess the value of the tasks we are given and have to take on vs. those we take on even though we don't have to. Particularly at the start of our careers, we might spend a great deal of time doing what can only be described as grunt work—tasks that feel unfulfilling and useless, especially in light of what we might see as our talent being wasted. While ambition and dreams might prompt us to fast-forward our careers and bypass this entry-level toil, we need to stop and recognize (with the aforementioned self-awareness) that these are not tasks that we can really say no to because they are very often (admittedly painful) rites of passage. The industrialist Andrew Carnegie believed that young workers ought to get "introduced to the broom." What he meant by this phrase was that hard work builds character and forges a good work ethic, so when young people enter the workforce, they should willingly take on the work that needs to get done, even if the tasks appear lowly and meaningless, because it is through doing these tasks that young people develop a work ethic that facilitates their later success. Consider, for instance, the transition a person makes when they go from doctoral student to professor, medical resident to doctor, or runner to film director. This is hard work that is not for the fainthearted or weak-willed. Clearly while it is not always fun to be a doctoral student (I can personally attest to this), medical resident, or a runner on a film set, when we are at that stage of our careers, we are assigned tasks that are impossible to say no to. In the throes of toiling through the time-consuming and tedious tasks that characterize these transitions, we will undoubtedly experience resistance and want to say no. However, we need to rely on our self-awareness to view the stage for what it is—a time period in our life when our mettle is being tested so that self-discipline and professionalism will be baked into our identities.

Consequently, empowered refusal is not a tool to be used to say no to things that are your responsibility, part of your job requirements at the phase of life you are in, or because you think you are too good, too talented, or too capable for the task at hand. Instead, empowered refusal is about saying no to things that we voluntarily take on when we don't want to *and* don't have to.

To summarize what we learned in this chapter, without self-awareness and without reflective practice, we are prone to say yes when we want to say no. With self-awareness, however, we can say no frequently and effectively. Both public and private self-awareness give us the insight we need to be able to say no without sacrificing our relationships or personal reputation. We can rely on private or internal self-awareness to keep us focused on what we truly want for ourselves and allow us to say no to requests that do not align with our values, priorities, and preferences. We can utilize our public or external self-awareness to help us discern the askers' perspective, understand why they asked us to take on the particular task, and attend to and respond to the request in light of this understanding.

Self-awareness helps us become trustees of our own life. It is when we develop a deep self-awareness that we can become wise to our truest interest (engage in purpose-driven good work) and develop the tools to enact what that wisdom dictates (calculate opportunity costs, assess trade-offs, and conduct a cost-benefit analysis of any request that comes our way). When we give ourselves the gift of self-awareness, we are less swayed by the swarm and more driven to follow the music of our hearts.

CHAPTER 5

Make Rules, Not Decisions

The ESPN sportscaster and show anchor Stuart Scott said, "Life consists of two dates with a dash in between. Make the dash count." Armed with self-knowledge about who you are, what you care about and find meaningful, and how you prefer things to be, it's time to set up some simple rules—what I like to call personal policies—that can translate this self-knowledge into how you live your life.

Productivity guru Brian Tracy wrote, "There is never enough time to do everything, but there is always enough time to do the most important things." While self-awareness identifies the most important things in your life, personal policies help you to make those things a priority. When we use the knowledge we have about ourselves to craft a better life, we do not simply live—we flourish and thrive.

Consider award-winning novelist Isabel Allende, who is a household name, at least for those of us who enjoy literary fiction. She regularly publishes rich, moving novels that convey a deep and profound understanding of human nature and the way the world can sometimes work. Some of these books have been made into movies that Allende has herself produced. She runs a successful philanthropic organization and speaks regularly about uplifting and empowering women. A few years ago, I had the privilege of seeing her speak to a huge audience of women at the annual Texas Conference for Women. She charmed the room with a riveting combination of humility, elegance, and storytelling. So, how does she do it? How does she do it *all*?

Fortunately for us, Allende has shared in numerous articles and interviews how she thinks about and manages her life to "make the dash count." Her writing takes center stage. It is her primary platform, and she makes the time and space for it. She has a personal policy that makes writing her novels a priority over everything else that might be going on in her life. In a *Harvard Business Review* article, she is quoted as saying: "My life is busy, so I need to save some months of the year to be in a retreat. I need time and silence, or I will never be able to write. Having a start date is good for me and everybody around me. They know that on January 8, I'm not available anymore."[1]

It turns out that this tradition began on January 8, 1981, when she began writing a letter to her dying grandfather that would evolve into the novel *The House of the Spirits*.[2] Having a personal policy to begin work on a meaningful project on a date that holds personal significance serves as a signal not only to herself but also to others who understand and respect Allende's dedication to her craft.

By instituting and enforcing a personal policy that she consistently follows year after year, and one that she can also share with others, Allende is able to say no to other engagements that come her way, without having to worry about her relationships or her reputation. This rule is one in what appears to be a system of rules that she has constructed to align how she lives to her identity as a writer. She follows a very exacting daily routine, working at her computer Monday through Saturday, 9:00 a.m. to 7:00 p.m. It is apparent that Allende is acutely aware of how she wants to spend her time and has a clear understanding of the kind of things she gets asked to do and how she intends to respond. Another indicator of this intense focus is easily found on her website. On the contact page (*isabelallende.com/en/contact*), she provides clear instructions on who to contact for the different asks people might have. Instead of having to respond to emails of all kinds, she has a delegation structure in place, one that might work for most authors, speakers, movie producers, and philanthropists. Notably she clearly also lays out a section titled "What I Don't Do," similar to the list from Edmund Wilson. It is this singularity of purpose that allows Allende not only to wear a bunch of different hats, but to wear them with the style and flair of her choosing.

It is clear to Isabel Allende, as it should be clear to each of us, that every choice we make in every minute of the day can shape how our lives turn out.

We are going to understand the power of personal policies to help achieve the excellence and meaning we seek. It is a way to use our resources—both time and energy—for the things that we want to do and, very importantly, to give us the platform from which to say no to the things we do not want to do. We will discuss the concept of personal policies and how grounding your refusal in personal policies that give voice to your values, priorities, principles, and preferences enhances the effectiveness of your refusal.

Personal Policies

Personal policies are an established set of simple rules that we make for ourselves, grounded in our unique identity, that guide our decisions and shape our actions. Through deepened self-awareness we become familiar and comfortable with our authentic self—the constellation of our values, priorities, principles, and preferences that make us unique. Just as our DNA makes us unique and is our biological fingerprint, our backgrounds, life experiences, belief structures, talent, skills, and experiences are distinctively ours, too, and constitute our *psychological DNA*.

Notably, a personal policy is different from other related ideas such as goals or boundaries. Gaining clarity on these differences is crucial and can shape the way you set up your personal policy. Goals are aspirations that you set for yourself, whereas a personal policy is a way of operating in the world. You could set up a personal policy to achieve a goal, but as George Leonard in his book *The Keys to Mastery* observed, true mastery is goal-less. Author and podcaster Ryan Hawk often mentions that he does not set goals; he simply puts processes in place and sets up procedures to get things done and then goes about doing them. Leadership guru John Maxwell similarly proposes that individuals need to focus on growth, not goals. Growth is a holistic and continuous process that transforms how we lead our lives.

Research shows that change is more effective when it is implemented in a gradual, baby-steps fashion. While goals are destinations you want to reach, personal policies are an operating manual customized to your psychological DNA—a way you do things, think about things, make choices, and enact behaviors that are important and personally meaningful.

My students often interchange the term *personal policy* with the popular use of the word *boundary*. Although personal policies and boundaries can appear to be similar, I see them as very different. Let me explain why. A boundary is a wall or barrier that you put up to keep someone or something out. In contrast, a personal policy is a rule that you make for yourself to live your life in accordance with what you deem meaningful and purposeful. Boundaries are about keeping other people out; personal policies are about giving yourself the opportunity to express who you are and achieve what you want to achieve.

Consider the following situation: If you were a farmer and you had some of your chickens stolen at night, you might put up some fences to protect your chickens from predators. Boundaries are a protection from threat; they help you avoid certain negative outcomes. In contrast, personal policies are designed by you for you. You set them up not in response to an outside threat but, instead, by looking inward and using your self-knowledge to arrive at sustainable and creative solutions to achieve the life you want to lead. To continue the farmer analogy, you would start by prioritizing the safety and well-being of your chickens as a personal policy. For that you might not only put up wire fences, but you would regularly check the wire netting to make sure the chickens do not have an escape route; you might also put up protective nets on top of the chicken coops to prevent chicken hawks from getting at your chickens; you might go natural by putting up bird houses for fiery little kingbirds who will fight hawks despite their tiny size; or you might go high tech by employing infrared cameras that would help you solve the mystery of the missing fowl. As this example illustrates, a boundary is a response to a specific external threat, but a personal policy forms part of an operating system designed to get what you deem most important done.

Consider the aforementioned stadium proposal moment. When an ask comes our way, we are faced with three overarching questions: (1) Should I say yes or no? (2) If I decide to say no, how do I communicate the no in a way that is empowered and does not invite pushback?

and (3) When I say no, how do I do so in a way that maintains my relationship and secures my reputation with the asker? As we have seen, we must say no to bake your famous lasagna asks (high-cost/low-benefit) and email-post-tweet asks (low-cost/low-benefit) and occasionally to pass the salt (low-cost/high-benefit) asks when they become too numerous and also to hero's journey asks (high-cost/high-benefit) when it is a journey that is not aligned with our purpose. But how? Our personal policies serve as a useful underlying infrastructure to make your responses to these different asks easier. Personal policies undergird your empowered refusal making it more persuasive.

To summarize, personal policies are simple rules you set for yourself that:

1. Stem from your identity
2. Reflect your values, priorities, principles, and preferences
3. Help direct your decisions and shape your actions toward achieving your unique purpose in a way that works for you

Because personal policies are grounded in what you want and pave the way for you to achieve your aims, they enhance the quality and experience of the journey. The Western novel writer Louis L'Amour observed that, "The thing to remember when traveling is that the trail is the thing, not the end of the trail. Travel too fast and you miss all that you are traveling for."

The DREAM Framework

The philosopher Jean-Jacques Rosseau said, "To be driven by our appetites alone is slavery, while to obey a law that we have imposed on ourselves is freedom." Inspired by this quote, we might consider personal policies to be rules that we impose on ourselves (or express to others) to live the meaningful and purposeful life that we desire. Put another way, a personal policy is a course of action that you adopt for yourself as your method of doing things that are important to you. Self-imposed rules are liberating, since they represent one's free will to live life according to one's own principles.

A few years ago, I developed a framework I called the DREAM (**D**iagnose—**R**eflect—**E**stablish—**A**ct—**M**onitor) framework to help participants in my classes systematically go through the steps of how to establish personal policies for themselves in order to lead and live better lives. Let's briefly go through the steps in this framework to learn how to set up personal policies for ourselves (see Figure 5.1).[3]

Step 1: Diagnose the pain point. We all want some things in our lives to change, but we do not always want to do the work it will take to make a meaningful change. For any change to occur, the first step is to pinpoint the area of our life that needs to change. Be as specific as you can about a pain point to create a targeted personal policy. Your pain point might be not having the time or energy to exercise or being distracted at work by Twitter or Slack. Consider the case of Jamie Bakal, a Los Angeles–based education consultant. She enjoyed her job and was good at it, but she was struggling with balancing work and home life in the early months of the COVID-19 pandemic. In a *Washington Post* article that I cowrote with Jennifer Wallace, we described how Jamie developed new rules to help guide how she lived and worked in a world where the boundaries between the two domains had blurred.[4]

When diagnosing your pain point, take care to distinguish between a real pain point and a phantom one. We may sometimes experience resistance to tasks that we find intimidating and want to avoid them or we deem a task too lowly to take on even if it falls within the purview of our responsibility. Stop for a moment to ensure that your pain is real and is not a phantom pain manufactured by your psyche to get out of fulfilling a responsibility.

Step 2: Reflect. This stage involves reflecting on what you would like things to look like after you have defined the general region where you wish to execute the change. To become more proactive, yet in a way that is both values-driven and authentic, you need to have a good sense of why you want that change. What values and principles are not being upheld in your life? For example, a desire to begin an exercise regimen could be linked to your values of maintaining good health and a desire to look good and feel good. To quit being consumed by your Twitter feed may be motivated by an increased desire to be more productive or to cultivate a more aware state of mind. In Jamie's case, she identified two areas of change based on her priorities (privacy during work calls) and stressors (kid interruptions).

It is worth noting a subtle difference between two sets of *why* questions that can come up during self-reflection. One is a *purpose-driven why* that reveals what we deem important and meaningful and the other is the downward-spiraling *situation-driven "why do I feel this way" why* that attempts to understand the reasons for our feelings. Let's understand the difference.

A default question people may ask themselves during introspection is *Why do I feel this way?* When we reflect, we instinctively try to understand our feelings and the situations we find ourselves in. We might wonder *why* we feel upset after that conversation or *why* we feel overwhelmed at work or *why* it is so hard to find time to exercise or *why* a stranger gave us a disapproving glance. Instead of ruminating on this flavor of *why*, consider replacing it with other more action-oriented questions: *What change do I seek? What would I prefer to happen?* Tasha Eurich writes, "I like to use a simple tool that I call *What Not Why*. *Why* questions can draw us to our limitations; *what* questions help us see our potential. *Why* questions stir up negative emotions; *what* questions keep us curious. *Why* questions trap us in our past; *what* questions help us create a better future."[5]

Asking a *situation-driven why* during self-reflection can lead to new unpleasant emotions and lead us to make baseless conclusions and unproductive assessments. *What* helps us focus on the reality of a situation, whereas *why* compels us to come up with a reason—any reason—to make sense of it. When we focus on a pain point and ask *what* instead of *why,* we take confusing emotions like guilt, fear, worry, and regret out of the equation.

An event I attended a few years ago featured Stephanie Cox, then North American president of the large oilfield services company Schlumberger. She was asked for some practical time management advice. She revealed a personal policy she upheld: "I don't say yes to a five-minute request." She described how quite frequently colleagues would catch her in the hallway to ask her a quick question, or "for just five minutes of her time." These small asks were distracting and stressful. Instead of dwelling on *why* the five-minute asks occurred, she thought about *what* she would prefer to happen instead. She came up with a way to handle them in a manner that suited her. She started asking her colleagues to email her for an appointment with a brief description of what they want to talk about. This simple rule helped Cox manage her time and enabled her to be better prepared for the meeting when it happened.

Use the DREAM framework's "Reflect" step (Figure 5.1) to gain the self-awareness you'll need to craft a successful policy for your life.

Figure 5.1: The DREAM Framework for Establishing a Personal Policy*

DIAGNOSE IDENTIFY PAIN POINTS

ASK
- Is there a habit I need to change?
- A behavior that is not working for me?
- Something I want to happen that is not currently happening?
- Something I want to stop happening, but it persists?

REFLECT LOOK WITHIN WITH UNDERSTANDING

ASK
- Why do I want a change?
- What values are not being upheld?
- What principles are being challenged?
- What priorities are being neglected?
- What preferences are not being met?

ESTABLISH FORMULATE POLICY

ASK
- What is the target? Do I need an announcement or self-talk or both?
- What form should my personal policy take? Should it be a decision rule? A ritual or a precept?
- Can I benchmark, copy, or borrow what works from someone else?

ACT GET STARTED AND IMPLEMENT

ASK
- What do I have to say **no** to?
- Am I experience pushback from myself or others?
- Is there something that is holding me back that I need to address?
- What do I need to tweak and adjust?

MONITOR UPDATE & CHANGE

ASK
- What is working for me and what isn't?
- Is there a pain point or conflict I need to address?
- Have my circumstances changed? Are my expectations (work or life) changed?
- Does success look different to me now?

---

* Adapted from: Vanessa Patrick, "Getting to Gutsy: Using Personal Policies to Enhance (and Reclaim) Agency in The Workplace," *Rutgers Business Review* 6, no. 2 (2021).

Step 3. Establish. Now that we understand *what* will diminish or even remove the pain point from our lives, we need to establish a personal policy to address the issues consistently over time. When designing a personal policy to say no, you need to consider *to whom* you have to say no—you need to identify the *target* of your personal policy. Let's call using a personal policy to say no to others *announcements* and using a personal policy to say no to yourself *self-talk*. We should agree that empowered refusal is a superskill that can be used to say no to others who are trying to get you to comply with what they want as well as to yourself (to steer you away from temptation, help you stick to your goals, manage your digital/virtual life by saying no to your devices).

Announcements are personal policies that you need to communicate to others because other people are pulling you away from what you believe is important and meaningful. If you find yourself feeling pulled in a direction other than what you deem "good work," you need to come up with announcements. Are you spending all day in meetings with no time to do the actual work you have to do? Then you need to carve out some time for "deep work" (*à la* author Cal Newport). Perhaps you can make this possible if you block out a chunk of time on your calendar to work on what you need to get done. You will also need to announce to people that you are unavailable, as you would for any other meeting on your calendar. (You could say, "Sorry, I will sit this one out. I have another event on my calendar at that time.") If you travel a great deal but have found that red-eye flights do not work for you, develop a personal policy by communicating that you do not take red-eye flights. (You might announce: "I don't take red-eye flights.") If you need to protect family time in the evenings, an example of an announcement would be telling your team at work that you are unavailable between 5:00 and 8:00 p.m. (You might say: "I don't take meetings between 5:00 p.m. and 8:00 p.m.," or "I am not available between 5:00 p.m. and 8:00 p.m.")

Self-talk is a personal policy that you set up for yourself to keep focused on tasks or behaviors that are important to you. We will do a deep dive into self-talk a little later in the book, but it is worth remembering that the most influential voice is often the voice in your head, the one that talks to you all the time, every day. If you want to develop an exercise regime, you could consider the advice author Gretchen Rubin's father gave her when she was in high school, "All you have to do is put on your running shoes and let the front door shut behind you." Rubin describes how she no longer debates about taking a run. Instead, at a designated time gets ready, laces up her shoes, steps out of the house and closes the door behind her. Having performed these essential first steps, she finds herself going for a run or heading to the gym. If you shy away from public speaking and you want that to change, you might make it a policy to offer to speak to prospective clients to overcome your anxiety. This personal policy might feel difficult at first, but the regular practice could give you the boost of confidence you need.

Some personal policies need to be both announcements we make to others *and* self-talk for ourselves. A professor friend works from home on Wednesdays. When she made that decision, she had to not only inform her faculty colleagues and doctoral students that she would not be available on campus on Wednesdays, but she also had to resist the temptation to drop by her office to get some work done on a day that she had designated a work-from-home day. Having the self-discipline to uphold your own personal policy serves a signal both to others and yourself of how important the values that underlie your personal policy are to you. I recall a long chat with a wise friend from graduate school who rhetorically queried, "Why would others take us seriously if we don't take ourselves seriously?"

It can also be helpful to share your personal policies with others so that they can help you uphold them. Carnegie Mellon University economics professor Linda Babcock identified a pain point. She was spending a great deal of her time at work engaged in doing favors and performing tasks that took away from the real work that university professors have to do to advance in their profession.

This is an all too familiar situation that often comes up in the leadership classes I teach tailored specifically to women in academia. Women are more likely to be approached to do things beyond research and teaching (these are promotable tasks in academia), like writing recommendation letters, chairing or serving on ad hoc college and university committees, or participating in countless task forces (these are invisible and non-promotable tasks). Many of these tasks are important and aligned with their purpose, but many times it can get too much (remember the mickles trap), and many times these tasks are not fulfilling and just have to get done. I once asked an academic leader why these enormously time consuming (being on a task force can be a weekly commitment for between six months and a year) and often inconvenient (speaking at a 6:00 p.m. student orientation on a Friday evening) tasks are not "counted" when it comes to raises and promotions? I was told, "We do not have a mechanism to count them, so we have to assume that you do them because you want to." Here is the stark reality: People make the assumption that you choose to take on tasks because you want to and because they are aligned with what you value when, instead, a lot of people (in my experience) take on many (unpleasant and inconvenient) tasks out of a sense of duty and responsibility.

Returning to how Linda Babcock approached this issue: she sensed that she was likely not alone in this dilemma, so she contacted a few friends who bonded over the struggles they face and also about how to turn down the requests that came their way. This was the genesis of what Babcock calls the "I Just Can't Say No" club. This self-created club created a support group of like-minded women who helped each other decide the "value-add" from saying yes to a request. Lise Vesterlund, one of the original club members explains how this helped her. She said, "The club made me ask each time: 'What will you give up to do this favor?' I wasn't good at that before." She also found that having the backing of the club helped her stop apologizing or offering long explanations when she said no to requests.[6] Borrowing from this experience, you might decide to form a "no club." It might be helpful to share what your personal policies are with the trusted club members. When you receive a request and share it with the group, it is likely that they are better able to see a misalignment between the ask and your priorities than you are.

Because they stem from our identity, personal policies are handy tools that provide us the lens with which to decide what to take on. They also provide the infrastructure ("It is my policy...") to support an empowered refusal response and ensure the consistency and longevity of that response over time.

Step 4: Act: Enacting our personal policies and making them come to life when we communicate our empowered refusal is something we will get to later in this book, so hang on. For now,

I will underscore the importance of putting a system of personal policies in place to help you eliminate the pain point.

Let's return to Jamie. Her announcement to her two children aged seven and nine was, "Unless you're injured or the house is on fire, please don't interrupt me during work calls." Since both girls did not have cell phones, she set up iMessage on their computers with both hers and her husband's numbers. The caveat was that they had the privilege of using iMessage *only* for homework or classroom help. By setting clear guidelines, Jamie was able to resolve a challenging issue faced by countless working parents during the pandemic.

Based on what we've learned thus far about personal policies, you'll probably agree that transforming your objectives, resolutions, or intended boundaries into personal policies makes them more likely to be achieved. For instance, I might set a *goal* to exercise for thirty minutes every day, or I might formulate a resolution that "Starting January first, I will exercise for thirty minutes every day." Translating these goals and resolutions into personal policies makes them more feasible and reasonable and hence easier to stick to. You might establish a personal policy that states, "I exercise for thirty minutes first thing every weekday morning." As you can see goals and resolutions tend to be generic, abstract, and impersonal while personal policies are specific, precise, and take into account what works for you. Just as you brush your teeth and drink a cup of coffee every morning, you will also exercise. A personal policy like this one could evolve into a daily ritual: "The first thing I do after I wake up is brush my teeth, change into my workout clothes, and get started with my exercise routine." However, this exercise plan might not work for someone who is not a morning person. For that person, perhaps exercise is better during their lunch break or after work instead. As you can see, a personal policy is a way of operating that is concrete and situationally triggered (more on that in a bit), and tailor-made to reflect what you value, prefer, and prioritize.

Step 5: Monitor. The rule of thumb about new habits is that it takes about sixty-six days—a little over two months—for a new habit to stick. If your personal policy has you doing things differently from how you were used to, then time is your best friend. Just stick with it.

However, if you established a personal policy in a particular form, you believe you have given it a fair shot, but for some reason it is just not working out, go back to the drawing board and reformulate it so that it suits you better. After all, it is your policy; you can adapt it and change it till it works for you. Take the time to reflect on these questions: *What personal policies am I upholding out of habit? Do I have personal policies that are no longer serving me?* Take a look at the "Monitor" step of the DREAM framework (Figure 5.1) to help ensure that you update your personal policies to reflect your current priorities.

Benefits of Personal Policies: As a Compass, a Magnet, and a Bridge

Let's unpack why personal policies are useful tools that help us communicate an empowered refusal. First, they serve as a *compass* to help us choose the path to take. Second, they act like *magnets* designed to keep us aligned with our values and serve our best interest. Third, they act like a *bridge* to achieving personal mastery and professional success to create a life of purpose and meaning.

1. PERSONAL POLICIES AS A COMPASS

Grounding your refusal in a personal policy conveys to yourself and others with conviction and determination where your priorities lie and what you deem important. Barbara Walters observed, "Most of us have trouble juggling. The woman who says she doesn't is someone whom I admire but have never met." Because we live such busy lives with so many competing demands, we very often have to juggle our different priorities. Having a personal policy in place can help us choose between different, sometimes equally important, options. Like a compass, personal policies guide the way.

Imagine that you have planned to leave your desk at 5:00 p.m. and head straight to the gym. Now, it is few minutes before 5:00 and a colleague stops by and asks if you would be open to a meeting at 5:00 p.m. today instead of tomorrow at 9:00 a.m. He says it would be nice not to have to deal with rush hour traffic to make a 9:00 a.m. meeting. We could all sleep in a bit, he jokes.

If you do not have a personal policy in place, here is the stream of different thoughts that might flood through your mind as you consider the request. First, you might be tempted to comply, rationalizing, *It would be nice to get the meeting over with. I could sleep in or maybe even go to the gym in the morning instead of now.* You might feel some annoyance at the ask and question, *Why did this guy set up a 9:00 a.m. meeting if he did not want it?* You could feel a tinge of conflict: *Should I say yes to this meeting now or should I go to the gym as planned?* You could feel regret: *I wish I had left a little early and headed to the gym so I wouldn't have had this encounter.* Or relief: *Ahh, a good excuse not to go to the gym.*

Consider what might happen if you had a personal policy in place.

You have a personal policy to leave the office on Monday,

Wednesday, and Thursday to head to the gym and get there at 5:30 p.m. In order to get there on time, you have to shut down your computer at work at 5:00 p.m. You have set up an accountability partner with whom you exercise, so your personal policy is designed to have some social time built in. Having this system in place ensures that you get in the gym time you need and sets you up to say no to anything else during that window of time.

You immediately know that you have to say no to this last-minute request. Like a compass, your personal policy helps you navigate the no and respond swiftly and with ease. You can simply respond that the 5:00 p.m. meeting would not work since you have a prior commitment. When you invoke a personal policy to say no, your no comes across as empowered.

2. PERSONAL POLICIES ACT LIKE MAGNETS TO SERVE YOUR BEST INTERESTS

To be human means to be concerned about the consequences of our choices and actions, for ourselves and for others. We are taught early on that our actions have consequences. We know our decisions impact both our reputation (i.e., our standing in the world) and our relationships. What we need are principles that draw us like magnets toward making the right decisions.

Tom Tierney, chairman and co-founder of The Bridgespan Group, which provides management consulting to nonprofits and philanthropic organizations, uses the term *magnet* to describe our commitments—the things in our life we want to be drawn to (family, friends, interests, and hobbies) and the term *sponges* to describe the things in our life that suck up all our time and energy and draw us away those commitments, leaving no time for anything else.[7]

At work, there are always more projects to complete, networking events to attend, and a plethora of ideas to pursue. By all means, we need to pursue those things, as long as they do not act like sponges and soak up every ounce of your time, energy, and enthusiasm. Exercise represented a magnet for Tierney and he set aside time each morning to workout. His wife and sons were another magnet, and so he prioritized his time for them by earmarking weekends as exclusively family time.[8]

What are your magnets? How do you identify them? To identify your commitments and prioritize them, we need to ask ourselves questions like: *What is my preferred way of operating? When do I work best? When do I find myself feeling lost and disoriented? What perks up my energy and motivation? What makes me smile and laugh? Who are the people I enjoy being around?* Set up personal policies to fill your own cup first, so you can, like actress Glenn Close, "deal with the world using the overflow."

We also need to identify the sponges in our life. You might have a boss who is a sponge—a person who believes you should always be available to 24–7 and who makes you feel terribly guilty any time you decide to focus on one of your magnets. Social media and technology can be a sponge if you cannot step away from it long enough to focus on getting work done. If you have a human (or nonhuman) sponge in your life, you have to control its influence and nip it in the bud.

3. PERSONAL POLICIES ARE A BRIDGE TO PERSONAL MASTERY AND PROFESSIONAL SUCCESS

Arête is one of my favorite words. It is an ancient Greek word that embodies excellence or virtue. We all want to achieve arête...and yet...when it comes down to it, our days blur into each other and years pass, and our quest for excellence remains a quest. Consider Twyla Tharp, the dancer and choreographer I mentioned in Chapter 1. In her book *The Creative Habit,* she proposes that it is daily habits and regular routine that shape and foster creativity. She writes, "Creativity is not a gift from the gods bestowed by some divine and mystical spark. It is the product of preparation and effort, and its within reach of everyone who wants to achieve it. All it takes is the willingness to make creativity a habit, an integral part of your life: in order to be creative, you have to know how to prepare to be creative." Since Twyla was a child, she has maintained a rigorous schedule centered around dance and music. In her book, she describes her daily ritual of waking up at 5:30 a.m., getting into workout clothes, and taking a taxi to the Pumping Iron gym on Ninety-First Street in New York. She writes, "The ritual is not the stretching and weight training I put my body through each morning at the gym; the ritual is the cab. The moment I tell the driver where to go I have completed the ritual." The rituals, routines, and habits Twyla Tharp has put in place has sustained her excellence and creativity over the years.

This is a hopeful message for us all: A productive and perfectly sane life full of passion and purpose is possible. It begins with self-reflection and self-awareness and involves putting systems in place to build a bridge from where we are to the personal and professional mastery we seek for ourselves.

Should You Use Excuses?

We all make excuses. We come up with reasons to explain why we did not do what we were tasked with (the dog ate my homework), why we are late (so much traffic), why we failed at a task (didn't sleep well the previous night), or why we can't say yes to a request (because I am swamped at work). Sometimes these excuses are grounded in truth, but sometimes we stretch the truth because we cannot muster the courage to say what we truly mean, and we definitely do not want to hurt other people's feelings. Being forthright seems to be a quality that was admired in Victorian novels but does not seem to easily translate into today's society.

Research finds that excuses serve as a buffer to protect ourselves from embarrassment, shame, guilt, and anxiety.[9] Excuses work because they shift the blame for negative outcomes from the individual to external factors beyond the individual's control. Psychologists have observed an enduring phenomenon referred to as the fundamental attribution error. Simply put, it goes like this: When explaining other people's behavior, we readily blame the person (they are late because they are lazy and slept in), but when explaining our own behavior, we are apt to attribute our failings to the situation we find ourselves in (we are late because there was a ton of traffic).

Imagine that someone rings your doorbell and asks you to buy a magazine subscription. Chances are you will never see that person again, so using an excuse to get out of buying the subscription might work. Imagine, instead, that the doorbell rings and it is your next-door neighbor and her little girl selling magazine subscriptions as an annual fundraiser for their school. Now, this is a dilemma: because you want to be polite, you come up with an excuse as to why you can't purchase one. But we know that excuses about why you can't do something begs the question why. If you used an excuse, you might have gotten out of buying the magazine subscription this time. *This time*. The interesting thing about excuses is that they are *short-run solutions to a long-term problem*. Research finds that giving an excuse works for the short run: you are less likely to succumb to consuming a tempting chocolate cake when you have a wedding to attend in two weeks.[10] But, once those two weeks are over, your excuse now disappears and you are stuck with dealing with the temptation once again. Using excuses is ineffective over the long run and leaves you grappling for reasons to back up your excuses.

You could offer a personal policy instead. You could say, here is ten dollars for your school, but "I don't subscribe to magazines." Chances are that when the next year rolls around, the little girl will not ask you to subscribe, because you have shared your personal policy.

In stark contrast to excuses, personal policies place the decision for an outcome squarely on oneself. This seems to fly in the face of all advice that says that as long as you don't make unpleasant outcomes about you, you will be okay. Personal policies take the deliberate stance of making things about you, even the bad things. In a research article, I pitch excuses against personal policies to say no to hard-to-refuse requests. I propose that instead of deflecting the causal attribution from yourself to the situation, you should own it. Owning the outcome is a signal of strength and courage and reflects your identity. Moreover, this has a longer-lasting effect than excuses, as I will share in the study that follows.

The Lasting Effects of Personal Policies: Evidence from the Lab

In a study I ran with university students, I wanted to compare the short-run and long-run impact of using personal policies vs.

good excuses.[11] I created a scenario in which the participant was told that an opportunity to rent an apartment of their own had come up, but they were $1,000 short of being able to pay the deposit. They were then told that they did not want to lose the opportunity, so they decided to reach out to their good friend, Pat, who they knew had the money in the bank. They pick up the phone, call Pat, and request the money. Study participants were then randomly assigned to one of the three experimental groups: explicit personal policies, implied personal policy, and good excuses.

For the "explicit personal policies" group, Pat declines the request saying: "I really would like to help, but I have a personal philosophy, 'Never a lender nor a borrower be.' My parents often quoted this golden rule from Shakespeare during my childhood, and I have adopted it as my personal philosophy about lending money to anyone. I am sorry and I wish you luck."

For the "implied personal policy" group, Pat declines the request, stating a belief but not providing a reason, saying: "I really would like to help, but loaning money to friends and family is often a hassle. I am sorry and I wish you luck."

For the "good excuses" group, Pat declines the request, saying: "I really would like to help, but I am saving to go back to graduate school myself, and every dollar counts toward the tuition I have to pay. I am sorry, and I wish you luck."

To assess how effective the refusal was, I asked participants to evaluate Pat's refusal as persuasive, convincing, and determined (all scale items where 1 = not at all; 7 = very much). Participants reported no significant differences on these variables, indicating that Pat had convincingly refused their request to loan them money. To evaluate whether they might push back or try to counter persuade to change Pat's mind, I asked participants whether they would try and persuade Pat to lend them the money and how likely they were to respect Pat's refusal. Again, there were no significant differences in how effective good excuses and personal policies were. In the short run, a good excuse will work as well as a personal policy.

However, I predicted that personal policies would be more enduring. To assess the long-lasting effects of personal policies vs. good excuses, I asked participants to imagine that it was ten years later, and they needed to borrow money for an important project. How likely would they be to ask Pat to loan them the money? Figure 5.2 below shows the number of people who were more vs. less likely to ask Pat to loan them money after ten years.

Figure 5.2

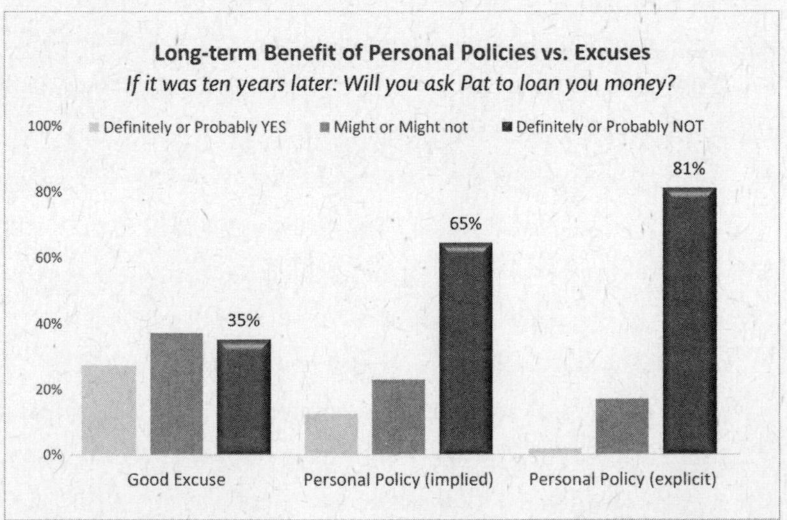

This study demonstrates that people are hesitant to reach out again when they know you hold a personal policy compared to when you give a good excuse. Significantly more study participants were likely to return to Pat ten years later to ask for another loan when Pat had given a good, but fleeting, excuse compared to when Pat had offered a personal policy. Even good excuses have an expiration date, but personal policies do not.

Remember, when deciding whether to offer an excuse or a personal policy to explain your refusal, choose the latter.

Creating Your Zone of Excellence

In his book *Good to Great,* Jim Collins writes, "Disciplined people who engage in disciplined thought and who take disciplined action—operating with freedom within a framework of responsibilities—this is the cornerstone of a culture that creates greatness. As a self-regulation and personal mastery researcher, this notion of a "culture of discipline" strongly resonates with me. In the same way in which Isabel Allende made writing a priority and created a culture of discipline around her writing work and Twyla Tharp made dance and choreography her focus and created a system of habits and rituals in order to achieve excellence, you can identify the most important things that you want to happen or even the pain points in your life that you wish did not happen, and develop personal policies around them.

Personal policies help create zones of operating excellence that allow you to flourish and thrive. In this, they remind me of the process of flame sterilization. One of the things you might not know about me (yet) is that I received a bachelor's degree in microbiology and biochemistry before I switched to business for my master's degree.

One of the first techniques I had to master as a microbiologist was flame sterilization, which is used when you want to transfer or grow microorganism cultures in the lab. First, you need to set up your workspace in a triangle shape with the Bunsen burner at the top of the triangle, your test tubes on the bottom left, and your sterilized agar plates on the bottom right (assuming you are right-handed). You then need to use the flame to create a zone of sterilization as you transfer, let's say, a streptococcus culture from the test tube to the agar plate in order to grow the culture. As a novice microbiologist, more often than you would like, you check your plates after the twenty-four-hour incubation period, and much to your dismay they are infested with fungi, all sorts of other colorful bacteria, and maybe some of the streptococci culture you were attempting to grow. Although your goal was to plate a pure culture, the air is so full of microorganisms that it is virtually impossible to do so without the keen mastery of flame sterilization. Skilled microbiologists learn to work close enough to the flame and use the zone of sterilization to transfer *only* the culture of interest onto the agar plate so that the plated microbial culture is pure and thrives without contamination.

Think about your personal policies as a Bunsen burner. They represent the way in which you can create a zone of excellence for yourself and a culture of discipline in which you can thrive without the interference of distractions and (dare I say it) the contaminating effect of others.

CHAPTER 6

Bringing Your Whole Self to Your Empowered Refusal

It was February 1993. The Gulf War had ceased about two years before, but the series of sanction resolutions at the United Nations were the loose ends that still needed to be tied up to declare the war officially over. At the time, the American ambassador to the United Nations, Madeleine Albright, had one singular charge: to make sure that the sanctions in Iraq stayed on. Sometimes this entailed criticizing Iraqi President Saddam Hussein for not complying with UN inspections or for failing to disclose information about the Iraqi weapons program. Needless to say, Albright was not popular among the government-controlled Iraqi media. So much so that a Baghdad newspaper published a poem titled "To Madeleine Albright, Without Greetings," describing her as, among other things, an "unparalleled serpent." Undeterred by this slight, Albright, who happened to have an antique gold snake pin, decided to wear it for meetings dealing with Iraq. The press quickly noticed this and asked her about her choice of the pin. This was the genesis of what Albright describes as her "personal diplomatic arsenal."

Albright's pins became a visual form of "plain speaking" to send a message expressing her position to staffers, reporters, and even world leaders, in a style and language of her own. When she was appointed the first woman Secretary of State in 1997, she become more intentional about her use of pins. In an NPR interview about her book *Read My Pins: Stories From a Diplomat's Jewel Box,* Albright said, "As it turned out, there were just a lot of occasions to either commemorate a particular event or to signal how I felt."[1] On good days she chose happy pins of suns, flowers, butterflies, and hot-air balloons. On those not-so-good days, she had a collection of bugs and carnivorous animal pins that she prominently displayed on her otherwise conservative dress suits; and on the slow, frustrating days filled with long and tedious diplomatic talks, she resorted to crabs and turtles.

Many stories tell of individuals who have used what *Smithsonian* journalist Megan Gambino describes as "nonverbal diplomacy—a means by which leaders can secure a powerful position, enhance their reputation, and forge close relationships with others."[2]

King Louis XIV of France flaunted his wealth to create an image of himself as "Le Roi Soleil" (the Sun King), the most powerful monarch around whom the world orbited. Not only did he want to secure his position as king, but he wanted to convey to the rest of Europe that if he could dress up in all his finery for a regular day in court and afford to build a palace like Versailles, he would be a formidable force to reckon with. In almost complete contrast, Apple cofounder Steve Jobs chose a signature look of a black mock turtleneck, Levi's 501® classic fit jeans, and New Balance sneakers. His choice of uniform conferred on him the status of a creative genius with "one less decision he has to make every day."[3]

One of my favorite illustrations of power dressing comes from

Zaha Hadid, a phenomenal Iraqi-born architect known as the Queen of the Curve for her architectural innovation and prowess. She became the first woman and one of the youngest persons to be awarded the famed Pritzker Architecture Prize. Despite the challenges of trying to make it in a man's world, which is what architecture was at the time, Hadid, who became a British citizen, defied the tendency that people had of putting her in box labeled with convenient categories like "female architect" or "foreigner." As she put it in one of her numerous interviews, "As a woman, I'm expected to want everything to be nice and to be nice myself. A very English thing. I don't design nice buildings—I don't like them. I like architecture to have some raw, vital, earthy quality." [4] Her bold design style that envisioned gravity-defying buildings was often reflected in her overall appearance. Her choice of creative fashion clothing and accessories memorably portrayed her confidence and authentic—"raw, vital, earthy"—self.

What each of these examples teaches us is that how we come across matters. Our nonverbal communication, often referred to as body language, involves not just visual cues like dress and jewelry, but also nonverbal cues like facial expressions, gestures, voice, and posture that signal our thoughts, feelings, and powerful (or powerless) status to others.

Together we will learn that for empowered refusal to be effective, we need to master our nonverbal communication to bring our whole selves to our refusal. Our nonverbals can serve as excellent complements to empowered "standing up" words, to boost their effectiveness. They can also be effectively employed to help cushion the blow of a refusal with warmth and kindness and secure our relationship with the asker.

It's Not Only What You Say, It's How You Say It

We have learned that empowered refusal involves a set of intentional steps that clearly communicate our no based on the personal policies we have set for ourselves, to make our refusal about us and what we want, and not about rejecting the other person. What this means is that we need to fully implicate our identity, not only with empowered words but also with empowered nonverbal communication cues. There are two important ways in which we can use nonverbal cues to increase the effectiveness of our empowered refusal: to boost empowerment and to secure our relationship bond with the asker.

NONVERBALS BOOST EMPOWERMENT

Our nonverbal cues can come into play even before any words are said. Think about the following: You are at a neighborhood get-together and Jess comes over to say hello. After a few minutes of chitchat, Jess says, "I have a favor to ask." You stop in your tracks, dreading the ask. Before you have even heard what she is about to ask, your mind is racing: *Gosh, I have so much on my plate right now. I wish I had not come to this event. No, no, no. Please don't ask me anything* As our brain is trying to anticipate what this request might be and then grapple with how to deal with any conflict that arises, our body in the meantime is revealing the dread we are experiencing. Our face might visibly change—it might tighten up, we might purse our lips and widen our eyes. Our body could signal disengagement—stepping back, folding our arms, looking away into the distance. We could signal our anxiety by physically clenching our fists to brace ourselves for what we think might be a big ask.

Have you experienced this anticipatory angst? Have you also

had occasion to sigh with relief when you hear the person out, only to realize that it was no biggie, just a simple "pass the salt" ask? Jess might just want to borrow your lawn mower for a day while she gets hers repaired—a request you can quickly and happily agree to. By allowing our imaginations to run amok, we have responded to Jess with our nonverbals. Even though we might ultimately say yes to her ask, our nonverbals most likely tinged the interaction with negativity. Our mental shrinking away, especially from situations we anticipate might be negative, often comes across loud and clear.

Receiving an ask and responding to it is a whole-body experience. It is quite common for people to say yes or no using only their words while completely neglecting their body language. If your words are saying no, but your body suggests you are unsure about your response, you are more likely to invite pushback. To wear your emotions on your sleeve, to leak power, and to have your face be a dead giveaway are phrases we have heard numerous times, because our body language readily cues our vulnerability. Managing nonverbal communication cues can impact the quality of an interpersonal interaction and the impression a person has of you whether they are able to consciously articulate it or not. For empowered refusal to be effective, we need to harness the personal power our body language affords.

Empowered refusal involves more than just words. Although saying no is primarily an act of speech, for a refusal to be empowered you need to enlist your entire body to bring your whole self to the refusal. As the old saying goes, "It's not only *what* you say, it's also *how* you say it." We have seen how the use of empowered words like I don't makes your refusal more effective. We have argued that if those words are grounded in our identity and convey a personal policy, we have won half the battle. Not only do we come across as more persuasive to others, we are also convinced in our own mind that saying no is the right thing for us to do. If you authentically believe in your stance on an issue, it is already less likely that your body will betray you. Indeed, there is a reason why we have referred to *I don't* as standing up words, because simply using empowering language like saying I don't spills over onto how you come across. It makes you stand taller and come across as confident and sure of yourself. When our verbal and nonverbal cues come together to convey an empowered stance, our refusal is more effective. When we communicate with our whole self, our strong and determined stance helps us gain greater compliance and get less pushback from the other person.

NONVERBALS CAN SIGNAL WARMTH AND SECURE OUR RELATIONSHIP WITH THE ASKER

A second benefit of using nonverbal cues in empowered refusal is to maintain harmony with the asker. *No* can be a harmony buster, so when you decide to refuse a request, nonverbal cues help buffer any harshness that your no conveys. Effectively employed, empowered refusal makes the asker feel that it is the request that you are rejecting, not the requester. Bolstering your communication with genuine body language more effectively conveys an "it's not you, it's me" stance on a matter.

People like to see that you live in accordance with your principles. The same way people do not enjoy a movie in which the picture does not match the sound, people want to see consistency and congruency in what a person says and how they say it. When you ground your refusal in a personal policy, you use empowering language accompanied by empowered, yet empathic, nonverbal support cues. In other words, when the audio matches the video, people think positively about you and hold you in high regard. Your refusal, however well-articulated, is unlikely to be effective unless your nonverbal communication suggests credibility, confidence, and trustworthiness. Even though you are saying no, if your strength of character, integrity, and authenticity shine through, you can leave the conversation with your relationship secure and your reputation untarnished.

Coming Across as Empowered, yet Empathic

Let's do a little exercise: Go to Netflix or your preferred movie streaming service and begin watching a foreign film in another language that you may not understand (I would recommend Iranian, Telegu, or Arabic because of their vibrant film industries). Chances are that within the first few minutes of the movie, you will be able to pick up on more elements of the film than you even thought possible: genre (drama, comedy, documentary), time period of the film (classic vs. contemporary), even production budget (blockbuster vs. independent). You may be able to intuit from the nonverbal cues the general tone of the film—is it eager and positive, characteristic of what you might see in a romantic comedy? Or is there a display of violence and tension, characteristic of a murder mystery or horror flick?

Now start listening to the dialogue and watching the facial expressions. Remember you don't understand anything of what is actually being said, but you can pick up on the flavor of what's going on, relying solely on the nonverbal cues. Pay attention to the vocal variety of the actor's voice. The six elements that contribute to vocal variety are volume (loudness), pace (rate of speech), pitch (highness and lowness), pause (the use of silence), timbre (resonance), and intonation (the rise and fall of pitch in spoken language, like the voice going up at the end of a question).[5] By attending to voice alone, you can pick up on emotions (who is mad and who is sad, who is happy and who is elated, who is upset and who is depressed) and also make more holistic assessments of the characteristics (who is the good guy and who is the bad guy, whom you can trust, or who is lying or might be hiding something). Furthermore, regardless of culture, when a person is happy they smile, and when they are angry or sad they scowl or frown. By shaking one's head from side to side we indicate no or disagreement, while nodding the head up and down indicates yes or agreement.

When we find ourselves in unpleasant situations, like a difficult ask, our body language reveals how we feel about this situation. We might look shell-shocked, roll our eyes or cast them down, droop our head and look away, or slouch as if we wished the earth would eat us up now. We might cross our arms, pick at our nails, or rub our palms together anxiously. If we say yes grudgingly out of fear or politeness, our true feelings of anger and resentment are often leaked through the tension in our face, the turned-away and often stiff upper body. Recognizing that our natural tendency is to respond to a request with avoidance[6] and to show grudging resentment to any ask that comes our way, we need to manage those feelings and the nonverbals that accompany them to be able to say no effectively. In other words, we need to know what an empowered refusal looks and sounds like and make sure we embody it consistently.

We have discussed the difference between empowered language

(I don't) vs. disempowered language (I can't). When people use empowered language they elicit more favorable attitudes and are more persuasive than when they use disempowered language. It does not matter whether this is only an audio medium like a phone call or a podcast, or an audio and video medium like a Zoom call, or an in-person chat.[7] We know the importance of boosting empowered language with absolutist words like *only* or *never* to convey greater conviction and avoiding submissive filler words *just, like* or er. Now let's get into how our nonverbals come into play, knowing that our body language and the nonverbal signals it sends conveys how empowered (or disempowered) we come across.

Signaling Empowerment (and Disempowerment) Using Nonverbal Cues

Organization behavior researcher John Antonakis and his colleagues define charisma as "the ability to communicate a clear, visionary, and inspirational message that captivates and motivates an audience." In their study of charismatic leaders, they identify twelve charismatic leadership tactics (CLTs), three of which are nonverbal: the expressions of our body, voice, and face.[8] The hopeful message from their research and fieldwork with managers is that anyone can master these CLTs to "become more influential, trustworthy, and 'leaderlike' in the eyes of others." I will draw on a variety of sources to share some ideas about how our body, voice, and facial expressions make us come across as empowered or disempowered. As we build our self-awareness, let's include gaining insight about how our body tends to react to different situations and try and replace those automatic responses with more intentionally powerful ones. After all, we human beings, like the apes we evolved from, tend to display our interpersonal power and dominance in a variety of nonverbal ways.[9]

Standing up tall: We need to accompany our "standing up" language with a body posture that signals empowerment. What does that look like? Own the space, whether while sitting or standing, to make yourself larger, not smaller. Mindfully stand with your back straight and shoulders back, feet slightly separated from each other with your weight evenly distributed between our feet. Claim more space by occasionally leaning forward with your palms open and your body relaxed. Occasionally, we might use gestures to make a point, casually rest our arms or elbows on a chair or table. Bad posture is a dead giveaway of low power, low energy, and submissiveness. Folding over with our chins tucked into our neck is a way of not drawing attention to ourselves, and it says, "don't look at me."

I believe that effective teaching is a whole-body activity. When I stand in front of a classroom filled with students, I do not simply share facts and material about the topic scheduled for the day. Central to the act of teaching (for me) is the use of nonverbal cues that convey care, confidence, credibility, and, dare I say it, charisma. The fact is that I am average height (for an Indian woman) but when I stand in front of 425 students in a huge auditorium, I look like a dot to the students at the back of the room. I know this for a fact because I once asked my teaching assistant to take a video of me from the back of the room so I could see what my students get to see. If I am honest, even after many years of teaching, I do feel anxious about my ability to command the attention of hundreds of pairs of eyes. So, I employ some intentional tactics that work for me.

I dress in business attire—usually plain dark colors accessorized with jewelry and the occasional scarf. Nothing loud or distracting. I am always early to class (my daughter's second-grade teacher instilled into both her and me that "being early is on time and being on time is late"). I am prepared with my notes so that I can casually chat with the students in the front rows and perhaps answer a question or two that my students might have before the class starts. When the class is about to begin, I switch on my lapel microphone and get into what I call *my* "tree pose" (different from the tree pose in yoga—that would not the best in-class posture choice for me!). My tree pose has me standing up straight and tall with my feet firmly rooted to the floor. This is the signal to the students (and me) that we are about to begin. I raise my right hand and the silence in the room radiates outwards from the students in the front of the room to the students at the back. I wait until the silence feels palpable. I begin with a warm smile and friendly nod and say, "Good morning!" The students are attentive. They know what follows is an interesting story relevant to the topic at hand.

Notice that before I speak a word, I use a sequence of *intentional* nonverbal cues to convey I mean business. When I speak, I am aware of the microphone. I lower my voice, modulate my pitch and speak slowly and deliberately. During the lecture, I walk around the auditorium with deliberate energy (taking care not to fall on the steps). As I move from one spot to another, I adopt the tree pose again. I am careful to engage the students by looking directly at them (eye contact conveys credibility) with open-body language. All of these contextual cues (how one comes across in a situation), including kinesic cues (displays of gestures, facial expressions, posture, and movement) and vocal cues (loudness, voice pitch, pauses) are learned behaviors that I have practiced (and tweaked till they work for me) over a number of years so they now come pretty naturally. I am confident that with self-reflection, noncritical observation, and practice, you can learn them too.

Attend to your voice: Voice coach Caroline Goyder in her book *Find your Voice* (and also in her engaging TED talk) shares how voice portrays confidence. She describes voice as "the ultimate human soft power"—a means by which we attract and persuade others. She draws on the metaphor of our voice as an instrument, arguing that an instrument itself is not bad or good, but really depends on how it is played. When I read that I recalled the beautiful poem about an old violin, written in 1921 by Myra Brooks Welch. In the poem, an auctioneer is getting bids of one or two or three dollars for a timeworn violin, till a grey-haired gentleman comes forward from the back of the room, wipes the dust off it, and plays a melody showing the beautiful sound the instrument could make with "the touch of the master's hand."[10]

One key takeaway from Goyder is the importance of learning how to breathe using your diaphragm to control your voice. When we are stressed or nervous, our breathing becomes fast and shallow and our breaths and the words we speak emanate from our upper body. Research supports the intuition that different emotions are accompanied by distinct breathing patterns.[11] For instance, what we need to do when we feel anxious is to intentionally lower our breathing into our diaphragm so that our voice can come across as strong and confident.

Research finds that *pitch* is an indicator of dominance.[12] To appear more dominant, lower the voice; to appear more submissive, raise the pitch of the voice. Both men and women need to lower their voice pitch when trying to appear in control, assertive, and dominant. High-pitched voices signal emotional speech and can convey a loss of control. Lowering the voice, on the other hand, signals dominance, which is a more natural way to create obedience. When emotions run high, the voice can rise. Practicing our speaking, in front of a mirror, can make the timbre of our voice sound confident.

A few years ago, one of my doctoral students came up with an innovative way to manage the pitch of her voice. We had discussed how when she was nervous or anxious during a presentation or when called on in class, the pitch of her voice went up drastically, which made her come across poorly. She took this feedback to heart and decided to join the university choir. It turned out that her newfound hobby was a thoroughly enjoyable break from her dissertation work, and it made a huge difference in how she came across as a speaker. Singing helped her learn to use her voice as an instrument under her control.

Even the speed of our speech and response times carries information. Faster rates of speech are thought to be more effective and make the speaker sound credible, confident, and competent. But remember, although a rapid tempo can convey confidence, it can also communicate recklessness in certain contexts, such as when the person is discussing sensitive or dangerous issues.

Watch what your body parts are up to: Very often our hands feel awkward. When we train our students for their job market presentations, they commonly ask, "What do I do with my hands?" When our hands are not employed, we tend to use them to self-soothe. Touching ourselves is reassuring when we are feeling uncomfortable, vulnerable, or scared. Self-touch takes many different forms—rubbing our hands together, biting our nails, fidgeting with jewelry or with our fingers, playing with our hair, or adjusting our clothes. When we are comfortable and relaxed, our hands move naturally.

Also, while we think *with* our head, we do not think too much *about* our head. A group of German researchers from Augsburg University, led by researcher Elizabeth Andre and her colleagues, identified a host of nonverbal associations based on the movement of the head alone.[13] I mention this one in particular because of the emergence of video conferencing in which the body language is largely limited to the upper body. Even head movements can convey meaning that goes from relatively straightforward to nuanced. While we might recognize a nod as acceptance and a nod with a smile as liking or approval, did you know that a nod with a slightly raised eyebrow signals genuine agreement? If you have been around teenagers, you are probably accustomed to eye rolls that signal their incredulous disbelief. In fact, a slight head tilt accompanied by a downward gaze can signal boredom, a head tilt with a frown indicates disagreement, but a head tilted to the right with raised left eyebrows says, “Tell me more, I am intrigued.” In the two-dimensional world of Zoom or Team meetings in which we all have worked for the past two years or so, learning to get attuned to these small nonverbal facial cues can make a difference.

Nonverbals Secure Our Relationships and Seal Our Reputations

“I’ve learned that people will forget what you said, people will forget what you did, but people will never forget how you made them feel." Consider this quote from Maya Angelou when formulating your refusal. How can you communicate your no response in a way that leaves the asker feeling valued? Despite saying no, can you do it with grace so that you leave a positive impression?

Across cultures, and since ancient times, two parties, often previously unknown to each other, might use nonverbal means and gestures of goodwill to signal to each other that they come in peace. The Japanese bow deeply, people from the Indian subcontinent fold their hands in a "namaste," medieval knights in armor would raise their visors, and in ancient Rome citizens would raise their hands to show that they were not carrying a weapon. These nonverbal cues are important signals of appreciation for the relationship and goodwill that one feels toward the other person. As William James, often known as the father of modern psychology, noted, "The deepest principle in human nature is the craving to be appreciated." Nonverbal gestures can be used to facilitate trust and reduce psychological risk in interpersonal interactions. Consider the following ways in which you listen, create rapport with the asker, convey warmth, and dampen any negative feelings that might arise from your refusal. I like to think of these tactics as ways in which you say an empowered no, but also leave the interaction with the other person better than you found it.

Active listening: As William Ury wrote in his bestselling book, *Getting to Yes*, "When you listen to someone, it is the most profound act of human respect." When we know a request is coming our way, instead of shutting it down or signaling our lack of interest at the outset, sometimes it pays to simply keep quiet and listen. Listening is crucial to empowered refusal. When we truly listen to the request the other person is making, we convey our sincere interest in what they have to say. This requires us to suspend judgment of the ask, even if we know from the outset that this is not something we want to do. Being in the spotlight is challenging enough, but letting go of our own feelings of anxiety and worry at having to say no, and just listening first, can work to diminish the spotlight, allow us to consider the ask and then respond in an empowered way. If you listened and it showed, this act goes a long way in securing your relationship with the other person. When people feel they have been heard, they are more receptive to your stance on an issue, even if it goes against what they want. This is the essence of mutual respect.

Active listening means that you devote yourself to the conversation. You cannot be watching a TV screen or looking at your phone if you want to connect with another person. You might assume that glancing at your phone every now and then will allow you to be just as present and engaged in a conversation. However, whether you mean to or not, you are conveying the message that the person you are talking to isn't as important as the text, tweet, or post that is on your phone. Not only are phones distracting,[14] research also finds that smartphones have become adult pacifiers. Wharton Professor Shiri Melumad's research finds that people have a close attachment and deep personal connection with our phones, so when it pings or rings we feel a compelling need to attend to it.[15] For our purposes, we need to set aside the psychological comfort of our phones to fully engage in our conversation with the person in front of us.

Build trust and create rapport: Some gestures, such as leaning back, crossing your arms, or putting your hands deep in your pockets, signal disengagement. Because our hands tend to do more "talking" than any other body part, they are often referred to as the vocal cords of body language. Hiding them or putting them away is equivalent to shutting up and choosing not to communicate. To come across as genuine and trustworthy, use open body language instead. When people begin to open up and tell the truth, they often open their palms or show their hands to the other person in some way. In the same way that most body language signals are unconscious, this one offers an "intuitive" sensation that the speaker is being truthful.

Research finds that the intensity with which we smile matters.[16] A wholehearted broad smile conveys warmth, but sometimes less competence. Perhaps we can forego a tad bit of perceived competence, if our goal is to make the other person feel better. Walking around to the same side as the other person, a light touch on the arm or shoulder, and a genuine compliment can forge a pathway of warmth and empathy.

What is pretty fascinating is that the nonverbal cues that come more naturally to us vs. the ones that don't can depend on our gender.

What Can Men and Women Learn from Each Other?

Men and women tend to have different strengths in how they come across from a nonverbal standpoint. Researchers attribute these different strengths to two behavioral differences between men and women: agency vs. communality.[17] Men tend to be agentic—aggressive, decisive, and strong—whereas women are predominantly disposed to be communal: caring, sympathetic, and sensitive. This same research documents that when it comes to touch, smiling, and other nonverbal cues, men tend to use them to remain in control, while women tend to use them largely to reassure the other person.[18]

The use of nonverbal cues in empowered refusal maps onto these two different uses of nonverbals by the two genders. Recall that we use nonverbals to convey an empowered stance (men are better at this because of their agentic dispositions) and to show warmth and compassion to the other person (women are better at this because of their communal dispositions). Each gender therefore has to learn to leverage their respective strengths, but also be open to learning from the other gender how to use the nonverbal behaviors that do not come naturally. Let's look at some of these differences and learn from these research-based insights to become more cognizant of how we come across.

While men are comfortable with and naturally use dominance nonverbal cues and do so more frequently than women, women tend to use more submissive cues.

In her book *Body Politics,* social psychologist Nancy Henley explains that men use subtle touch cues to try to control. They might try to calm a woman down (e.g., grabbing arms or shoulders), silence her (e.g., putting their finger to the woman's lips), or show control over them (e.g., putting an arm across a woman's shoulder, patting them).[19] Research has shown that men touch more than women, often to control or dominate.

Men also tend to swagger more than women do. Men's body language is more expansive than women's, and men occupy more physical space with their bodies. Women tend to make themselves smaller by keeping their legs and hands together, slouching, and sitting back in their chairs. When Sheryl Sandberg encouraged women to *Lean In,* she meant it literally—taking a seat at the table and conveying through verbal and nonverbal cues a woman's right to be there.

Invading a person's personal space is a dominance cue. It can be used negatively—yelling and spraying droplets of spittle in their face without even touching them. In fact, the personal space bubble that men create for themselves and occupy is larger than that of women. Women occupy less space, withdrawing within themselves, and men often comfortably invade women's space bubbles.

As we discussed, touching our body and face signals anxiety, nervousness, and lack of confidence. In the book *Calmfidence,* a nice combination of the words *calm* and *confidence,* the author Patricia Stark, describes the "hand to throat" and "fig leaf" poses that give away feelings of discomfort and being threatened. Reaching for the neck dimple—the hollow of the neck—either to place one's hand over it or to fidget with a necklace or pendant—is a classic signal in which a woman is saying, "Oh, no." The demure pose in which the hands are clasped in front of us is what body language experts dub the *fig leaf pose*. It turns out that we subconsciously cover this part of our body when we are concerned or worried. Women very often do what is called the *partial-arm cross*: standing with one arm crossed and hugging the other arm. Don't do it. The arm cross is seen as a partial hug, a comforting position that indicates the person is trying to soothe nerves and calm themselves. It might also show discomfort with one's own body image. Using rapid but meaningless gestures with the hands is what is referred to as hand dancing. Women are twice as likely as men to do this.

Looking directly at someone is a dominance cue. It could be accompanied by feelings of rage and anger on one hand or with feelings of pride and confidence on the other. While women are observant and pay attention to other people's behavior, they often do not hold a person's gaze, or they even avert their gaze, coming off as more submissive.

Women are more likely to invest in relationships, and their use of nonverbal cues provides evidence of that. Women are more likely to listen with empathy and use interpersonal touch to reassure the other person. When women enter the other person's space, it is usually used positively to reach out and gently touch an arm or a shoulder. Women also tend to smile more. This is good in moderation to create a feeling of warmth. It is important for women to remember, however, that if you smile a bit too much, your words are not taken seriously. It is no wonder that women are more likely to suffer Zoom fatigue (a feeling of being drained and lacking energy following a day of virtual meetings) than are men. Cameras increase self-awareness and provide ample opportunity for self-criticism.[20] This insight, I relate to! Women are also more liberal in their use of emojis in texts, email, social media, and other forms of computer-mediated communication. Women tend to be more sensitive to the emotions portrayed by the emoji, especially negative emotions.[21] Emoji (particularly smileys) are used liberally by women to signal warmth and buffer the harshness of a negative response.

"The most important thing to keep in mind with nonverbals is congruence—that what you say and what your body looks like are aligned," said Carol Kinsey Goman, author of *The Nonverbal Advantage*. "Incongruence will throw people."[22] Research using fMRI brain scans shows that when first-time moms saw the smiling face of their infant child, the reward centers in the brain lit up.[23] Smiles are contagious, even among adults, for a similar reason.[24] We mirror each other's emotions, and it is natural to respond to a smile with a smile.

Make Your Mess Your Message

Robin Roberts, co-anchor of *Good Morning America,* recalls a specific moment in her career when she responded with authenticity and honesty, instead of following journalism textbook instructions on what is considered professional on-screen reporting.

It was August 2005 and Hurricane Katrina had just hit Mississippi. ABC flew Roberts down to report on the story. Roberts's mother, sister, and close family members still lived in the area, so while the crew were setting up, she sought them out before she went on the air to make sure they were out of harm's way. They were okay. She then readied herself to get on air and began reporting on the devastation that was being wrought by the battering winds and the heavy rain. As is common in such broadcasts, Roberts, as the journalist on location, was in conversation with the anchor of the show in New York, Charlie Gibson. Knowing of her personal connection with Mississippi, one of the questions Gibson asked Robin was if she had been able to find her family. Having just witnessed the wreckage first-hand, Roberts's response was punctuated by sobs. She broke down on live TV and wept.

Roberts was sure that on her return to New York, she would be fired from the show for her inability to be stoic and steely. Isn't that what we are taught—professionals do not display emotions at work? Crying, of course, especially for women, is a textbook no-no. Later she wrote, "Just the opposite happened. I was being authentic. I was being in the moment. I was speaking from the heart. People sensed that, rallied around me, and adopted my hometown, which was decimated." Roberts learned something that day that she often shares: "Make your mess your message."[25] Nicknamed Rock'n Robin, what Roberts learned in her career was that realizing dreams is not without hardship, but by responding to events with one's whole authentic self, you can turn a messy situation into a magnificent one.

As Robin Roberts's story illustrates, when we communicate, we need to do so in a way that is authentically our own. Michelle Obama, for instance, is known to be a hugger. She is often seen hugging her husband and her daughters. In her memoir, *Becoming*, she describes how she broke royal protocol to hug Queen Elizabeth, who happily hugged her back. She even hugged a rather contented George W. Bush, captured in a photograph, later described as "genuine bipartisanship."[26] A *New York Magazine* article described her hugging tendency saying, "When not busy curling dumbbells, the First Lady's arms have acted as tools of diplomacy."[27]

Owning our distinctive nonverbal behavior can be very powerful, indeed. Barbara Jordan, an attorney by profession, is a household name associated with championing the Civil Rights Movement in 1960s Texas. She had a distinctive, unforgettable voice that she used throughout her career to give a voice to those who didn't have one. Even as a child, growing up in Houston's Fifth Ward neighborhood (adjacent to the University of Houston, by the way), her big, clear, and confident voice made teachers and friends sit up and pay attention. Later in her career she became a congresswoman who used her rich and commanding voice to deliver a speech during the Nixon impeachment hearings that is widely recognized as one of the finest speeches in twentieth century American history.[28]

To communicate with our whole self requires us to become astute observers of how we use and understand nonverbal cues. We need to become committed practitioners of effective body language—including, like Barbara Jordan, the tone and timbre of our own voice—as we pursue our practice of the A.R.T. of empowered refusal.

Putting Empowered Refusal into Practice

There is a reason why January 17 officially marks "Ditch Your New Year's Resolution" day. We have first-hand knowledge from our own lives, not only in January but also throughout the year, that the chasm between planning and implementation is often wide and deep.

In a research article I wrote with my coauthors, Alex Tawse and Dusya Vera, we proposed that planning has a flavor of optimism, excitement, and positive energy, which quickly dissipates when faced with the stark reality of doing. We identified the need for strategies that aid the transition from a thinking (planning) mode to a doing (implementation) mode. We wrote, "Like the coaching staff of a football team, the work does not stop with the development of a draft strategy, playbook, or game plan. The hard work of communicating, training, motivating, and developing teamwork must accompany the strategy in order to actualize the plans and achieve strategic goals."[29]

The rest of this book is designed to shift you from merely thinking about empowered refusal to addressing the practical realities of using empowered refusal in your daily life. I am going to guess, rightly I hope, that you did not pick up this book on empowered refusal to simply learn about the idea but not to glean its benefits. Reading about the A.R.T. (**A**wareness, **R**ules, not decisions, **T**otality of self) of empowered refusal is not enough: we need to face head-on the practicalities of implementing empowered refusal in our lives. In the chapters that follow, we will take the neat and tidy concept of empowered refusal and look at how it plays out in the messy reality of life.

Let's begin by addressing the eight-hundred-pound gorilla in the room: What if, despite my empowered refusal, the other person does not take no for an answer? How do I deal with the pushback? Let us, for this purpose, accept the likelihood of this eventuality. With the tools I will provide, our eyes will be trained to spot situations of influence and the pushback strategy being employed. We will also learn the value of a resolute mindset and acquire a repertoire of counter-persuasion strategies to fight fire with fire.

PART 3

THE PRACTICALITIES OF EMPOWERED REFUSAL

CHAPTER 7

Managing Pushback from Difficult Askers

There is wisdom in the natural world that can teach us a great deal about how to live. Consider the village of mother trees that work together to raise saplings and sustain and nurture younger trees by sharing their nutrients via a rich underground network of roots and fungi.[1] If you visit a vineyard in Épernay, in the heart of the Champagne region in France, you will see rose bushes adorning the perimeter of the vineyards. While rose bushes add a certain aesthetic to the region, they also serve a crucial function as an early warning signal of an impending aphid infestation or fungal attack. The susceptibility of rose bushes to black rot and powdery mildew serves as a harbinger to wine growers who can then do what they need to do to protect their crop. Ubiquitous and happily colored marigolds add a lovely splash of color to a garden, but when planted on the border of vegetable patches, they also display a unique superhero-like protective power. Marigolds produce a chemical called *alpha-terthienyl* that safeguards the roots of vegetable plants from attack by microscopic worms called nematodes.[2]

For hundreds of years, farmers have paid attention to nature and drawn on its wisdom to foster nurturing relationships among different plant species, a practice commonly referred to as *companion farming*.

Our own lives likely flourish in no small part because of the marigolds that care for and nurture us and the rose bushes that protect us from misfortune. Our family members, friends, coworkers, and mentors are like these good plants. These people help us succeed, cheer us on, hear us out, and support us in what we do. They are the ones who have our best interests at heart and serve as excellent sounding boards to help us make decisions that focus on what is good for us. These marigolds are most likely lifetime members of our "no club." We rely on these good people to protect us from unnecessary and unimportant commitments when we are unable, or sometimes even unwilling, to say no to the requests of others.[3] In my leadership classes, we often spend a few minutes listing the marigolds and rose bushes in our lives to acknowledge with gratitude that we do not achieve success without the support of others.

However, superheroes often have evil supervillain counterparts. Sadly, in the garden of our lives, some of us might fall under the deadly shade of a walnut tree or two.

Identifying Walnut Trees

Walnut trees, in particular the black walnut species native to North America, sport a luxuriant canopy, and their rich-colored wood can be crafted into beautiful furniture. But these trees have a dark side. Black walnut trees flourish at the cost of other plants. Their roots can spread fifty feet or more away from their trunks and exude a natural herbicide—a chemical called *juglone*—that kills or stunts the growth of many other plants in the vicinity.[4]

If you have ever taken one of my classes, you have heard me use the moniker "walnut tree" as a euphemism for the not-very-nice people we encounter in our personal and professional lives.[5] These are the people whom one would categorize as jerks, assholes, tyrants, and bullies. Walnut trees are those downright mean-spirited individuals who do their damnedest to sabotage our success; make us feel worthless and disempowered, annoyed, frustrated, anxious, and fearful; drain our energy with their overwhelming negativity; and make us cringe at the thought of any interaction with them. Walnut trees make our otherwise peaceful lives a living hell.[6]

Presumably like you, I have dealt with my own fair share of walnut trees—the most devastating of whom are the ones who will not take no, even an empowered no, for an answer. Let's face facts—the reality is that sometimes we will encounter a walnut tree who will push back on our empowered refusal. Regardless of how empowered our no is, and even if it is grounded in our identity and conveys our personal policies, these individuals completely disregard the "you" in you to enforce the "me" in themselves.

Since it is inevitable that we will encounter walnut trees in our lives at one point or another, we need to recognize the six main techniques walnut trees use to push back against your empowered refusal. Although you would prefer a magic wand to wish them far away, I hope to offer you the second-best option: the tools to develop a resolute mindset to deal with walnut trees and some common-sense strategies to hold them at bay. Remember, empowered refusal is taking responsibility for saying no because it is the right thing for you. When you take responsibility for your empowered refusal, you don't simply cave under pressure. Instead, you use your empowered stance to recognize pushback for what it is, spot the pushback tactic being employed, and confidently respond with courage and grace.

Feeling Powerful vs. Powerless in Our Relationships

Do you remember a time you felt on top of the world? Maybe you made a fantastic point in a meeting at work, wowed an audience with a stirring speech, successfully landed a client, or even posted something on social media and received an overwhelmingly positive response. These positive feelings are empowering: You feel blissfully content (happy); strong in mind, body, and spirit (healthy); and, to borrow from the catchy tune by the Carpenter siblings, you "won't be surprised if it's a dream."[7]

Our feelings of empowerment or personal power can have a profound effect on our daily lives. Our feelings of power are fueled by having a meaningful purpose that drives us (we know what we want and how to get there), the self-knowledge to make wise choices and decisions (we know ourselves, our strengths, and our weaknesses), and the self-confidence to handle what comes our way (we know that we have amassed the skills, talent, and experience we need to deal with what gets thrown at us). Research finds that how powerful we feel can shape how we think, what we feel, and the choices we make.[8] Feeling powerful helps us construe a difficult situation as a challenge or an opportunity, not as a personal threat. A healthy dose of personal power puts us in the driver's seat of our own lives.

But empowerment and disempowerment are two sides of the same coin. Our feelings of power can quickly turn to panic when we find ourselves in a difficult situation that we have never encountered before and are not equipped to deal with. Dealing with a walnut tree who catches us off guard can disempower us, especially if the walnut tree operates by undermining our purpose, questioning our self-knowledge, or knocking the bottom out of our self-confidence by making us feel inadequate and worthless.

Although we have immersed ourselves in the three core competencies we need to develop for empowered refusal, what if a walnut tree just will not take no for an answer? Walnut trees are not happy when we are empowered. They like the people around them to be submissive, compliant, and agreeable. They like the old you, not this newly empowered you, and they will try their best to keep you in that vulnerable spot by pushing back.

When we feel overpowered by a walnut tree, the guaranteed way to get out of the line of fire is to reach for the easy button and passively conform to the walnut tree's demands and expectations.[9] Going back to where we started in this book, when we feel disempowered, we are more likely to say yes, even if we want to say no, just to remove ourselves from the unbearable toxicity of the walnut tree.

What we need to do instead is to recognize what pushback looks like and employ counter-persuasion to push back against the pushback. As Peter Bregman, in a *Harvard Business Review* article, wrote: "Be as resolute as they are pushy. Some people don't give up easily. That's their prerogative. But without violating any of the rules above, give yourself permission to be just as pushy as they are."[10]

How Walnut Trees Cast Their Shade

The goal of the walnut tree is to control the situation, render you powerless and vulnerable, and, ultimately, manipulate you to backtrack and say yes to what they want. Let's first look at some common techniques walnut trees might use to take charge of a situation and disempower you.

Walnut trees will most likely approach you *face-to-face* with their request. Research finds that a face-to-face request is thirty-four times more successful in obtaining compliance than making the same request via email. Do you find it harder to say no when someone asks you for a favor in person vs. by phone, email, or text? If your answer is yes, you are not alone. Researchers show that even when the asker used the exact same script, they got greater compliance when that request was made in person as opposed to via email. Remember this: face-to-face is thirty-four times more effective in getting you to say yes![11]

Walnut trees will also seek a *home-court advantage* and set up to meet with you in a physical environment where they can comfortably exert greater dominance and control: their office or home, among their friends or family, or even at a restaurant where they are going to foot the bill. It is worth watching out for any situation in which the walnut tree feels at ease and in a dominant position, but you do not.[12]

Walnut trees will often insist on an *immediate response*. It is not uncommon for walnut trees to manufacture situations in which they create artificial pressure on you to submit to their demands. They might just happen to run into you in the hallway when you are in a rush and get you to say yes. They might enter the elevator with you and engage in some casual banter, but then hold the elevator door just as they are leaving and seek your agreement to their request while the alarm is buzzing and the elevator lights are flashing. They might catch you as you are dropping off your kids at school and ask you to take on some significant responsibility, knowing full well that your number-one priority in the moment is getting your kids, with their lunchboxes and their class projects, into their classrooms on time without a hitch. Do these instances resemble the stadium proposal moments we reflected on early in the book? Begin to observe with self-protective vigilance the ways in which walnut trees create high-arousal, high-pressure situations to get you to cave. Keep this in mind when, later in this chapter, we discuss two common traps walnut trees lay for us by using time to their advantage.

Walnut Tree Pushback Styles

Walnut trees employ two broad styles to obtain compliance: *active pushback,* in which a walnut tree might use their dominant position to put pressure on you to conform to their wishes, and *passive pushback,* in which they subtly manipulate your thoughts and feelings so that you yourself decide to change your mind and comply.

Before we get into the specifics, let's remind ourselves that regardless of the pushback strategy a walnut tree might employ, every single one of these tactics implicates the walnut tree and not you. I do not in any way want to diminish how negative or uncomfortable it feels to deal with a walnut tree, but I do want you to remember that your vulnerability stems from your goodness, sincerity, and feelings of responsibility. Rightfully, being assertive about what your priorities are and responding with empowered refusal should not elicit pushback, but sometimes it does. Together let's develop the expertise to spot the different ways in which a walnut tree will resist empowered refusal.

ACTIVE PUSHBACK USES EXTERNAL PRESSURE

Active pushback occurs when the walnut tree confronts your refusal directly. They typically employ three broad techniques to create *external pressure* to get you to change your mind: the enraged "How dare you?" response, the insistent, "I will wear you down," response, and, the bargaining, "I will do this for you in exchange," response. Let's understand how each of these works.

Enraged "How dare you?": Some people respond to your refusal with anger and aggression. They might challenge your decision with intimidation, name-calling, and threats. They might react with rage and hostility and even raise their voice or swear. Their flying off the handle can even be accompanied with physical aggression (banging doors, hitting the table, breaking things). Well-known individuals Steve Jobs and G.E.'s Jack Welch, recognized for their visionary leadership and business success, yelled at work. Yelling, it appears, was part of their competitive and demanding management style.[13]

Researchers Donald Gibson and Ronda Roberts Callister define anger as "an emotion that involves an appraisal of responsibility for wrongdoing by another person or entity and often includes the goal of correcting the perceived wrong."[14] Anger is often described as a social emotion that tends to be in response to another person's actions or response. In other words, when a walnut tree responds to you with anger it might stem from their belief that you are wrong in saying no. Here is an example to understand the enraged response.

Sarah works as a hostess at a restaurant. Pat, the restaurant manager, calls Sarah in and tells her that one of the servers has called in sick and that she will need to forfeit her day off the next day to fill in. Sarah responds saying, "Sorry, but no, that will not be possible." Sarah feels justified in saying no. It is her day off and she has things she needs to take care of. Plus, her job is as a hostess, not a server. Pat responds with anger. Pat yells at Sarah for not being a team player and threatens her that she could lose her job if she did not come in to work the next day in a server uniform. During the tirade, Pat calls Sarah "lazy," "selfish," and "entitled." Pat storms out of the office, slamming the door behind her.

Research finds that displays of anger occur for different reasons and can be triggered by different thought processes. Consider the following reasons to explain Pat's angry pushback.

→ Pat might have taken Sarah's refusal as a *personal offense.* Pat might think, *Sarah does not respect my authority. I am the boss. How dare she say no to me?*

→ Pat might see Sarah as being uncooperative and unhelpful in keeping the restaurant running smoothly. Pat would in this case view Sarah's no as *interfering with Pat's goal to run the restaurant well.* Pat might think, *I have to run the restaurant tomorrow. How do I do it with one less server? Sarah really needs to chip in for me to do my job.*

→ Sarah saying no feels *unfair and unjust* to Pat. Pat has her own problems to deal with and is angry that the server falling ill is adding to them. Pat thinks, *I was hoping for some cooperation from Sarah, but now I have to figure out how to manage the situation. This is so unfair*

→ Research also finds evidence for *trait aggression,* in which Pat simply has an aggressive personality and cannot take no for an answer. In this case, Pat's default response to someone disagreeing with her is to respond with anger and aggression.

Insistent "I will wear you down": When a walnut tree insists that you do what they ask and persists in their ask, their insistence stems from a belief that they are right and they can pressure you into agreeing with them. Some walnut trees tend to take on an authoritarian stance, implying that they know what's best for you and deny you your right to decide for yourself. Walnut trees hold strong beliefs in how they think things should be, so they persist and haggle till you see the light and respond in a way they think you should. When walnut trees use insistence, they turn a deaf ear to your protests and refuse to listen to your no. By simply not acknowledging your no, they attempt to coerce you to comply against your will.

Furthermore, with constant access to digital technology, a walnut tree's insistence and pushback can transition from the initial face-to-face encounter to a slew of emails and a barrage of texts that carry on for days till they finally wear you down. Consider how a woman in one of my studies described her mother's "I know what's best" walnut tree response: "I told her a very bold NO. She spent days trying to convince me to change my mind. She called my phone MANY times and texted me even more often. I just kept repeating my no and my reason for it."

Bargaining, "I will do this for you in exchange": Occasionally a walnut tree will use a refusal as an invitation to negotiate. Bargaining research experts define bargaining as "the process whereby two or more parties attempt to settle what each shall give and take, or perform and receive, in a transaction between them."[15] Keeping this definition in mind, the walnut tree does not see your no as a firm decision that allows you to walk away. Instead, they try to engage you in a dialogue and keep you invested in what they want. A walnut tree might sweeten the deal, offering you something they think is valuable to you in exchange for your compliance. The implicit assumption behind the "If you do this, I will do that" offer the walnut tree is making is that you can be bought off with something better.

Consider a typical COVID-19 pandemic dilemma: Jackie invites you to a restaurant for her fiftieth birthday party. You don't want to go because you are worried about contracting the virus. Your mutual friend Norah insists you both go together, reminding you that it is Jackie's special day. Norah also offers to go to the party early and help find a table with relatively few people. She even says that she would pick you up so that you wouldn't have to drive or find parking.

A walnut tree like Norah will entice you with money, convenience, a promise to return the favor at a later date, or an offer of loyalty and friendship if you convert your no to a yes. When bargaining, some people switch between a hard sell and a soft sell. They might balance out their negotiation by tugging at your heartstrings to make you change your mind. They might beg, cajole, or plead and make promises like, "Do it just this once," or "This is the last time. I will never ask again."

It might be useful here to draw on Adam Grant's definitions of "takers" from his book *Give and Take*, for walnut trees are undeniably takers.[16] He describes takers as those who "like to get more than they give" who "tilt reciprocity in their own favor, putting their own interests ahead of others' needs. Takers believe that the world is a competitive, dog-eat-dog place. They feel that to succeed, they need to be better than others."

Now that we have looked at some of the active ways in which walnut trees push back and demonstrate "taker-like" tendencies, let's look at some more passive means walnut trees employ. They may be passive, but they are no less taker-like.

PASSIVE PUSHBACK CREATES INTERNAL PRESSURE

Passive pushback occurs when a walnut tree does not confront your refusal directly, but instead uses indirect means to make *you* want to change your mind yourself. Walnut trees know that saying no is undeniably hard, and they realize that if they can make you feel bad about saying no you might change your mind. Do you recall the dominant emotions we feel when we are in the spotlight? These negative feelings of guilt, shame, obligation, and regret are what walnut trees intuitively leverage to get you to change your no to a yes. Social psychologists have explored in depth how walnut trees can make us feel bad about ourselves, often describing the use of these aversive techniques as "the underbelly of social interaction."[17] The main strategies that walnut trees employ for passive pushback are: the guilt-tripping "How *can* you?" response, the you'll-regret-this "FOMO"(fear of missing out) response, and the you'll-be-sorry "silent treatment" response.

Guilt-tripping "How can you?": Walnut trees tend to view your decision to say no as morally wrong. By treating your refusal as a transgression, they make you feel guilty about your decision and encourage you to repair your wrongdoing and comply with their request. Friends might remind you of your social obligations, and family members might use their relational ties to get you to do what they want. They implicate your identity, saying, "How can you find it in your heart to?" or "You aren't being a good friend."

A senior executive in one of my classes, let's call her Sandy, mentioned that she had been trying to get out of being president of her neighborhood association. She had been an active member for years and then took over as president. Her involvement and leadership had resulted in some positive changes to the neighborhood, from new bike paths to improved street lighting and enlightened parking regulations. But in recent years, with her work responsibilities mounting, she was having a hard time keeping her head above water. However, every time she decided not to stand for reelection, her friends and neighbors convinced her otherwise, saying, "It is for the good of the association," "You are the only one who has such a good relationship with the city officials," and, "If you don't do it, no one else will." She felt responsible for the neighborhood after so many years of dedicated service to the association and felt guilty for saying no. If you were in Sandy's place, what would you do? Are there steps you could take to manage your transition out of your leadership position without feeling racked with guilt?

FOMO "You'll regret missing out": FOMO is a common experience, especially with the emergence of social media. Today it is so easy to know about all the activities—both online and offline—that one could be engaging in. Researchers describe FOMO as "a pervasive apprehension that others might be having rewarding experiences from which one is absent."[18] FOMO taps into our human need to belong and our desire to stay connected with others and participate in social activities and events.

Walnut trees can be astute exploiters of FOMO, reminding you of everything you might miss out on if you stick with your no. They might trigger feelings of anticipatory regret, saying, "This opportunity may not come again, and we should enjoy it while it lasts." When you say no to going to an event, they will remind you that "it will be fun and the food will be good."

It is true that when you say no, it usually means that you are passing up an opportunity. However, as you consider your options, keep in mind that by saying no to the walnut tree's request, you are saying yes to something else that you value more highly. Opportunities can be found in both. You're simply picking one option over the other. Walnut trees who use FOMO will try and make you look outwards and think about what you might be missing out on rather than letting you look inward and decide what is right for you to do.

Silent Treatment "You'll-be-sorry": An ominous, stony response to your refusal is almost as intimidating as outright yelling. Walnut trees might display this response as a warning of the disaster that will befall you if you persist in your position of saying no. Silent treatment is a form of social ostracism in which a walnut tree punishes you with "avoidance of eye contact and absence of verbal communication."[19]

Research finds that giving someone the silent treatment is a different, more passive, expression of anger.[20] You might observe silent yelling in the walnut tree's body language and facial expressions. The body language warns, change your mind or you will be sorry. Walnut trees punish you by ignoring you at social events or by pretending they did not see you at a gathering until you come around and change your mind. Walnut trees try to create doubt and uncertainty in your mind by deliberately not responding to your calls, texts, and emails in a timely manner.

One woman from one of my studies described the silent treatment she experienced this way: "This person did not necessarily say anything to change my mind but did start treating me very, very differently from the moment I said 'no.' This person started to purposely be rude and mean to me, as well as exclude me in public settings to in a sense show me how that 'no' I said affected her, and how (she) wanted me to feel bad about my decision."

In an online environment, the walnut tree can easily even ghost you. Ghosting occurs when one individual in a relationship abruptly disappears from the life of the other. For the ghoster, it is easy to ignore your calls, texts, messages, and emails, or just actively block you on their devices to show their anger or disapproval. What do you feel if you are the ghostee? It turns out that ghosting has a negative impact on self-esteem, leaving the ghostee feeling insecure, vulnerable, and unwanted.[21] Radio silence is the worst kind of silence. Making someone feel like they don't exist is a cruel form of ostracism.

PREVALENCE OF ACTIVE VS. PASSIVE PUSHBACK

Psychologist Bill Knaus suggests that people who are pushy and manipulative usually have an agenda. They might need or want certain things to get done and they want those things to get done in a certain way.[22] To further their own agendas, walnut trees resist your refusal, using both active pushback strategies and passive pushback strategies to get you to comply.[23] But which of the strategies we discussed are most prevalent in everyday situations?

To understand the social pressure that people experience when they say no, I conducted a survey with 332 business undergraduate students (60 percent female; age range nineteen to forty-two years old) who were enrolled in a professional program. I requested them to "please think about a time that someone (a friend or family member) made a request of you, asked you a favor, or invited you to go somewhere you did not want to go. You said no to that person, but the person did not want to take no for an answer. They tried to convince you to change your mind. People push back against our decision to say no in different ways; we want to understand your experience."

The stories were coded to reflect one of six pushback strategies. The results of this survey revealed a representation of all the types of pushback strategies we discussed, but to varying degrees. As Figure 7.1 shows, the participants reported the highest incidence of insistence (active pushback) and guilt-tripping (passive pushback).[24]

Figure 7.1: Pushback Styles

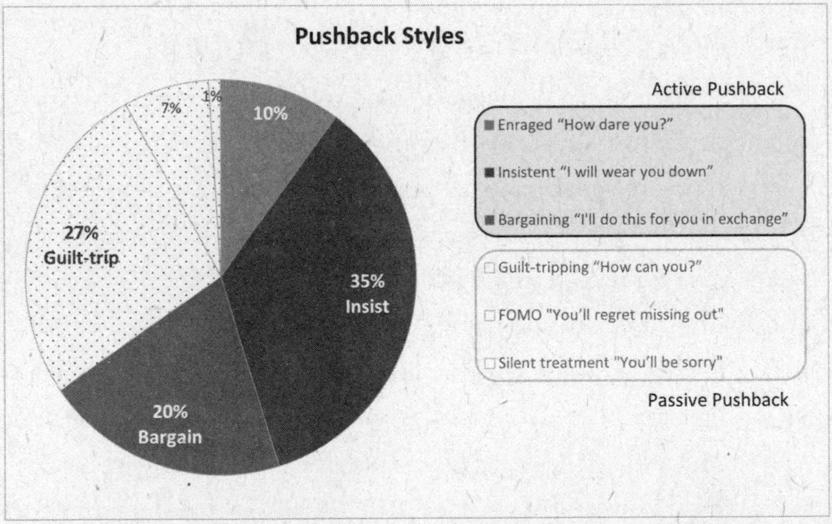

Since this survey was based on the recall of a pushback episode, I also wanted to capture how people felt after receiving pushback to saying no. I measured the emotions participants experienced after recalling the pushback episode by asking them to respond to the question, "How did this experience make you feel?" I assessed the extent to which the participant reported experiencing a list of negative emotions (1 = does not describe my feelings; 5 = clearly describes my feelings). It is probably no surprise that getting pushback is a negative experience, leaving people feeling angry, resentful, upset, and guilty. Interestingly, the use of passive pushback techniques did not diminish the negativity of the experience. The intensity of anger and resentment, as well as feeling upset and guilty, were reported in equal measure across both pushback styles.

Now that we have understood how walnut trees push back and how we respond, let's move on to learn some strategies to lessen the impact of pushback.

Making Ourselves Steadfast and Strong

When we must deal with a walnut tree, perhaps especially when we have to say no to one, it is quite natural to feel anxious and vulnerable. It is worth reminding ourselves that "we either make ourselves miserable, or we make ourselves strong. The amount of work is the same."[25] Instead of lamenting about the walnut trees in our lives and feeling miserable, we need to direct our energy to learning to respond to a walnut tree's pushback with strength and grace. Psychologist Knaus advises, "Knowing where you stand on important issues, and where you control the agenda, simplifies dealing with agenda-driven people whose pushiness can put you off but where you may ordinarily capitulate to avoid causing bad feelings." [26]

DEVELOP A RESOLUTE MINDSET

How we approach walnut trees stems from how we think about them and their motivation. As we have previously seen, the way we think about things—our mindset—matters. To effectively counter a walnut tree's pushback against our empowered refusal, we need to develop a resolute mindset fueled by the conviction we have for the stance we have taken and our decision to say no. What are some ways to regard a walnut tree's attempt at manipulation to win the battle against them? First, and of foremost importance, is that we need to attribute the pushback we receive from a walnut tree to be about them and not about us. As much as a walnut tree might try to change our mind, remember it is their walnut tree essence that does not allow them to accept your refusal—it has little to do with you.

Another useful perspective to adopt is to accept pushback as normal and expected. It is wisest to accept that you will occasionally get pushback when you say no to others. When I sense resistance, I have learned to tell myself something that the architect/designer Maya Lin once said: "Resistance is what makes birds fly." Framing pushback positively, even normalizing it as something you will sometimes encounter, lessens some of the negative emotions that accompany pushback and aids in your quest for personal mastery.

Let's also try and view the pushback we might receive from walnut trees as a challenge or a hurdle that you simply must overcome. For most people the path to personal and professional success is an obstacle course. We cannot let the obstacles stop us; we need to empower ourselves to figure out a workaround. Author, educator, and speaker Stephen Covey once wisely observed, "We develop our character muscles by overcoming challenges and obstacles."

Finally, the greater self-awareness we have about what enables us and what disables us, the better equipped we are to manage the pushback from walnut trees. One of the first exercises my friend, co-instructor, and Professor of Management Dusya Vera does in our leadership trainings is an exercise in which participants come to class having thought about two stories from their own lives. Participants are instructed to think about times that they felt vulnerable at work. For their first story, they have to think about a time in which they overcame their vulnerability and dared to move forward with courage. For their second story, they have to recall a time they backed down and succumbed to their vulnerability. This self-reflection exercise is designed to increase the participant's self-awareness about how they respond to difficult situations. When we understand for ourselves the factors that *enable* us to stand our ground even when we are feeling vulnerable, we feel empowered and are better equipped to counteract the pushback of a walnut tree. Let's discuss some enabler strategies (some of which you might already use, and some of which you can learn to employ) that help us deal with pushback from walnut trees.

ENABLER STRATEGIES FOR EMPOWERED REFUSAL

Two broad sets of enabler strategies can be employed to deal with pushback from walnut trees. The first set of enabler strategies *reinforces our position* to respectfully stick to our decision to say no. These strategies help us counter the active and passive pushback we receive in the moment. The second set of enabler strategies can be used to limit the toxicity of the walnut tree and counter our impulse to say yes by *creating distance* from the walnut tree. Let's first discuss how the *reinforcer strategies* might work for you.

Spell It Out: If a walnut tree is pushing too hard and making you uncomfortable, you can tell them exactly how you feel by spelling it out. You can say several things you have learned in this book, like "I'm the one who decides whether I do something or not," or "I have already told you where I stand. Please respect my decision." You can describe the situation by saying, "Please don't keep on asking. All you are doing is making me say no five times instead of just once." You can even express your vulnerability: "It is making me very uncomfortable to have to keep saying no to you." Or you can put the ball in your own court by saying, "If I change my mind, I will let you know."

State Your "No Means No" Personal Policy: Sometimes it helps to share your personal policies as announcements. You can simply state your policy to the walnut tree to reinforce your stance on the matter. For instance, you might tell a work colleague who is trying to guilt-trip you into taking on a new project, "I have a policy not to take on a new project until I complete what I already have on my plate." If a friend is repeatedly trying to get you to do something you do not want to do, ensure that you communicate that your refusal stems from your values.

Sometimes we need to give a walnut tree a compelling reason that they cannot push back on. Research finds that although we often decline an invitation by citing a lack of time, while the real reason could be because we don't have the money and can't afford the expense. Research finds that saying, "I don't have time," can lead the asker to feel undervalued, while telling the truth about not having money can be more sincere and readily accepted.[27] Of course, if you use the "I don't have the money" reason, then you should be willing to accept the invitation if the asker offers to cover the cost or change the activity to something within your budget.

For some walnut trees, you need to stubbornly repeat your refusal by channeling your five-year-old self. If they are going to insist that you change your mind, then you must keep saying no. Remember, "no" is a full sentence. If you want to mix things up, and perhaps diffuse some of the tension, consider repeating your no in different languages or in different voices. Some language options to consider include: the German *nein* (nine), the Hindi नहीं (nah-hee), the Russian Нет (nyeht), and the Chinese *bù shì* (boo-shih). Some voice options to consider depending on your style, talent, and humor: Sing out your no. Spell out your refusal, "en oh." Or borrow from the unique cadence and tone of a robotic Wall-E voice, a cartoon-like Bugs Bunny or Mickey Mouse voice, or the charming and versatile voice of Aladdin's genie.[28]

Draw In for Buy-In: One counterintuitive strategy to deal with walnut trees is to bring them closer rather than push them away. We all have people in our life who make repetitive, sometimes burdensome, requests of us. Sometimes we can draw a walnut tree onto our side by preempting their request and coming to an agreement before they can actually make the ask. For instance, if you know that it is your turn to host Christmas lunch at your home, then do it on your terms by planning the menu and assigning responsibilities before a walnut tree family member tells you exactly how the holiday should be spent. If you know that a demanding colleague will want to take a red-eye flight to "make the most of the day," be sure to fill in your travel request paper in time to account for daytime travel.

Sometimes walnut trees need you to say yes so that they do not lose face when you say no. In these cases, it can be better to decline the request before it even arrives. At work, you can inform the person that you are hyper-focused on a few things in your life and are attempting to lessen your duties in all other areas. If your boss is the one who makes the request, try and create an agreement with her up front on how you should use your time. When the requests start coming in, you can refer back to your previous interaction.

Now let's move on to *strategies that create distance* between you and the walnut tree.

Buy Time: When dealing with walnut trees, we need to use time to our advantage. Earlier in the book we discussed the spotlight effect. One way to diffuse the spotlight is to buy time. If you are feeling in the spotlight and like you are being coerced to do something against your better judgment, choose to delay. Make it a personal policy to never say yes on the spot. Ask for the time to consider your response before making a commitment.

One handy practice to embrace is, before saying yes to something, pull out your calendar and schedule exactly when you are going to do it. If you look at your calendar and the task looks impossible to accomplish, you probably have given yourself a heightened conviction for why you are responding with a no. If you do have time on your calendar, book that time right away. In fact, reserve twice as much time as you think it will take to do it right. These scheduling rules are helpful because they force you to recognize that saying yes, even to a walnut tree, has a very real cost. Also remember, just because you have time on your calendar does not mean you should say yes to every request that comes your way. Consider the opportunity costs—the something else that might come your way that is a more interesting and important way to spend your time.

Delegate Your No: Transitioning from doing to leading is one of the hardest shifts a leader has to make. This is compounded by the fact that leaders are often asked, quite frequently by walnut trees, to roll up their sleeves and do even when what they need to focus on is to lead. When a walnut tree gives you an assignment that is of a more tactical nature, you first need to identify whether that task is better delegated to others. Although the last thing you want to do is foist a walnut tree on someone else, you need to counter the walnut tree's pushback and clearly communicate the mismatch between your priorities and the task at hand.

When you occupy a leadership position, you can even delegate your no response to someone else. It is quite common for a leader to maintain a friendly, pleasant, and agreeable stance (the good cop) and have someone else in their office be the tough one, the person who asks for money, or the one who says no (the bad cop).

If you are going to delegate your no, consider having an Emily Wilson–like individual on your team. In his autobiography, *A Life in our Times,* the renowned economist John Galbraith narrated a tale of his devoted housekeeper of forty years, Emily Gloria Wilson. It was an afternoon in 1965 when the noted economist was taking a nap and asked not to be disturbed. The phone rang and Emily picked it up, and it was President Lyndon Johnson on the other end of the line. She told the president, "He's taking a nap and has left strict orders not to be disturbed." In a huff, President

Johnson replied, "Well, I'm the president. Wake him up." Before she hung up, she responded, "I'm sorry, Mr. President, but I work for Mr. Galbraith, not for you." After Galbraith woke up from his nap, he promptly returned the president's call, somewhat mortified. The first thing President Johnson wanted to know was the identity of the woman who had firmly told him no. The economist reluctantly shared her name. His pleasure uncontained, the president said, "Tell that woman I want her here in the White House working for me."

Technology as a Buffer: Because a great deal of our communication today is done in the digital realm, we get pushback via email, texts, WhatsApp, Facebook, LinkedIn, etc. At least two things help us stand our ground when we deal with pushback in an online space: (1) it is a technology-mediated environment, so the social pressure of a face-to-face interaction is diminished, and (2) it is asynchronous, so we can strategically and thoughtfully craft our response.

With online requests, we are less likely to feel the same intensity of the glare of the spotlight than we would with an in-person request. With this diminished spotlight, you can consider the request more carefully. This does not mean that you will not agonize over whether you should say yes or no. But you can use the time to be able to think through the request, evaluate the trade-offs, and make a decision that suits you. You also can consult your "no club," and run through your pros and cons list. The best thing about online requests is that you can craft an effective refusal in writing.

A number of people keep a repository of nicely phrased refusals that use empowering language and emotive words. In a brilliant essay titled "Wives of the Organization," strategy and innovation expert Anne Sigismund Huff recommends that we keep a file of no letters to become more effective at denying requests to "become involved in secondary activities." Here is what she writes about a letter template she used (we might have to adapt this to email): "One of the early ones has had wide circulation as a model among my colleagues. It says: Thank you for asking me to become involved in X, which is an important contribution to this community and one that I value. However, I must decline. As an untenured assistant professor, I feel the interests of the university, as well as my own interests, are best served by focusing on my research." She asks the reader to consider crafting similar correspondence "that can be adapted to the many demands made of you and one that needs to be rewritten and rephrased at every stage in one's career." The idea that Huff proposed is that it is not in our best interest, nor in the best interest of the organizations that we work for, to take on work that is not rewarding.

As we have learned we need to use "standing up" phrases like "I don't," "I won't," "I have a policy that," that are sometimes easier to write than to say. Also use words that convey a strong and secure position, like absolutist words (*always, never, certain, absolutely*) and emotive words (*deeply, delightful, confident, unique, grateful, fulfilled, genuine*).

Beyond the words you can have access to, technology has also introduced a new digital nonverbal language: emojis, emoticons, and gifs. In the same way that there is no playbook for how to harness nonverbal cues, there is no perfect set of recommendations out there for interpersonal digital communication. Studies show that the use of emojis and emoticons has increased significantly. These devices serve several functions, with emojis being most effective in conveying the meaning of a statement by signaling emotion.

Sharpening Our Persuasion Knowledge

As human beings, one of the most valuable domains of knowledge that we can invest in is understanding other people and how they operate. One reason why middle school can be so daunting is that it is the stage of socialization when children begin to independently relate to their peers without parental influence and get to see the good, bad, and ugly sides of others. From this time on, we need to become adept at understanding the agendas of others, the way bullies operate, and learn to see through manipulative tactics, even though they might be couched in praise and flattery.

Researchers Marian Friestad and Peter Wright term this unique sociocognitive resource *persuasion knowledge* and describe it as an "interpretative belief system because it tells people about situations where an intelligent, purposeful outside agent is skillfully trying to alter their inner self (their beliefs, their emotions, their attitudes, their decisions, their thought processes) and thereby alter the course of their lives."[29]

In the context of pushback, those intelligent, purposeful outside agents are the walnut trees whose alterations are not valuable or desirable to us. I shuddered when I read Friestad and Wright's ominous conclusion: "Individuals who allow unnoticed or uncontrolled invasions of their internal psychological world, and consequently changes in their behaviors, do not survive and prosper."

One way to develop and skillfully employ persuasion knowledge is to gain from our experience with walnut trees and learn from our mistakes. Consider the walnut trees in our lives. Thus far, our interactions with them have likely been negative, and it is also likely that on occasion we have caved in to their demands. Recall that walnut trees will try their best to trap you into saying yes and lock you in to a commitment that you might have a hard time getting out of. There are two traps to be aware of as you think about how to deal with walnut trees:

THE "YOU CAN'T BACK OUT NOW" TRAP

A walnut tree strives to get you to say yes in the moment. Why? Saying no is not easy, but it feels virtually impossible to say no after you have said yes. Once you have uttered that one little word, you think of your yes like a contract that is signed and sealed.

Has this happened to you? Perhaps a colleague has asked you to join a new project team. Maybe a friend has asked you to go on a weekend trip. In the moment it sounds exciting and fun, so you say yes. But then later you realize that taking on the new project or going on the weekend trip is not the right thing for you to do. You have other deadlines and commitments to deal with, but you worry that you cannot back out. Executive coach Melody Wilding says this: "Whether you have overbooked yourself, realized you have a conflict, or otherwise can't or don't want to participate in a project, it's essential to uncommit gracefully."[30] Here's the thing: If you were gracious and explained your situation, most decent people (like marigolds and rose bushes) would understand, empathize, and be gracious in return. Walnut trees, on the other hand, are less likely to give you an easy pass. They thrive on making it as painful as possible for you to leave, so when you know you are dealing with a walnut tree, go slow. Go very slow. Once you are ensnared, they will not let you go very easily.

THE TIME-RICH FUTURE TRAP

Research shows that we tend to think we will have more time or energy or space in our calendar in the future than we have now. Given our susceptibility to the belief that the future is time-rich, walnut trees very often ask us to do things well into the future. This is one surefire way in which a walnut tree can push back against your refusal. Since the request is not for another three months or six months, they refuse to take your no for an answer because you have time to plan. They might even leave it open for you to take the time you need to decide, and in the meantime, they are sure that they will be able to wear you down. Resource slack manifests itself in our lives like this: While three months ago, it seemed fine for you to say yes when it felt like you had infinite time, the reality is you will be as free three months from now as you are today. Which, sadly, is not very free!

When you get a "well in advance" request, imagine that the ask is for something three days away and not three months away. Also, remind yourself that your values are not going to change, so just because you might have time in the future, you still do not want to spend that time doing something that is not aligned with your purpose.

Gaining from Our Exposure to Walnut Trees

It should come as no surprise that research shows that we would much rather avoid the request of a walnut tree than engage with one. But consider this: we do not get to practice how best to deal with a walnut tree if we spend our entire lives dodging them.

If you were terrified of snakes, crocodiles, or spiders, you would want to avoid them at all costs. If your fear became debilitating, you might go to a psychologist, who would likely recommend greater, not lesser, exposure to the source of fear. Exposure therapy is grounded in the idea of desensitization. If you expose yourself to the object of fear, it becomes less ominous and more manageable. In the same way, when you find yourself shrinking away from the ask of a walnut tree, consider whether you might use the opportunity to employ empowered refusal to ward them away once and for all (and remember the studies on excuses vs. personal policies).

In my own research, I have found that occasionally people are prone to describe pushback by a walnut tree, followed by them giving in, and then finally concluding that it was "not so bad" or that they are glad they did it. While this can sometimes be true, we need to also be aware of a nifty trick our minds play on us when dealing with negative situations. We tend to make sense of a negative experience by identifying a silver lining.

Researchers at Harvard refer to our collective coping responses as a *psychological immune system*. Like the immune system that gears into action when a bacterium or a virus enters our body, the psychological immune system kicks into action when something negative occurs.[31] Let's imagine that we said yes to something when we wanted to say no. Now we feel miserable about that stinking pile of garbage that has become our responsibility. We are frustrated and angry with ourselves for not saying no.

How do we cope with these negative feelings? We find a silver lining.

We seek out the one good outcome that might have occurred from taking the task on and latch onto that. We might convince ourselves that we will reap the rewards in the future or that we will be recognized and rewarded for this. Don't get me wrong! This is great and it is adaptive. The psychological immune system is good for our mental health and well-being, but it is terrible for learning from our mistakes. Silver linings actually make us prone to repeating them. When we inadvertently say yes to an ask, we need to allow ourselves to languish in the pain. We need to calculate the opportunity costs of our reluctant yes and understand how much saying that reluctant yes has cost us. We need to painfully account for the late nights we put in or the sleep-ins we had to forgo to deliver on our promise. When we stop adaptively coping with our reluctant yeses when they should have been a resounding no, we begin to break the vicious cycle of mindless compliance and sharpen our persuasion knowledge.

The trick to learning from our negative interactions with walnut trees is to underscore, not undermine, the huge costs we bear for saying yes to "bake your famous lasagna" asks or from agreeing to take on "email, tweet, posts" tasks simply because a walnut tree pushed back against our refusal. Embrace the pain now so that you will not have to endure it again. Keep in mind Roman poet Ovid's words: "Be patient and tough; one day this pain will be useful to you."

CHAPTER 8

Getting Out of Our Own Way

"O powerful Goodness! bountiful Father! merciful Guide! Increase in me that wisdom which discovers my truest interest. Strengthen my resolution to perform what that wisdom dictates. Accept my kind offices to Thy other children as the only return in my power for Thy continual favors to me."[1] This is the morning mantra that set the tone for Benjamin Franklin's day for most of his adult life.

Nowhere, I believe, is Franklin's "truest interest" more evident than amidst the things he created, tinkered with, and acquired over his lifetime, now displayed at the Benjamin Franklin Museum in Philadelphia. I spent a rainy afternoon a few years ago in the museum that was designed, I thought, in a way that would very much appeal to Benjamin Franklin's sensibilities. Organized into five rooms, each of which reflected the particular set of values that Franklin abided by (ardent and dutiful, ambitious and rebellious, motivated to improve, curious and full of wonder, and strategic and persuasive), the museum brought to life the way Benjamin Franklin lived: with resolute intentionality.[2]

He started each day at 5:00 a.m. pondering the question: "What good shall I do this day?" And he kept himself accountable by ending the day with the question: "What good have I done to-day?" By rigorously monitoring his daily choices and actions, Franklin made every day count. More than three hundred years after his birth, many of Benjamin Franklin's practical contributions to the world—the lightning rod, the catheter, bifocals, and the household stove—still impact our lives. No less intriguing are some of his lesser known, yet fascinating, inventions: the divided soup bowl (for eating soup less messily while on a ship in a turbulent sea), the glass armonica (an enchanting instrument with glass bowls fitted with cork one inside the other in a decorated shell that can be closed and handily transported around), and, of course, swim fins (invented when Franklin was only eleven).

As I wandered around the museum I remained in awe of how much he had accomplished, and I couldn't help but wonder: *How in the world did he get so much done in one lifetime?* Spending time in the room dedicated to Franklin's motivation to improve, I was struck by the realization that this singular value likely enabled and facilitated the other four. Luckily for us, Benjamin Franklin practiced "thinking on paper" (a "writing things down" habit I often recommend to my students) to clearly articulate his list of thirteen virtues and the precepts he lived by; record his daily schedules, including his daily wine consumption; and document in various ways the thoughtful and deliberate way in which he lived his life.

I asked myself that rainy afternoon the question I ask you now: If you had to create a set of "rooms of your own" that represent what you value, what would your rooms be? Could you, at this point in your life, legitimately fill your rooms with tangible proof that you have lived in accordance with those values?

Benjamin Franklin's rooms reflect his self-discipline and

singularity of purpose, but this also naturally implies that he had to narrow his playing field and focus his attention on the things that mattered to him. Franklin, for instance, did not care to pursue wealth and ownership for its own sake. He chose not to patent his inventions and make money off them; instead he shared them so that they could be widely used. He prioritized his thirteen virtues in order of importance and systematically tackled them one by one. About this strategy he wrote, "I judg'd it would be well not to distract my attention by attempting the whole at once, but to fix it on one of them at a time, and, when I should be master of that, then to proceed to another, and so on, till I should have gone thro' the thirteen."

He dedicated his mornings to his own intellectual pursuits and refused to meet anyone until he got his most important work for the day done. In fact, on Wednesday, May 27, 1778, John Adams, future second president of the United States, wrote complainingly in his diary about Franklin's unavailability during the morning hours. He wrote, "I could never obtain the favour of his Company in a Morning before Breakfast which would have been the most convenient time to read over the Letters and papers, deliberate on their contents, and decide upon the Substance of the Answers."[3] Clearly what was a convenient time for John Adams did not quite work for Benjamin Franklin!

Like Franklin, we need to turn inward and take ownership of the rooms of our life with compassionate self-discipline. We will learn to use self-talk—the voice in our heads—to motivate us and guide our actions and behaviors. We will ponder the systems we need to set up to nudge ourselves to live a life of passion and purpose. We will walk away recognizing that inner order shapes our outward success and profoundly influences how we show up in the world.

Temptations and Distractions Are Everywhere

"If we cannot say no to ourselves, how can we say no to others?" This is the question a woman named Kristin posed to me more than a decade ago that first propelled me into the study of empowered refusal. I often like to say, "It all began with Kristin." Here's the story.

Kristin, like most working moms, had become adept at juggling home and work responsibilities. Every evening, however, after a long day at work and after she had rushed to pick up one daughter from kindergarten and the other one from day care, Kristin found herself heading to a drive-through on her way home. She did not want to resort to eating fast food for dinner every night, and she felt really guilty afterward, but she was so tired at the end of the day that the thought of cooking a meal was daunting. This pattern of behavior had become a habit, and one that she really wanted to break. This was her pain point (recall the DREAM framework, and the importance of clearly identifying a pain point).

Like Kristin, many of us are plagued with unhealthy or unproductive patterns of behavior that have gone unchecked for so long that they have become a habit that we really want to break but don't know how.

Based on some early observations on the power of self-talk, I offered her some friendly advice. It was a germ of an idea at the time (one you will now likely recognize) when I made the casual recommendation: Tell yourself "I don't" instead of "I can't." I explained that when she was driving home she needed to literally put herself in the driver's seat of her own life. She needed to recognize that fast food drive-throughs were a pain point and that she needed to tell herself, "I don't pick up dinner from drive-throughs after work." To support this self-talk, Kristin also had to set herself up for success. For instance, she could spend thirty minutes on the weekend doing some meal planning, she could invest in learning some easy and tasty weeknight recipes, she could enlist her husband and children in preparing the meal, and when she had some time in the morning, she could consider getting some dinner prep done: defrost some chicken or fish before work or chop vegetables for a stir-fry.

At the time Kristin seemed skeptical that such a simple switch in language would actually work, so I left it at that. About a month later, I met Kristin again. She was gushing. She told me that what we now know as the "standing up" words that characterize empowered refusal had really worked well for her. She said that she told herself, "I don't eat fast food on weeknights," and that decision triggered her motivation to get herself out of the rut she felt she was in. What Kristin discovered was the power of self-talk and personal policies. What she needed was to put a system in place that worked for her and to use self-talk that made her feel empowered to operate within that system.

Responding to Temptation with Deprivation

We have to acknowledge an obvious human dilemma: temptation is all around us, luring us away from our best selves with short-term promises of pleasure. French novelist Marcel Proust wrote, in *Remembrance of Things Past, Volume II: Within a Budding Grove,* "It is always thus, impelled by a state of mind which is destined not to last, we make our irrevocable decisions."

When I met Kristin, I was an assistant professor working on a number of projects that dealt with how to resist temptation. At the time, the study of self-regulation was a hot research topic, and researchers were looking at new ways to manage temptation, given the proliferation of abundant food options, entertainment choices, and of course the ever-present draw of social media. The academic literature at the time was brimming with research articles describing our helplessness at the hands of desire and the different ways the pull of temptation rendered us powerless to resist. The powerful pull of desire that activates the release of the dopamine (often dubbed the "happy hormone") gets us hooked, so we begin to crave the feeling of pleasure. Eating a doughnut or even the ping of a notification of a new email or tweet can trigger a surge of dopamine, leading us to succumb to grabbing the tasty treat or abandon our work to check email or Twitter. The world we live in is so full of candy of every stripe, being offered to us at every turn, that it becomes irresistible.

A battle takes place within us between willpower and desire. Each time we are faced with a temptation or need to say no to ourselves to reduce or stop a behavior, we use up willpower. If you want to reduce your sugar intake, each craving for a sugary treat utilizes willpower to stay on track. If you are at work, every Instagram, WhatsApp, or Twitter notification makes you feel curious about what is going on in the world that you are not engaged in (remember FOMO?). Being tired, hungry, or sleepy can make our ability to resist a temptation even weaker, making us more likely to give in and give up. This was exactly what was happening to Kristin. She simply did not have the energy at the end of a long workday to regulate her behavior and stop doing the easiest thing—picking up dinner and getting that chore over with. Are there easy things you default to when you are tired, hungry, or sleepy?

To vividly illustrate the human struggle to manage temptation, researchers commonly draw on stories like the trap of the sirens' song from Homer's *Odyssey*. Consider the sirens. In classical mythology, the sirens were part bird and part beautiful woman. They had voices so lovely that they lured unsuspecting sailors toward their islands, shipwrecking their boats, and causing their deaths. To avoid the lure of the sirens' song, Odysseus plugged his crew's ears with wax and had himself tied to the mast of the ship. It was imminently clear to Homer a few thousand years ago, as it seems to be to us today, that the solution to temptation appears to be holding yourself back, tying yourself down, exercising restraint through deprivation.

However, research shows that deprivation does not work in the long run.[4] If you tell yourself you can't eat something or do something, when that thing does becomes available the temptation to indulge becomes so strong that it can be impossible to resist. Depriving yourself of what you desire only makes the desired thing more desirable. You become more fixated on that object and begin to crave it. Researchers find that objects that have the potential to satisfy a craving, such as a cigarette when in a state of nicotine withdrawal, increase in perceived value, resulting in people being willing to pay more for a cigarette when in a state of nicotine deprivation than when they have recently satisfied their need for nicotine.[5] Remember that our default behavior is to yield to temptation,[6] so the desire and craving induced by deprivation almost guarantees that self-control will be sabotaged. In one of my own research articles, we show that depriving ourselves of a desirable opportunity (discounted amusement park tickets or a weekend trip to Las Vegas with friends) increases our desire to avail of that opportunity when it comes along again. My coauthors and I find that we leap with greater enthusiasm to grab with both hands a forgone pleasure when given a second chance.[7]

It is more than a cliché that when you can't have something, you desire it more. So, instead of relying on deprivation, which feels bad and often does not work, in my own work, I have been drawn to a more compassionate form of self-regulation.

Compassionate Self-Control

To introduce this idea, I will share a story about the Buddha that profoundly influenced the way I think about self-regulation.[8]

After the Buddha renounced his wealth, position, title as a royal prince, and all the earthly pleasures that go alongside, he retreated into the forest to seek enlightenment. He sat under the Bodhi tree and meditated along with five other men also seeking wisdom and enlightenment. Each day, they consumed only a small fruit for sustenance and nothing else. The belief was that wisdom and enlightenment is bestowed upon people who deprive themselves of the daily sustenance needed by mere mortals. As the story goes, one day the Buddha was walking into a nearby town but he was so weak from lack of food that he collapsed. He was found by a villager whose name was Sujata. Sujata revived him by giving him a cup of milk. He was revived and refreshed and asked her for another cup. By and by, he shared with Sujata his mission to seek enlightenment, and she wanted to support him and offered him her help.

The Buddha asked her to bring him a small bowl of rice every day.

So entrenched was the notion that deprivation is the key to

divine illumination, that the five friends of the Buddha who saw him eating a bowl of rice every day now regarded him with disdain. They deemed him weak and needy and undeserving of enlightenment, so they moved on without him. Left alone in the forest, with the exception of the daily visit by Sujata who brought him his bowl of rice and the occasional cup of milk, the Buddha settled under the Bodhi tree and soon attained enlightenment—a deep and profound understanding of, and compassion for, all beings.

Inspired by this story and drawing on the notion that there had to be a better way to self-regulate than deprivation, the way I study how to live the best possible life and achieve one's version of success and personal mastery does not involve pain, guilt, deprivation, anxiety, or fear. I believe from the bottom of my heart that one can manage temptation through compassionate self-control. In my research and in the classes I teach, I have adopted this positive and sustainable approach to managing temptation that does not require a person to feel deprived, guilty, depleted, or upset.

To live a successful and fulfilling life and thrive, we need to do what I suggested to Kristin all those years ago: (1) harness our self-talk and the way we frame and think about temptations to manage the pull of desire, and (2) design our lives to set ourselves up for success with the knowledge that our own thoughts, feelings, actions, and behavior can, and likely will, influence our future selves. At the risk of confounding ancient religious teachings, I recall a pronouncement in the *Bhagavad Gita* (an ancient Hindu text) that says "A man's own self is his friend. A man's own self is his foe." To be a good friend to ourselves, we need to set ourselves up for success, as Benjamin Franklin did when he put in place a set of systems that worked for him. Let's look at some ways you can get started.

IT GOES THE WAY YOU SAY

We may as well admit it: we all talk to ourselves. Research finds that self-talk, when done right, is an effective way to self-regulate.[9] It involves both the words we use and the tone and manner with which we speak those words to ourselves (similar to the verbal and nonverbal communication we use when we talk to others) that shape our thoughts, feelings, actions, and behavior. After all, the person we spend the most time with, and the most important person we will ever coach, is ourself.

Research finds that self-talk falls into two buckets: instructional self-talk and motivational self-talk. When we want to get things done (task performance), we rely on instructional self-talk, and to keep ourselves going we use motivational self-talk. Instructional self-talk prompts us to action: we might talk ourselves through doing a specific task, like practicing a golf swing or rehearsing a script for an upcoming negotiation. Motivational self-talk keeps our spirits up: we might tell ourselves: "You can do it," "Come on, get up and get going," or "You look good."

Positive self-talk can help enhance self-control, increase self-direction, and make hopes and dreams a reality. When we do not actively frame our thoughts in a positive way, our mind becomes flooded with negative chatter that can diminish and demotivate us. When we tell ourselves, "You are an idiot," "What a foolish thing to do," "You look like sh*t," or "It's pretty obvious you don't belong here," the negative self-talk acts like a feedback loop in which we begin to feel what we say to ourselves. When we sound angry in how we talk to ourselves, we feel angry with ourselves. If we sound depressed, we feel depressed. If we sound cheerful, we feel cheerful... It goes the way you say.

An interesting insight that is the cornerstone of using the empowered *I don't* to help manage temptation, as we saw earlier in the book, is that self-talk that implicates our identity is more effective in shaping our behavior. If we implicate positive aspects of our identity, it leads us to do things that are good for us rather than procrastinating or postponing doing those things. As I mentioned in Chapter 3, research found that when people were given stickers that said, "I am a voter," using a noun (voter) to implicate their identity as a voter, it was more likely to prompt people to go out and vote. Instead, when the sticker used a verb to describe a behavior saying, "I vote," individuals were less likely to go out and cast their vote.[10] You are best served by framing your self-talk as a positive enactment of your identity.

INSTRUCTIONAL SELF-TALK FOR POSITIVE ACTION

To coach ourselves better with our self-talk, we need to train the trainer. Our inner coach needs to deliberately practice using language that makes instructional self-talk effective. Here are a few evidence-based strategies that your inner coach might employ.

Instructional Self-talk for Better Self-control: One research article I published on what I just described as compassionate self-control was with my friend and coauthor Nicole Mead, on a topic we fondly labeled *strategic postponement* I distinctly remember discussing with her an experience that laid the groundwork for our paper. Since I love learning about the background story of research articles, I'll share this one for mine.

I spent some time on a flight from Atlanta to Los Angeles talking to a wealth manager about his job (I was on my way to spend a week or so with my husband in LA; ours was a commuter marriage at the time). We spoke primarily about his job, until the conversation turned to Athens, the college town where I lived. He excitedly asked me if I had eaten at "the best fried chicken place in Georgia." He described the spot and told me it was right on the main street, and I realized that I probably drove past it every day on my way to work. Unbeknownst to him, this gentleman had just strewn temptation on my path to and from my work!

I love Southern fried chicken, I really do, but I don't eat it very often. Pretty frequently during that LA trip, I thought about the fried chicken place and considered that I might pick up a meal from the restaurant or maybe plan to head there with a friend for lunch. I had a plan when I got back to Athens, and it involved fried chicken.

On the first day I got back, I drove past the place and I told myself, *Another time, perhaps*. Another time I drove past, I said *Sure, but not today*. I did this almost every day for a month or so. I gave myself the permission to eat it, but not at that time. This formed the idea that motivated the paper Nicole and I together wrote: Giving yourself the permission to indulge in pleasure, but not actually doing so, feels way better than depriving yourself. The best part is that after postponing the pleasure for a while, your craving diminishes and you no longer want it as badly as you did in the heat of the moment. The bottom line: Using instructional self-talk to say, "Not now, later" is more effective in warding off temptation than saying, "Not ever."[11]

Instructional Self-talk to Improve Performance: A study conducted by a team of researchers examined two different types of self-talk on the performance of a basketball shooting task.[12] The researchers divided the study participants, all students in sports-related subjects—physical ed or sports science—into three groups. One group was the control group not given any instructions. One group was the "relevant trigger group" who were asked to tell themselves to relax before shooting the ball into the basket and the last group was the "irrelevant trigger group" who were told to say the word fast before shooting the ball into the basket. The study revealed that cueing the word relax improved player performance. When we use the right cue word, we can harness the energy, motivation, and drive needed for peak performance.

Find the relevant trigger words or phrases that resonate with you and your priorities. Some useful mantras people in my classes employ are, "Not my circus, not my monkeys," "Chip, chip, chip away," "I can do all things through Christ," "This too shall pass," and, "Always be improving." Do you have something you say to yourself on a regular basis? Perhaps when you use that phrase as self-talk, it gives you the lens you need to make a confident and empowered decision and spur you on to meaningful action.

I began writing this book during the COVID-19 pandemic. Like many working moms, I had a lot going on—from homeschooling to learning to teach fully online to putting three meals a day on the table for my family—coupled with my increased administrative and research responsibilities. I had no choice but to ruthlessly prioritize.

I adopted a phrase to manage the stress of the COVID-19 pandemic: "Be in demand, stay in control." To be in demand captured my gratitude for being seen as a valuable resource both at home and at work, and the positive feeling of contributing to the success, health, and wellbeing of my friends, students, colleagues, and family. The cautionary stay in control was a reminder of the importance of self-preservation. For me, stay in control meant that I had to, with courage and grace, walk away from things that came in the way of what I deemed professionally rewarding and personally meaningful.

Instructional Self-talk to Change Your Perspective: Viewing yourself and the situation you are in as if you were a fly on the wall helps you tackle it more calmly and effectively. Ethan Kross, University of Michigan social psychologist and author of the book *Chatter*, found that talking to yourself in non-first-person terms (using your name or he, she, or you) is more effective than talking to yourself in the first person (using me, my, or I). The research finds that speaking to ourselves other than in the first-person distances us psychologically and gives us more perspective—very much as if it is someone else were speaking to us.[13] This calms us down and allows us to better handle anxiety-provoking social situations. Another study conducted by Lindsey Streamer and her colleagues had participants prepare to pitch themselves for a dream job.[14] Before they delivered their pitch, the researchers had participants write for a few minutes, either using first person pronouns (I, me, or my) or non-first-person pronouns (own name or he, she, or you). Subsequently, when the participants were actually pitching themselves for the job, as you would during an interview, the researchers recorded their cardiac vitals. It turns out that when the non-first-person group approached their dream job pitch they did so in a calmer and healthier way, as reflected by their less constricted blood vessels. To be more effective in your self-talk, consider talking to yourself using your own name, like a coach or mentor would talk to you.

MOTIVATIONAL SELF-TALK TO KEEP US GOING

Reese Witherspoon, one of Hollywood's highest paid actresses, has used her position to empower women through various endeavors.

She said, "If you're one of those people who has that little voice in the back of her mind saying, 'Maybe I could do [fill in the blank],' don't tell it to be quiet. Give it a little room to grow, and try to find an environment it can grow in." One of the key benefits of motivational self-talk is to guide ourselves to become the best versions of ourselves. We can use self-talk as a reminder of the values we hold and why these values are important to us. As the examples to come illustrate, generating personally meaningful self-talk and speaking to ourselves with compassion and understanding is the way to go.

Motivational Self-talk as Personal Reinforcement: One wonders what keeps people going, even when the going gets tough. Think about Diana Nyad, who in 2013 at the age of sixty-four became the first person to swim the 110-mile stretch from Havana, Cuba, to Key West, Florida, without the use of a shark cage for protection. What's incredible about her story was that the first time she attempted to swim these waters teeming with jellyfish and sharks was in 1975. Her previous attempts were thwarted by storms or venomous jellyfish stings, but her commitment remained unwavering for nearly forty years. Undoubtedly, Diana Nyad had to overcome numerous physical, emotional, and mental obstacles over the years, but the steady voice in her head repeated, as she narrated in her inspiring TED talk, "Never, ever give up," "Find a way," and "You never are too old to chase your dreams."[15]

When I read Secretary of State Colin Powell's book *It Worked for Me,* I was struck by his reflection, "I love old movies and get from them lots of examples that I use for personal reinforcement." He describes the opening scene of *The Hustler,* one of his all-time favorite movies, in which Minnesota Fats, reigning pool champion, defeats the overconfident upstart Fast Eddie. Powell uses a line from that scene as a reminder that it's not over until it's over. He writes, "Many times when facing a tough meeting, an unpleasant encounter, a hostile press conference, or a vicious congressional hearing, the last thing I would do beforehand was go into the restroom, wash and dry my hands and face, look into the mirror, and say softly to myself, "Fast Eddie, let's play some pool... I may be down, but never out."[16] Are there some words from a popular song or a movie that resonate with you and serve as a motivator to keep you going, even when the going gets tough?

Motivational Self-talk to Give Voice to Your Values: We can develop our own personal philosophies or mantras that can guide the way we live our life. In my classes, many leaders describe the different words they use to prevent being overwhelmed, improve confidence, and say no to fear and discomfort. One woman shared a story of what she told herself when she had to make a difficult decision at work: "I am my father's child. I know what is right." This mantra was rooted in the way she saw her dad—an upstanding citizen and a devoted Eagle Scout. Knowing she was his daughter gave her both courage and comfort that she was making the best possible decision grounded in her deep-rooted value system.

We have discussed how people-pleasing often requires us to put other people's desires higher than our own values and preferences. One way to avoid this is to make sure your self-talk is not unconsciously driving you to prioritize other people above yourself. Research on directionally motivated reasoning finds that our unconscious motivations affect the decisions we make and the conclusions we draw.[17] To avoid motivated reasoning and adopt a perspective contrary to what we naturally fall into, we need to change the question we ask ourselves. Instead of succumbing to social pressure and giving in to our (sometimes unconscious) motivation to be seen as nice, cooperative people, we need to shift our questions from "Can I do this?" or "Can I assist?" to "Must I do this?" or "Should I assist?"

When we ask ourselves, "Can I?" we are channeling our ideal self and searching for reasons to accept the request and say yes. Perhaps, occasionally, at the cost of the values and priorities we hold dear. In contrast, when we ask, "Must I?" or, "Should I?" we are adopting a more realistic view of our lives and searching for reasons to reject the request on the basis of our values, priorities, and preferences.[18] Consider the self-talk we engage in when an ask comes your way. Sometimes writing down answers to the "Can I....?" question (sure, I can do a lot of things) and then the "Must I...?" or "Should I...?" questions (But do I have the energy, time, motivation, bandwidth? Is this aligned with my purpose and what I find meaningful?) can feel like you have considered all sides of the issue. Make sure that when you speak to yourself you do not favor an unrealistic ideal and perfect self over your real self who has to deal with what is actually possible.[19]

Motivational Self-talk to Silence Your Inner Critic: Our minds can sometimes be like a ball of yarn with limitless unravelling potential. It unravels and then reravels (if that is a word). The nature of worry and rumination is negative and self-critical. Our thoughts can veer toward making harsh self-judgments, amplifying shortcomings, taking blame, and fretting over minor mistakes. Research shows that these self-critical thoughts can leave us demotivated[20] and less goal-oriented.[21] In contrast, compassionate thoughts motivate self-improvement and higher achievement.[22]

Learn to use self-talk to manage the negative voice in your head. If you watched the movie *Luca*, you might recall the scene in which the pair of friends Alberto and Luca have jumped on their home-made Vespa ready to ride it down a cliff. Luca is nervous about joining Alberto in this dangerous stunt, but Alberto encourages him to silence the apprehensive Bruno in his head. As the Vespa begins careening down the hill, Luca yells the memorable line, "*Silenzio, Bruno!*" It is not uncommon in many of the discussions that we have in our classes about our inner critic that individuals have given that mean and nasty voice who chatters away in our heads a name that typifies their tone. When you give your inner critic a name, its power over you decreases, because you have distanced that voice as distinct from your own identity.[23] Each time your inner critic tries to bring you down, your inner coach can tell it to pipe down in no uncertain terms—and with the choicest of language.

Our Inner Dialogue

A vast amount of research on self-talk has been done in sports psychology to help athletes improve their performance by willing themselves to push harder. Athletes refer to this coaching as the "athlete's mindset" while psychologists call it "self-talk" or "chatter." In his TED talk titled "Inside the Mind of Champion Athletes," sports psychologist Martin Hagger points out that at the highest level of performance, one athlete does not differ very much from another in terms of physical capability, skill level, and conditioning. The difference maker in what leads them to success is believing in themselves and their abilities. He says, about self-talk: "It's an extremely important strategy, because it enables athletes to go through in their mind and use mantras to try and boost their motivation, but also to try to manage the competition and the situation.

So, self-talk might have motivational components, but it also might help athletes focus on important things that are relevant to performance, so-called cues, and also might have a calming effect. Things like breathe and relax."[24]

Consider Muhammad Ali, one of the greatest heavyweight boxers of all time. He regularly used self-talk for both instruction and motivation.[25] He relied on these instructional words to steer himself away from the fear of failure: "Inside a ring or out, ain't nothing wrong with going down. It's staying down that's wrong." Or these that kept him focused on his aspirational goals, free from the pressure from his peers: "It isn't the mountains ahead to climb that wear you out; it's the pebble in your shoe."

He also regularly used motivational self-talk, like, "I am the greatest! I said it even before I knew I was," and, "Don't count the days; make the days count," among many other affirmations that kept him going. Even when he was fighting a losing battle with Parkinson's disease, he conceded, "God gave me this illness to remind me that he is the greatest."

The way we speak to ourselves can fill us with feelings of personal power and motivation to get things done, or it can make us feel down in the dumps. Your self-talk is how you speak to you, so choose to make your self-talk positive, empowering, and motivating. You will find yourself filled with motivation and drive and will see a marked improvement in your performance.

Become an Architect of Your Life Experiences

One of my favorite fables is the old Cherokee legend known as "The Tale of Two Wolves." A grandmother explains to her grandson that inside each of us there are two wolves. One wolf is positive, gentle, and kind, while the other is negative, destructive, and hostile. The wolves battle each other to control us. With curiosity, the little boy asks: "Which wolf wins?" to which the grandmother replies, "The one you feed."

We previously discussed making rules, not decisions, to shape our actions and behaviors. Since our thoughts shape our feelings, the way we set up our personal policies matters. What you have probably realized is that if we do not have clear systems in place to feed the good wolf, we can very easily be overpowered by the bad one. The basic idea is this: by putting a system in place, you can make undesired behavior less likely and harder but desired behaviors or actions more fluent and easier.

St. Francis of Assisi is often quoted as saying, "Start by doing what's necessary, then do what's possible, and suddenly you are doing the impossible."

Personal policies create a system of discipline instead of quotas or bans on your consumption or activities. Because of their concrete nature, personal policies help you control yourself without depriving yourself entirely. At the very core of personal policies is the notion that cutting out something completely that you enjoy and derive pleasure from can be hard, and so you have to set rules up and put systems in place that keep the temptation at bay.

I will admit to knowingly tricking myself into getting my daily steps in. I have made it a daily routine to wear walking gear when I get ready to drop my daughter off at school in the morning. This outfit makes me more likely to stop by a park or a neighborhood close to her school (not close to my house) and get in my daily quota of steps before I start my work day. This becomes even more likely when I use the walking time to do something pleasurable—either listening to an engaging podcast or chatting with a friend from India (it is midevening in India at the time I walk). I have conditioned myself to look forward to my morning walks, because I associate them with pleasurable activities, and I see the benefits of my morning exercise for the rest of my day.

Setting up a system of default behaviors takes away making decisions in a "hot" state when faced with a temptation, but simply following a rule you have set for yourself when you were in a "cool" state. It is human to succumb to temptation, especially when our ability to resist temptation is at its lowest in the heat of the moment when we act on impulse rather than with thoughtful deliberation. When we are in a cool state our mind is calm and relaxed and capable of thinking about what is best for us and our future, so we make different choices than when we are in a hot state (when we are fatigued, angry, or agitated).[26] Anyone who succumbs to the habit of a late-night snack in front of the refrigerator or a repeated snooze button routine knows that the pull of temptation can be very strong. Resisting this pull requires mental resources, and if we are hungry or tired, we are less likely to have the mental resources needed to resist temptation. It is at these points, when we are most likely to veer off a path that we have set up for ourselves, that we need to incorporate a system of personal policies. Indeed, to achieve anything within a system, you need multiple subcomponents in place that work together synergistically to get things done and to keep you going.

The late actress Betty White maintained the same desired weight for years. She had a simple system in place. She weighed herself every morning, and if she was a pound over her target weight she did something immediately to lose that pound that day. She recognized that letting herself gain two or three or five pounds would make it harder to do something about her weight. Gaining a pound and then losing a pound is a much easier endeavor, and one that worked for Betty White for decades.

Embellish Your Life with Red Velvet Ropes

Wayfaring is a design principle that is focused on orienting an individual within a design space. It shows the way and helps one navigate an unfamiliar space. At night, a light at the doorway of a home guides a visitor from the street or driveway to the front door. A lighthouse guides ships away from the rocks. This is wayfaring in action. When something is navigable, it means that the navigator can successfully move in the information space from his present location to a destination, even if the location of the destination is imprecisely known. It turns out that there are three criteria that determine the navigability of a space: first, whether the navigator can discover or infer his present location (Do you have a sense of where you are?); second, whether a route to the destination can be found (Is there a viable pathway forward?); and third, how well the navigator can accumulate wayfinding experience in the space (Do you have the knowledge, skills, and motivation to get from here to there?). These are the same three questions that determine the navigability of your life.

One of my favorite wayfaring devices is the stanchion—the red velvet rope that cordons off an area in a movie theater, a sports event, and at some Trader Joe's stores. At many venues the red velvet rope subtly guides people to their destinations. It is a barrier that commands respect and affords compliance. Although it is not barbed wire or electric fencing, the soft and pretty red velvet rope effectively directs people to their destination and prevents them from straying into forbidden areas.

What we need in our lives are red velvet ropes. Ropes that say, this is my family time, this is the work that I truly care about, this is what makes me happy, this is what I am good at, this is my time for self-care. Personal policies give you the platform and the permission that you need to be able to say no and feel the freedom of that no response to see increased productivity and happiness in what you truly care about. Your personal policies are the red velvet ropes in your life. They are guides that help you achieve a meaningful life. They also act like a psychological barrier that prevents you from taking on things that detract from your purpose. While barbed wires could hurt you and others, velvet ropes gently guide you to where you need to go.

But remember, your personal policies are not a prison sentence. Because they are your rules, you get to change them when they are not working for you. While personal policies should reflect your preferences, they are not etched in stone. They are yours to change, modify, and adapt based on circumstances. With each day that passes, we evolve and change, as do the people we interact with and the challenges we encounter. Our self-talk and our systems of personal policies need to similarly adapt and be updated to reflect our changing circumstances. The most valuable gift we can give ourselves is to adapt in a way that nurtures our unique spirit.

CHAPTER 9

Harness Your Trailblazing Potential

In 1968, with the slogan "unbought and unbossed," Shirley Chisholm, a former schoolteacher, ran for the seat in New York's Twelfth Congressional District in Bedford-Stuyvesant to become the first African American woman elected to Congress. Chisholm's first assignment was to the House Agriculture Committee, on the subcommittee for rural development and forestry, a panel that dealt with the farmlands of America. Upon learning about this assignment, she indignantly responded, "Apparently all they know about Brooklyn here in Washington is that a tree grew there."[1]

Unwilling to take on work that did not directly impact the people she represented, Shirley Chisholm first approached the Speaker of the House of Representatives, John McCormack, to ask for a change of subcommittee. Speaker McCormack brushed her request aside, saying, "Mrs. Chisholm, this is the way it is... You have to be a good soldier." Chisholm knew that although assignments ought to be made based on district needs and relevant experience, they were often made based on seniority instead, resulting in the choice assignments being given to the more senior representatives. Her response was swift and direct: "All my forty-three years

I have been a good soldier... The time is growing late, and I can't be a good soldier any longer."[2]

Her next bold move was to make a motion on the floor of the House and address the issue directly. She made her case stating that "...it would be hard to imagine an assignment that is less relevant to my background or to the needs of the predominantly Black and Puerto Rican people who elected me, many of whom are unemployed, hungry, and badly housed, than the one I was given." Finally, after much discussion and debate, an amendment eventually passed, and Shirley Chisholm was assigned to the Veterans' Affairs Committee, which she accepted. After all, she said, "There are a lot more veterans in my district than trees."

Even though it meant a potential risk to her political career, Chisholm refused to accept an assignment based on a flawed system. Her persistence and determination established her as a force to be reckoned with and solidified her nickname, "Fighting Shirley." Later in her life she said, "I'd like them to say that Shirley Chisholm had guts. That's how I'd like to be remembered."

Shirley Chisholm was driven by the belief that, "At present, our country needs women's idealism and determination, perhaps more in politics than anywhere else." She spent seven terms in Congress, during which time she made significant progress on behalf of the "have-nots" of the country, dealing with issues of pay equity and the upliftment of poor families. In 1972, she became the first Black Democratic candidate to run for president of the United States. (She was excluded from the campaign's first three debates and had to fight to be included.) Not everyone on Capitol Hill, especially the men, applauded Shirley's accomplishments. To them, she gutsily countered, "If you can't support me, or you can't endorse me, get out of my way."[3]

In 2015, ten years after her death, President Barack Obama posthumously awarded Shirley Chisholm the Medal of Freedom, to showcase her service to the nation. He said, "There are people in our country's history who don't look left or right, they look straight ahead. Shirley Chisholm was one of those people."[4]

No Is a Gendered Issue

You don't have to look far before you find evidence, both anecdotal and research-based, that unlike Shirley Chisolm, most women have an especially hard time saying no, and they hesitate to push to get what they want.[5]

Women are more likely than men to think in people terms. If you are a woman, ask yourself when was the last time you said no to anyone—a friend, your partner, a colleague, or your children. It turns out that girls more than boys tend to be socialized into believing that it's important to be nice, agreeable, likeable, and caregiving.[6] Research finds that women are more likely than men to say yes to both professional and personal requests.[7] Research also shows that some people or groups have a higher need to belong than others. For instance, people who are more communal or empathic (women tend to fall into this group) tend to be able to take the perspective of the person in need, recognize the negative impact their refusal might have, and go out of their way to help.[8] However, socialization needs to account for both the needs of others and of oneself. To be a responsible adult, one needs to be aware of one's own values and priorities and act authentically from that place of empowerment to help others in need.

I conducted a survey with 1,902 people (58 percent female), to understand the difficulty women and men experience with saying no using the same questions in the quiz I introduced in Chapter 1. The survey contained the four questions (out of a total of sixteen—including the six items for concern for relationships and six items for concern for reputation) that dealt with the difficulty of saying no. Participants responded to these questions on a scale of 1 to 7, where 1 = not at all true of me at all and 7 = very true of me.

Figure 9.1*

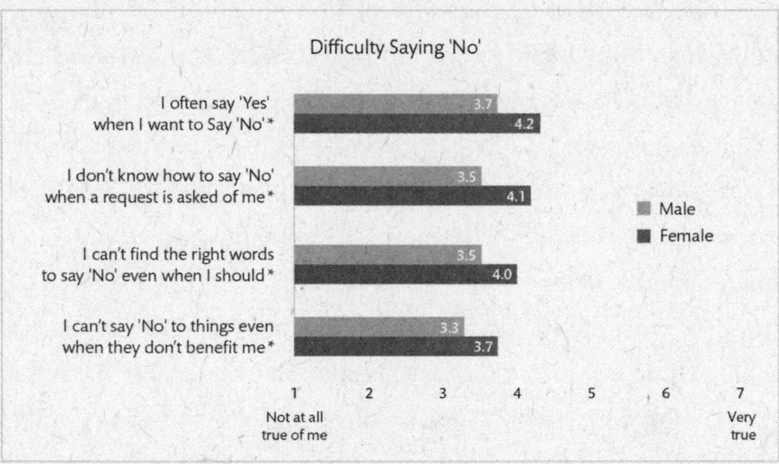

As Figure 9.1 shows, women have a harder time saying no than men do. Many women seem to think that to be seen as a good person requires putting your needs on the back burner for the sake of others around you. Being considerate and polite—so that others are not embarrassed and do not lose face—can often result in women saying yes when they want to say no. The stronger the perceived benefit to the other party, the more likely women are to diminish the cost to themselves and say yes to the request. As the

* Significant gender differences

figure reveals, women are more likely to struggle with the words to say no. Indeed, saying no is like speaking a foreign language, and to avoid speaking this language, women tend to debate with themselves—fighting to say yes instead of saying no. This needs to change, and the time is now, and the solution is empowered refusal.

When women receive a request, they feel that they ought to be cooperative and helpful in their response and feel guilty if they respond in a way that appears uncooperative and selfish.[9] From this same survey, we see depicted in Figure 9.2 and Figure 9.3 that women report that they care more deeply about their relationships with others (higher concern for relationship scores) and want others to think highly of them (higher concern for reputation scores), which explains why women find it harder than men to say no (higher difficulty to say no scores).

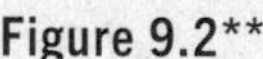

Figure 9.2**

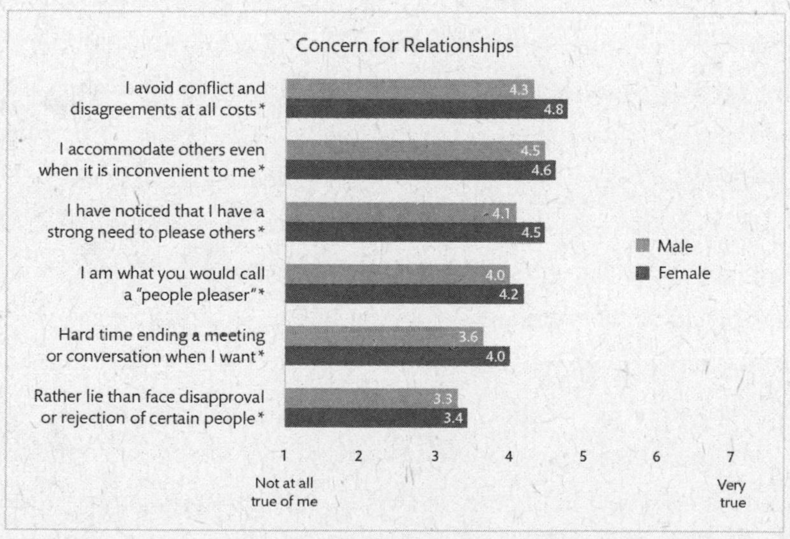

** Significant gender differences

Figure 9.3*

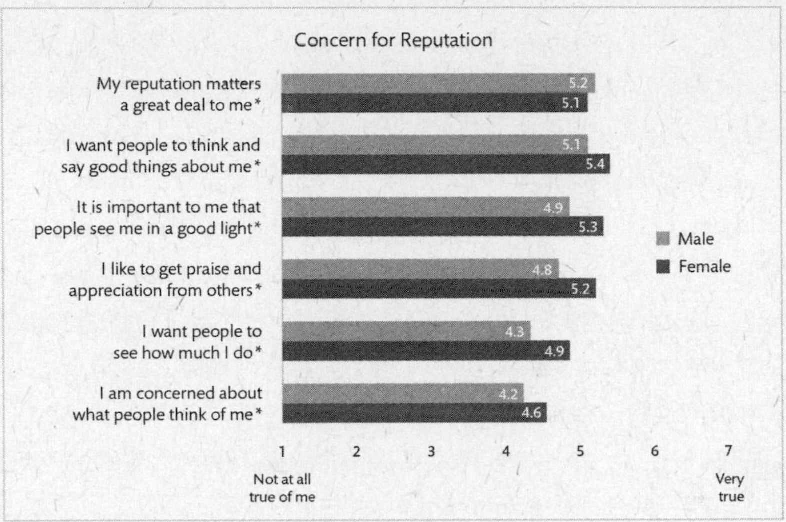

Women fear the consequences of not helping others, and unfortunately their fears are not without a basis. Research finds that society expects women to be more altruistic than men and punishes women severely for eschewing communality; however, society does not mete out the same harsh consequences to men.[10] All you have to do is turn to the number of movies that capture the distraught and exhausted working mom (like Michelle Pfeiffer in *One Fine Day*) or the shunning (and even bullying) of the overworked and overwhelmed mom striving to do it all (think Mila Kunis in *Bad Moms*).

When it comes to receiving a request, women experience more intense negative emotions when the request is something they want to say no to. The spotlight glares more intensely on women,

---

* Significant gender differences

whether the request is made in a social setting (social asks) or whether it is a one-on-one exchange (solo asks). Earlier I suggested that women appear to conjure up the intensity of group pressure, even when it is just the asker and them interacting with each other. In the studies I've shared in this book, women feel intense guilt for saying no (but they also feel guilty when they say yes). It seems that no matter what women do, comply or not comply, they are racked with guilt. Since guilt is a handy weapon of self-torture, when walnut trees want others to do their bidding, they effectively rely on guilt-tripping to obtain compliance.

I have briefly mentioned research that examines how women respond to non-promotable tasks in the workplace. Let's expand on that here. While promotable tasks are those that drive revenue, are challenging and valuable for the organization, and rewarded in performance evaluations, non-promotable tasks are those that do not drive revenue, are time-consuming but not challenging, and not recognized or included in performance evaluations. In other words, non-promotable tasks are the housekeeping tasks that include chores like cleaning out the break room fridge, organizing the office picnic, bringing in coffee and bagels for the Monday morning meeting, writing up a report, planning a retirement party...the list is endless. Clearly someone has to do them, but let's face it, no one gets promoted because they took on coffee and bagels duty!

Despite this, researchers find that the burden of non-promotable tasks falls disproportionately on the shoulders of women. Not only are women more likely to be asked to perform non-promotable tasks in the workplace (managers asked women to do these chores 44 percent more often), women are also more likely to say yes to performing these tasks (they said yes to 76 percent of the requests that came their way, while men said yes to 51 percent).[11]

But this is not a workplace issue alone. If you look around the room in a PTA meeting, a neighborhood association gathering, the organizing committee of a church social, a high school dance, or an annual community Christmas get-together, the volunteers are disproportionately female. Women feel obliged to help out as an unspoken rule of friendship, even if they really do not want to. The movie *27 Dresses* captures this in a very real context. Jane, played by Katherine Heigl, is the completely selfless, perfect bridesmaid. She is at each of her brides' dress fittings, she goes wedding shopping, attends cake tastings, organizes the bridal shower, handles the last-minute mishaps, so much so that her entire life pretty much revolves around "other people's Kodak moments."[12] And all she has to show for all that effort is a closet full of twenty-seven outrageous bridesmaid dresses!

Deeds of a Feather Stick Together

In the classes I teach, I hear, first-hand, stories from female leaders about their experiences in the workplace. These are also corroborated by research findings:

- They regularly get bypassed for promotion and recognition[13] and often stay out of the spotlight.[14]
- It is often lonely at work (it's a man's world), and it is not uncommon for women to be left out of lunches, golfing Saturdays, hunting trips, and midafternoon basketball games (this "structural exclusion" is attributed to homophily—the tendency of

people to be more comfortable with others like themselves—and work-home conflicts).[15]

- Women tell stories of their ideas being stolen or appropriated by others.[16]

In addition to these institutional barriers that are external to themselves, women also narrate instances in which their own self-doubt, lack of confidence, and hesitation to advocate for themselves hold them back:

- They experience greater internal conflict between their work selves and home selves.[17]
- Stress and burnout afflicts more women than men.[18]
- Many women struggle with negotiating a better deal for themselves.[19]
- They deliver on time and tend not to ask for an extension on a deadline no matter the personal cost.[20]

In the workplace, women, it seems, have pulled the short straw.

Besides the reluctance and inability to say no, there are a cluster of similar behaviors that likely stem from the same source—a place of low confidence, poor self-worth, and feelings of fear and guilt connected to self-advocating and self-promoting. In dealing with the practicalities of empowered refusal, let's not only try and understand how women can become better at saying an empowered no, but also how building up empowerment to say no might help decrease the incidence of these other self-handicapping tendencies.

Women tend to be less self-assured than their male counterparts,[21] and this decreases career aspirations and thwarts professional advancement.[22] Take for instance, one study that showed that women will apply for a job only if they fully meet all the job criteria and check every box. In contrast, men will apply for the job when they meet only 60 percent of the needed job qualifications.[23]

Women also feel torn between work and home. They feel inadequate and guilty regardless of where they are and fear being seen as unprofessional at work and not a good wife, daughter, sister, or mom at home. Indra Nooyi, ex-CEO of PepsiCo and author of the recent book *My Life in Full: Work, Family, and Our Future,* does not sugarcoat the work-life challenges that women face. She is candid about the difficulties she faced in managing intense professional and personal demands. She recommends: "The first thing I'd say to women is put aside the guilt. I think we're all genetically programmed to feel guilty for not giving total effort at the job."[24] As we embrace this advice, let's look at three ways in which this cluster of behaviors (which we will soon learn are symptomatic of low personal agency) play out in the workplace.

Women Undervalue Their Own Contributions: Women often brush aside compliments, attributing their success to luck instead of hard work. They are harsh critics of their own capability and beat themselves up when things go wrong. In fact, studies show that women often talk down their accomplishments when working alongside men in a successful team.[25] Pervasive among successful women is what we commonly refer to as the "imposter syndrome"—the extent to which successful women struggle to internalize their success and attribute achievements to external factors, even in the presence of evidence to the contrary.[26] This stems from a belief that accomplished women often hold about themselves: that they are frauds, unworthy of promotions, recognition, and rewards. Researchers attribute this devaluation by women of their own abilities as one reason why incompetent men occupy leadership positions,[27] especially in competitive environments.[28] Grounded in the belief that they are not good enough, women settle for less influential positions and lower-paying jobs.[29]

Women Shy away From Asking for What They Want: Whether it is a promotion, a raise, a new job, or even time off, women are less likely to ask for what they want or even deserve in the workplace.[30] Studies on salary negotiations show that men are four times more likely to initiate salary negotiations than women are. When women do ask for a salary increase, they ask for 30 percent less money than men do.[31] Astoundingly, a 2020 study found that 60 percent of women report that they have never negotiated salary with an employer, and an enormous 72 percent of women would rather leave their job to get a salary bump elsewhere than negotiate a raise at their current job.[32] Perhaps the silver lining is that when empowered by others, women do overcome their reluctance to ask for what they deserve. If women are informed that they can negotiate their salary, they are more likely to do so.[33]

Women Don't Like to Brag: I teach a course on personal branding in which I draw on marketing principles to help students showcase what they uniquely bring to the table. Many people, especially women, dislike the idea of personal branding because they see it as pushy, arrogant, and show-offish. This disregard is grounded in the misguided belief that other people will just see your talent and reward you for it. The fact is, nobody is paying attention to you unless you make it worth their while to do so. I think the fabulous Flying Flapper of Freeport, Elinor Smith (a pioneering American aviator) put it best when she said, "It had long since come to my attention that people of accomplishment rarely sat back and let things happen to them. They went out and happened to things."

Self-promotion is an essential skill by which you convey information and provide evidence about what you uniquely bring to the table. Yet research demonstrates a persistent gender gap in the act of self-promotion.[34] Both women and men are socialized to think that people look down on those (read women) who brag. In concert with this belief, research finds that women who self-advocate or self-promote face severe backlash for not behaving with the stereotypically expected modesty.[35] Women may perceive this backlash as more costly to their reputations than the opportunities foregone, resulting in their being less likely to advocate for themselves and showcase their accomplishments. In her book *Brag! The Art of Tooting Your Own Horn without Blowing It*,[36] author Peggy Klaus dispels the misperceptions around self-promotion to argue that "bragging is an art, an individual form of self-expression and communication that, once mastered, is the key to opening doors."

Getting Ahead vs. Getting Along

Researchers find that there are two cardinal axes along which people chart their lives: agency and communion. We tend to describe ourselves (and others) in terms of these two sets of qualities: "agentic" (e.g., assertive, ambitious, capable, clever, confident, and decisive) and communal (e.g., cooperative, empathetic, friendly, generous, sincere, and trustworthy).[37] Our agentic qualities result in our acquiring social status and power, gaining dominance and influence over others and setting ourselves apart as unique and distinct.

In contrast, communality results in our caring about and nurturing others, cooperating with others for the greater good, and sharing connections with others.

Stereotypically, men are seen as more agentic while women are seen as more communal. Agentic motivation is concerned with "standing out" and "getting ahead," while communal motivation has to do with "fitting in" and "getting along."[38]

These drives have biological underpinnings and are associated with different hormones and neurotransmitters. Unsurprisingly, perhaps, testosterone activates agentic motivations[39] while oxytocin activates communal motivations.[40] Some research suggests that testosterone can simultaneously enhance agency and weaken communality, which might help to explain the difference in relative importance placed by men vs. women on agency vs. communion.[41]

How does this play out in the real world? Consider two brothers, Frodo and Freud. Although siblings, the two had very different leadership styles. Freud gained control by fostering strong alliances and cultivating friendships, while Frodo resorted to aggression and brute strength. Researchers label Freud's strategy as a *prestige* route to power while Frodo's strategy is termed a *dominance* route to power, both equally viable ways to gain status and get ahead in a social hierarchy (for men).[42] Now consider Hope's rise to the top in her community. As a female, she is less likely to gain power through aggression and violence (the dominance route) but readily does so more through building relationships and developing a winning personality (more likened to a prestige route to power).

Would it surprise you that Freud, Frodo, and Hope used to live in the chimpanzee community in Tanzania's Gombe National Park and had their lives documented by renowned primatologist Jane

Goodall?[43] Their striving for power and the means by which they achieve status bears startling resemblance to any regular workplace or community.

However, when it comes to personal and professional advancement, men and women differ in a key ingredient: personal agency.

The Tale of Gender Stereotypes

Alice Eagly and her colleagues assembled a database of sixteen nationally representative U.S. public opinion polls on gender stereotypes that captured the views of 30,000 U.S. adults between 1946 and 2018. Using a meta-analysis, they wanted to compare how males vs. females are perceived on three sets of traits: competence traits (e.g., intelligence, creativity, good at your job, well-trained), communal traits (e.g., emotionally intelligent, warm and caring, good listener, compassionate, empathetic), and agentic traits (e.g., ambition, confidence, self-focused). The goal was to determine whether poll participants thought each trait was truer of women or men or equally true of both.

Some perceptions don't change. Over the entire time period from 1946 to 2018, women ranked higher in *communal stereotypes:* they were viewed as more communal than men.

Where women see the greatest improvement is in the *competence stereotypes.* Over the time period, there was a dramatic change in how women were perceived. In the early portion of the period, women were viewed as less competent than men (they were less likely to pursue advanced education or work outside of the home), but today they are seen as equally, or even more, competent than men. This is not surprising, since women are entering the workforce at equal or higher numbers[44] and score higher than men on some critical leadership skills (like relationship-building, inspiring and motivating others, taking initiative, and practicing self-development).[45]

Clearly, the combination of high communality and high competence is very good news for women when it comes to *getting* a job. If a candidate can demonstrate both competence (they can do the job well) and congeniality (they are nice to be around and have lunch with), they are a shoo-in at any organization. As the authors of the meta-analysis write, "These current stereotypes should favor women's employment because competence is, of course, a job requirement for virtually all positions. Also, jobs increasingly reward social skills, making women's greater communion an additional advantage."

But while they might get the job, the combination of competence and communality *on the job* can sometimes be a double-edged sword. For women, walking this tightrope between nice and competent is the "double bind" that women face. Sheryl Sandberg writes, "If a woman is competent, she does not seem nice enough. If a woman seems really nice, she is considered more nice than competent. Since people want to hire and promote those who are both competent and nice, this creates a huge stumbling block for women."[46]

Here is more not-so-great news. When it comes to the last bucket of traits—*personal agency* stereotypes—women lag significantly behind men. Men are consistently perceived as more confident, ambitious, and self-promoting than women. Even though both genders are equally competent, women today are not much more agentic than they were in the 1940s.

This might explain why women might get the job and be able to do the job, but their careers are also likely to advance more slowly. As Eagly and her colleagues write, "On a less positive note, most leadership roles require more agency than communion. Therefore, the lesser agency ascribed to women than men is a disadvantage in relation to leadership positions."

Although some results of this analysis are heartening, they also clearly identify the shift in mindset women need to harness their full potential: women need to *increase* their agentic motivation to accept and embrace leadership positions and learn to consistently *convey/communicate* evidence of their competence and accomplishments with emotional intelligence.

Bridging the Agency Gap

Looking at the cluster of behaviors symptomatic of low personal agency reinforced by gender stereotypes people hold about personal agency helps us understand why, despite women's competence, the pathway to professional advancement is rarely straight or easy. Spotting low agency behaviors in ourselves is a crucial step in learning how to sidestep them. Brené Brown writes in her book *Daring Greatly* that we sometimes need a permission slip to dare greatly.[47] The research is clear: we need to bridge the agency gap. Women need to exercise their "agentic muscles" to assert themselves with less hesitation and get more comfortable advocating for themselves with empowerment, banishing feelings of fear and guilt.

How to do this is at the heart of this book. While agency is formally defined as assuming strategic perspectives and/or taking intentional actions toward goals that matter to oneself,[48] I would encourage you to think of agency as a purposeful drive to wholeheartedly pursue what *you* deem to be meaningful and important.[49] When you think about agency in this way and reframe it as the drive to do what is meaningful and important, then agency does not so obviously become an alien concept for women or a prerogative of men.

There are undoubtedly numerous institutional barriers that need to be eliminated (some mentioned previously) and gender-friendly policies put in place to advance equity, inclusion, and belongingness in the workplace and in society at large. However, as Shane Parrish, founder of Farnam Street Media, pointed out, "You don't control the mountain, only the climb." In this vein, we need to set ourselves up for success by controlling how we climb—how we wholeheartedly pursue what we deem meaningful and important. When we put our values, priorities, preferences, and beliefs in focus, we are more likely to act, and influence others, with greater personal agency.

Personal Policies to Enhance and Reclaim Agency

In 1922, Lord Beaverbrook wrote the book *Success*.[50] He began a few years before by sharing his thoughts in a newspaper column that became so popular that the articles he wrote were circulated as pamphlets and were ultimately compiled into a book. According to Beaverbrook, the "temple of success" is held up by three pillars—judgment, industry, and health. Industry is what we commonly refer to as effort and hard work, and good health is the physical capability to exert effort in the service of doing good work. Beaverbrook deemed judgment to be a critical pillar, arguing that good judgment comes from knowing what to take on and what not to take on in the pursuit of one's passion, success, and purpose. When I read the book, I fully agreed with Beaverbrook on his aforementioned three pillars, but I do believe that his temple of success is missing a pillar.

An essential ingredient that drives success today, and perhaps that which fuels it for at least half the workforce, is personal agency. It is possible that at the time Beaverbrook was writing, when success was deemed a masculine endeavor, this fourth pillar of agency remained unstated, because it was a given. However, based on the emergence of women in the workplace and the apparent agency gap that exists, I believe that personal agency is a necessary pillar for success in contemporary society.

Based on this conviction, my work with leaders centers around helping them develop personal policies to intentionally enhance and reclaim agency based on their authentic selves. What these individuals find is that when they develop and enforce personal policies that reflect their values, priorities, preferences, and beliefs, they are more likely to act with enhanced agency.

To follow your own dreams you need agency. Most things do not fall in our laps or stay there unless you are very lucky. If you believe that a life full of passion and purpose is possible, you will strive your damnedest and do what it takes to make it so. Since personal policies reflect our truest interests (remember Benjamin Franklin), we can intentionally use them as a tool to set us up to act with greater agency.

We have seen examples of unwavering passion and purpose elsewhere in this book—in Isabel Allende's commitment to writing, in Shirley Chisholm's devotion to the "have-nots" she represented, in Rosa Parks's refusal to leave the bus, and in Maria Tallchief's dedication to her American Indian roots.

What are you passionate about? What is your purpose? How can you channel your purpose into action? What personal policies can you come up with that lend themselves to using what you are passionate about to fuel agency? And how can saying no help you achieve your life's purpose?

A woman in one of my classes shared that she chose real estate as a career because she was committed in her belief that everyone should have the security of a roof over their heads. When she was a little girl, her father had died prematurely, leaving her, her mother, and her siblings with nothing, not even a home to live in. Fueled by her passion, she worked tirelessly on behalf of her clients to ensure that they could have a roof over their heads. She ultimately led the real estate association in her community and took on other service-related projects. Standing up for yourself and what you believe is agency, and as Maya Angelou said: "I not only have the right to stand up for myself, but I have the responsibility. I can't ask somebody else to stand up for me if I won't stand up for myself."[51]

Harnessing Our Full Potential with Empowered Refusal

Ralph Waldo Emerson's beautiful aspiration for himself and for all humankind is captured in his 1841 essay titled "Self-Reliance." In it he identifies the need for each of us to avoid blindly following society's rules and conforming to the expectations others have of us. Instead, we need to do what we believe is right and that which brings us joy. In Emerson's words, our goal should be to "...do strongly before the sun and moon whatever inly rejoices me, and the heart appoints."

Let's revisit some of the broad themes of this book that will allow us to lead a life in which we "inly rejoice."

Begin with You. As Robert Pirsig, the author of *Zen and the Art of Motorcycle Maintenance,* wrote, "The place to improve the world is first in one's own heart and head and hands, and then work outward from there." We need to invest in self-reflection and gain deep and valuable self-awareness. One of the things you might notice in this book is that I do not offer you a set of fixed rules to follow. Instead, I have provided principles, frameworks, and insights and encouraged you to develop your own rules based on your distinctive (sometimes quirky) constellation of values, priorities, principles, preferences, and beliefs. To create an improved future, one in which we feel empowered and in the driver's seat, we need to have a crystal-clear view of our purpose (the why of our existence) and a vision of what a meaningful and authentic life looks like for us.

Say No to Things That Don't Matter. This bears repeating one last time. Accept that every decision we make entails trade-offs. We need to protect our time and energy to do what we were put on this earth to do. Remember that people who do significant things in their lifetime have a keen singularity of purpose and practice the superskill of saying no to the things that do not align with this purpose. Sometimes it might feel a bit selfish, but that's okay. As opera singer Sarah Brightman pragmatically stated: "You do have to be fairly selfish when you have a gift. You can't afford to let too many outside things get in the way."

To be human is to be concerned about the consequences of our choices and actions, for ourselves and for others. Instead of looking outward to please others, empowered refusal involves looking inward to evaluate each request by considering whether it is aligned with our purpose and will involve doing something meaningful. We need to separate the "good-for-me" activities that energize us from the "not-good-for-me" activities that drain us. When we do this using a purpose-driven lens, the decision to say no becomes obvious, and its underlying rationale is compelling.

Use Empowered Refusal. Empowered refusal is a way of saying no that gives voice to our values. Because it stems from our identity, it conveys conviction and determination, we don't get push-back, we remain secure in our relationship with the asker, and our reputation remains intact. I have shared research-based insights to explain how to use "standing up" words like I don't, to employ non-verbal cues to enhance the effectiveness of your refusal and to rely on personal policies, not excuses, to explain why you are refusing the request. Empowered refusal is a *justified* and *purpose-driven* no response that reflects who we are and what we care about, not a rejection of the other person.

Regularly Revisit the A.R.T. Competencies. The three competencies of **A**wareness, **R**ules, not decisions, and **T**otality of self need commitment and practice. These are skills that we can and must hone, develop, and master. We need to refine our Napoleon-like *coup d'oeil* to help us rapidly categorize requests that come our way. Let's become adept at identifying those "bake your famous lasagna" asks or those "email-tweet-post" duties that suck up our time and drain our energy with little to show for the effort. Let us also choose only the hero's journey asks that spark joy. You will find that when you embrace self-awareness, create a system of meaningful personal policies that shape how you live, and become adept at utilizing both verbal and nonverbal communication to reflect your values, preferences, priorities, and beliefs, this formidable trio of competencies will help you navigate the most difficult of circumstances.

Develop a System of Personal Policies. You might also find it worthwhile to invest in developing a system of personal policies that work for you based on the DREAM framework to advance your personal agency in all areas of your life. You will find that having a personal policy in place is liberating. It can make your decision to say no guilt-free and can refocus your energies on things that are meaningful for you. When are lives are embellished with the red velvet ropes of personal policies to guide our decisions, the toxicity of walnut trees is less likely to get to us.

Huddle Together. Helen Keller reflected, "Alone we can do so little; together we can do so much." One of the greatest strengths that women can leverage to increase their personal agency (including the ability to say no) is their communality. Journalist and book author Brooke Baldwin calls groups of women supporting each other a "huddle," describing this as "a place where women can become energized by the mere fact of their coexistence. A huddle is where we can uplift each other to succeed, thrive, and if I may—get amazing shit done."[52] In a *Harvard Business Review* article, Brian Uzzi raised the question: "Is there a difference between the networks of successful male and female leaders?" The answer was a resounding yes. What that research found was that for men to succeed they needed to have a central location in the social network—connected to key people (hubs) who in turn have many contacts across different groups. The research finds that women need dual networks: successful women have both centrality and an inner circle of close friends on whom they rely for information and support. In other words, successful women need a huddle to support their rise to the top.[53] Consider finding a huddle of your own. It could be a Lean In circle or a No Club or a book club. It might even be a WhatsApp, LinkedIn, or Facebook group. Find the marigolds in your life to help you flourish and thrive and the rose bushes to protect you from the dangers of overcommitment. This is what huddles can do.

Graciously Accept the Empowered Refusal of Others. This is my penultimate call to action. Let us learn to accept the noes we receive with grace, generosity, and compassion. This is crucial if we want to replace a culture of reluctant yeses with a culture of the empowered no. Of course, it is easy to be annoyed when someone says no to something we request of them. But we also need to take a step back and avoid spontaneously responding to others' refusals with walnut tree–like toxicity. Instead, we need to respect the person who is willing to own their no based on a personal policy they hold. When someone says no, thank them for considering your request and try to determine with genuine interest how they prefer to employ their time and energy so you might better fit your requests with their talents and interests. As we develop ourselves as leaders in our workplaces and communities, we will benefit from employing the "First Who, Then What" rule: get the right people on board the bus, help the right people find the right seats, and then take the driver's seat to get to somewhere great.

Achieve a New Harmony. Mahatma Gandhi once observed, "A 'no' uttered from the deepest conviction is better than a 'yes' merely uttered to please, or worse, to avoid trouble." Mohandas Karamchand Gandhi, who is commonly known as "*Mahatma*" (meaning "Great Soul") was a central figure in India's struggle for independence from British rule. He introduced the novel concept of *satyagraha,* a Sanskrit word meaning "holding onto truth," which involved taking a determined but nonviolent path to seek truth in a spirit of compassion and peace and resist evil and wrongdoing. What is interesting about *satyagraha* and why it attracted the attention of leaders from Nelson Mandela to Martin Luther King Jr., is that it was not merely a tactic that Gandhi used to oust the British from India, it was a philosophy that pervaded all aspects of his life, and that stemmed from deep reflection and self-scrutiny. His book *The Story of My Experiments with Truth* illustrates how Gandhi's lived experiences of discrimination as a young lawyer in South Africa, as well as the religious roots sown in his childhood, fueled his conviction to "conquer through conversion: in the end, there is neither defeat nor victory but rather a new harmony."

With the art (and science) of empowered refusal I hope we will find a similar harmony. A workplace in which bosses do not dictate the final outcome of things. Homes and communities in which the burden of work is shared, and happiness redoubled. A society where everyone has a say in their own future. By saying no to the things that don't matter and by accepting the noes of others without resentment, we can create a workplace, a community, and even a world in which people live more positively and productively because they are doing their best work on the things that they do best—the things that matter to them most.

GLOSSARY OF EMPOWERED REFUSAL TERMS

Using shared language to describe and label our experiences increases our expertise, reinforces our own learning, and facilitates smoother communication with others. Participants in my classes describe their own rules as personal policies, tell stories of frustrating "email-tweet-post" tasks, use walnut tree as code for the not-very-nice people they encounter, and refer to their supporters and protectors as marigolds. Now, having read this book, you can too. I hope this handy list of lingo will aid in your mastery of the art of empowered refusal.

Acquaintance Trap: The difficulty of saying no to people with whom you have an arm's-length relationship.

Bake Your Famous Lasagna Requests: Requests that are disproportionately tedious and time-consuming (high cost to us) in comparison to the impact that they have (low benefit to others).

Email-Tweet-Post Requests: Requests that are relatively easy to perform (low cost to us) but make no discernable difference to the world (low benefit to others). (Alternative: Bullshit job)

Empowered Refusal: A persuasive way to say no that reflects your identity, conveys conviction and determination, and does not invite pushback.

Hero's Journey: Requests that require effort to perform (high cost to us) but they may be worthwhile because of the actual or potential impact they can have on the world (high benefit to others).

House of Cards Trap: Taking on more things than you can feasibly handle.

Marigolds: The people in our lives who help us succeed, cheer us on, hear us out, support us in what we do, and have our best interests at heart.

Mickles Trap: Saying yes to several low-cost asks that begin to add up and become overwhelming.

Non-Promotable Tasks: Workplace chores that do not drive revenue, are time-consuming but not challenging, and are not recognized or included in performance evaluations.

Only You Can Do It Trap: The use of flattery and praise to get you to say yes to a request.

Pass the Salt Requests: Requests that are easy enough for us to do (low cost to us) but can make a big difference to others (high benefit to others).

Personal Policies: Established set of simple rules that we make for ourselves, grounded in our unique identity that reflect our values, priorities, preferences, and beliefs to guide our decisions and shape our actions.

Spotlight Effect: The feeling of being the center of attention with all eyes on you.

Stadium Proposal Moment: A situation that puts you in an awkward position so that you feel unable to say no.

"Standing Up" Words: Empowered language like "I don't" or "I never" or "I always" that convey conviction and determination, also make you stand up taller.

Time-Rich Future Trap: The mistaken belief that we will have more time in the future than we do now.

Red Velvet Ropes: The personal policies we set up for ourselves that serve as gentle psychological barriers that shape the direction we want our lives to take and steer us away from taking on things that detract from our purpose.

Walnut Trees: Those mean-spirited individuals who sabotage our success, make us feel worthless and disempowered, drain our energy with their overwhelming negativity, and make us cringe at the thought of any interaction with them. (Also, code for jerks, assholes, tyrants, and bullies).

ACKNOWLEDGMENTS

As a person who loves books and enjoys reading more than pretty much anything else, writing a book of my own is a dream come true!

What I did not know when I began this journey was how rewarding it would turn out to be, largely because of the many marigolds in my life who did what marigolds do—warm you with kindness and support, safeguard you from negativity, and generously share their knowledge, stories, resources, and wisdom. This note of acknowledgment will not adequately capture how transformative this book-writing experience has been for me or how grateful I am to all those who made it possible. But I will try.

The impetus for writing this book came from the leaders who participated in my classes over the years. Their interest in and curiosity about empowered refusal, and their desire to craft personal policies to live and lead better, inspired me to put pen to paper in a way that is (hopefully) implementable and useful. I thank them for saying "I need your book," because it is the nudge that *I* needed to start writing it and the reason I kept on going.

This book is grounded in research, and my perspectives have been shaped by innumerable research conversations I have had with co-authors, doctoral students, and seminar participants. I owe immense gratitude to my self-regulation research co-authors from whom I have gained so much: Julia Bayuk, Nicole Mead, Debbie MacInnis, Anirban Mukhopadhyay, Sonja Prokopec, Melanie Rudd, and Alex Tawse. A special thanks to my first doctoral student and long-time research collaborator, Henrik Hagtvedt, who co-authored the empowered refusal papers with me. I would also like to thank my other doctoral students who have taken me in different research directions and consequently enriched my intellectual life: Anoosha Izadi, Mahdi Ebrahimi, Zhe Zhang, and Rita To.

I have benefited immensely from the supportive environment at the Bauer College of Business, where I serve as the Associate Dean for Research. I am grateful to work in Houston (a fantastic city, IMHO!) in a vibrant research community in the company of incredible people: Dean Paul Pavlou, previous Dean Latha Ramchand, Ed Blair, Roger Barascout, Norm Johnson, Amy Vandaveer, Saleha Khumawala, Tom George, Jessica Navarro, Amanda Sebesta, Marla Molony, Adina Dawoodi, Marie Tighe, Linda Monita, and Jennifer Coppock, to name just a few. A special shout-out to my Women in Leadership co-conspirators and friends: Dusya Vera, Jamie Belinne, Je'Anna Abbott, and Erika Henderson. Y'all make working both meaningful and fun!

There are a number of people who had a direct hand in making this book a reality. A warm and special thank you to Jonah Berger, Dolly Chugh, Ryan Hawk, Peter McGraw, Mike Norton, Dave Nussbaum, Raj Raghunathan, Sunita Sah, and Zoe Chance for providing valuable insight into the book publication process and for generously sharing their knowledge and experience. While I wrote the words in the book, I did not always write them alone. I am so thankful for the support and camaraderie (especially during the COVID-19 pandemic) of my virtual writing buddies from the UH FED (Faculty and Engagement) and the WOB (Women of Organizational Behavior) writing groups, in particular the session hosts whose positive and amiable dispositions always set a wonderful tone to our writing mornings—Leslie Coward, Rita Shea-Van Fossen, Beth Campbell, Phani Radhakrishnan, Bobbi Thomason, and Mai Trinh. I greatly appreciate the effort invested by Tom Tolan and Simone Patrick, who read early drafts of the manuscript and provided thoughtful, constructive, and creative feedback. For their excellent research assistance, I would like to thank Kota Nagase, Michael Fulfs, and Elizabeth Sells.

In terms of my core book publishing team, I think I hit the jackpot! It has been an absolute delight to work with Laurie Abkemeier—agent extraordinaire—who showed me the ropes and whose astute insights helped me navigate this new world of publishing. I am incredibly thankful to Anna Michels at Sourcebooks, who shared my vision for the book. Her suggestions, guidance, and ideas have made the book much, much better. I am indebted to the talented Sourcebooks team who shepherded the publishing process in a seamless and professional manner, including Lauren Harms and Jillian Rahn for the cover design, production editor Emily Proano, and the marketing and publicity team with Liz Kelsch, Brittney Mmutle, and Madeleine Brown.

For their unwavering support and friendship over the years, many long walks and even longer chats, for their prayers and text messages, I am so thankful for my dear friends: Seemantini Pathak, Naina Barretto, Deepa Chandrasekaran, Cathy Horn, Candice Hollenbeck, Lorraine Paul, Olivia Miljanic, Reshma Khemlani, Cheryl-Ann Monteiro, Melanie Larsen, Kamal Hirani, Swathi

Balaji, Nina Godiwala, Ryan Lobo, Shashi Matta, Mary Lou Daly, and Tina Carpenter. I have greatly benefited from the stimulating interactions in the CCLA leadership group, led by the wonderful Idahlynn Karre, the WiBE (Women in Business Education) group with the lovely Lisa Leander, and the GHWCC (Greater Houston Women's Chamber of Commerce) thought leader group with Houston's phenomenal women leaders, including Bambi McCullough, Suzan Deison, Janette Marx, Tracey Shappro, and Cindy Jennings.

Last, but certainly not least, I am thankful for my extended—Patrick, Ralhan, Rodrigues, and Kawauchi—family. I am who I am because of my mom, Ruby (whom I miss every day and who would be so proud!), and my dad, Ashley. Over the past couple of years, my dad took on the mantle of cheerleader, and in our daily chats gently steered me back to writing whenever my attention strayed. I am grateful to my husband, Sanjay, who offered his steady and pragmatic "mind of a strategist" perspective to every major book-related decision I had to make and for his detail-oriented design of the charts and figures in the book. I have been blessed to be surrounded by strong, resilient, and amazing women who inspire me and drive me to become the best version of myself: my grandmothers Maria and Queenie, my mom, Ruby, my mother-in-law, Hiroko, my incredible sisters (and best friends), Nicole and Simone, and the young lady to whom this book is dedicated, my sweet daughter Zoe.

NOTES

Chapter 1: Why We Say Yes When We Want to Say No

1 This story is taken from a George Orwell essay, "Shooting an Elephant," first published in 1936. Whether it is autobiographical was never definitively revealed, but for the purpose of illustration, I am going to assume that it was. After his stint in lower Burma, Orwell (his pen name; at the time of this story he was Eric Arthur Blair) went on to have a brilliant literary career.

2 The Urban Dictionary introduced the word *downthumbing* as the act of disagreeing online, and a downthumber as a person who disagrees. Aaron Peckham, "Downthumber," *Urban Dictionary: Fularious Street Slang Defined*, n.d. http://downthumber.urbanup.com/4862925.

3 Russell Cropanzano and Marie S. Mitchell, "Social exchange theory: An interdisciplinary review," *Journal of Management* 31, no. 6 (2005): 874–900.

4 Roy F. Baumeister and Mark R. Leary. "The need to belong: Desire for interpersonal attachments as a fundamental human motivation." *Interpersonal Development* (2017): 57–89.

5 Mark R. Leary, Kristine M. Kelly, Catherine A. Cottrell, and Lisa S. Schreindorfer, "Construct validity of the need to belong scale: Mapping the nomological network," *Journal of Personality Assessment* 95, no. 6 (2013): 610–624.

6 Robert B. Cialdini, *Influence: The Psychology of Persuasion,* rev. ed. (New York: William Morrow, 2006).

7 Ernst Fehr and Urs Fischbacher, "Third-party punishment and social norms," *Evolution and Human Behavior* 25, no. 2 (2004): 63–87.

8 Xinyue Zhou, Liwei Zheng, Lixing Zhou, and Nan Guo, "The act of rejecting

reduces the desire to reconnect: Evidence for a cognitive dissonance account," *Journal of Experimental Social Psychology* 45, no. 1 (2009): 44–50.

9 Natalie J. Ciarocco, Kristin L. Sommer, and Roy F. Baumeister, "Ostracism and ego depletion: The strains of silence," *Personality and Social Psychology Bulletin* 27, no. 9 (2001): 1156–1163.

10 Jaishree Umale, "Pragmatic failure in refusal strategies: British versus Omani interlocutors," *Arab World English Journal* 2, no. 1 (2011): 18–46.

11 Nick J Enfield, *How We Talk: The Inner Workings of Conversation* (New York: Basic Books, 2017).

12 Derek D. Rucker, Adam D. Galinsky, and Joe C. Magee, "The agentic–communal model of advantage and disadvantage: How inequality produces similarities in the psychology of power, social class, gender, and race," *Advances in Experimental Social Psychology* 58 (2018): 71–125.

13 Classic studies in social psychology on obedience and compliance consistently demonstrate people's willingness to obey authority and to comply with their social group. Summarily referred to as the Milgram Experiments, these studies show that when an experimenter ordered participants to harm other people, by giving them electric shocks, they would do so, under the power of authority. In Solomon Asch's studies on compliance to group norms, participants were tricked into giving wrong answers about which line is the longest of a set of three lines. Instead of trusting what they saw and identifying that line as the longest, a notable number simply followed the group's lead (the experimenter's confederates, by the way, who were instructed to provide the wrong answer) demonstrating the human tendency to distrust one's own judgment and conform to group opinion.

14 Jia Jiang, "Day 3 Rejection Therapy—Ask for Olympic Symbol Doughnuts. Jackie Delivers!," *Rejection Therapy with Jia Jiang* (blog), November 18, 2021, https://www.rejectiontherapy.com/blog/2012/11/18/day-3-rejection-therapy-ask-for-olympic-symbol-doughnuts-jackie-delivers.

15 Amy J. C. Cuddy, Susan T. Fiske, and Peter Glick, "Warmth and competence as universal dimensions of social perception: The stereotype content model and the BIAS map," *Advances in Experimental Social Psychology* 40 (2008): 61–149.

16 Roy F. Baumeister and Mark R. Leary, "The need to belong: desire for interpersonal attachments as a fundamental human motivation," *Psychological Bulletin* 117, no. 3 (1995): 497.

17 Adam Grant, "8 Ways to Say No Without Hurting Your Image," LinkedIn, March 11, 2014, https://www.linkedin.com/pulse/20140311110227-69244073-8-ways-to-say-no-without-hurting-your-image/.

18 Gail M. Williamson, Margaret S. Clark, Linda J. Pegalis, and Aileen Behan, "Affective consequences of refusing to help in communal and exchange relationships," *Personality and Social Psychology Bulletin* 22, no. 1 (1996): 34–47.

19 Raveena Tandon, "Women's Day 2021: Raveena Tandon writes about adopting and raising daughters at 21," *Free Press Journal*, March 7, 2021, https://www.freepressjournal.in/entertainment/womens-day-2021-raveena-tandon-writes-about-adopting-and-raising-daughters-at-21.

20 Robert Zinko, Gerald R. Ferris, Fred R. Blass, and Mary Dana Laird, "Toward a Theory of Reputation in Organizations," *Research in Personnel and Human Resources Management* (Bingley, West Yorkshire: Emerald Group Publishing Limited, 2007); This group of researchers defines reputation as "a perceptual identity formed from the collective perceptions of others, which is reflective of the complex combination of salient personal characteristics and accomplishments, demonstrated behavior, and intended images presented over some period of time as observed directly and/or reported from secondary sources, which reduces ambiguity about expected future behavior."

21 Erving Goffman, "The moral career of the mental patient," *Psychiatry* 22, no. 2 (1959): 123–142.

22 Jari J. Hakanen and Arnold B. Bakker, "Born and Bred to Burn Out: A Life-Course View and Reflections on Job Burnout," *Journal of Occupational Health Psychology* 22, no. 3 (2017): 354.

23 Vanessa Van Edwards, Captivate: *The Science of Succeeding With People* (New York: Penguin, 2018).

24 To protect the privacy of individuals, I have changed all names. Unless it is an author whose book I reference or a person in an article I reference, all the names I use in the examples are not real names.

25 Oprah Winfrey, "What Oprah Knows for Sure About Saying 'No,'" Oprah.com, accessed March 16, 2022, https://www.oprah.com/omagazine/what-oprah-knows-for-sure-about-always-saying-yes.

26 Mara Reinstein, "Educated Author Tara Westover Reflects on Her Success, Her Regrets and Her Advice from Oprah," *Parade*, February 6, 2019,

https://parade.com/777230/maramovies/educated-author-tara-westover-reflects-on-her-success-her-regrets-and-her-advice-from-oprah/.

27 Paulo Coelho, Twitter post, March 5, 2014, 11:47 a.m., https://twitter.com/paulocoelho/status/441268849871454208?lang=en.

Chapter 2: The Spotlight Effect

1 Roy F. Baumeister and Mark R. Leary, "The Need to Belong: Desire for Interpersonal Attachments as a Fundamental Human Motivation," *Psychological Bulletin* 117, no. 3 (1995): 497.

2 Elliot Aronson, ed., *Readings about the Social Animal* (New York Macmillan, 2003).

3 Robert B. Cialdini and Melanie R. Trost, "Social influence: Social norms, conformity and compliance," *The Handbook of Social Psychology* (Hoboken, New Jersey: John Wiley & Sons, 1998).

4 Ibid.

5 Thomas Gilovich, Victoria Husted Medvec, and Kenneth Savitsky, "The Spotlight Effect in Social Judgment: An Egocentric Bias in Estimates of the Salience of One's Own Actions And Appearance," *Journal of Personality and Social Psychology* 78, no. 2 (2000): 211.

6 Michael Ross and Fiore Sicoly, "Egocentric Biases in Availability and Attribution," *Journal of Personality and Social Psychology* 37, no. 3 (1979): 322.

7 Miron Zuckerman, Michael H. Kernis, Salvatore M. Guarnera, John F. Murphy, and Lauren Rappoport. "The egocentric bias: Seeing oneself as cause and target of others' behavior," *Journal of Personality* 51, no. 4 (1983): 621–630.

8 Allan Fenigstein, "Self-Consciousness and the Overperception of Self as a Target," *Journal of Personality and Social Psychology* 47, no. 4 (1984): 860.

9 Martha Beck, "The Cure for Self-Consciousness," Oprah.com, July 2007, http://www.oprah.com/spirit/Martha-Becks-Cure-for-Self-Consciousness#ixzz2WMHdNyT4.

10 For the researchers among you, the scenarios were successful in conveying that the goal was to say no and that the ask was a social versus a solo ask. In other words, the experimental manipulations worked.

11 Katharine Ridgway O'Brien, "Just Saying `No': An Examination of Gender

Differences in the Ability to Decline Requests in the Workplace," (2014) Diss., Rice University, https://hdl.handle.net/1911/77421.

12 Linda Babcock, Maria P. Recalde, Lise Vesterlund, and Laurie Weingart, "Gender Differences in Accepting and Receiving Requests for Tasks with Low Promotability," *American Economic Review* 107, no. 3 (2017): 714–747.

13 Chris Argyris and Donald A. Schon, *Theory in Practice: Increasing Professional Affectiveness* (San Francisco: Jossey-Bass, 1974).

14 Audre Lorde, *Sister Outsider: Essays and Speeches* (Berkley, California: Crossing Press, 2012).

Chapter 3: The Art (and Science) of Empowered Refusal

1 Her story is taken from *Maria Tallchief: America's Prima Ballerina* by Maria Tallchief(New York: Henry Holt and Company, 1997). In addition, I referred to: Jack Anderson, "Maria Tallchief, a Dazzling Ballerina and Muse for Balanchine, Dies at 88," *New York Times,* April 12, 2013, https://www.nytimes.com/2013/04/13/arts/dance/maria-tallchief-brilliant-ballerina-dies-at-88.html; Sarah Halzack, "Maria Tallchief, Ballet Star Who Was Inspiration for Balanchine, Dies at 88," *Washington Post,* April 12, 2013, https://www.washingtonpost.com/local/obituaries/maria-tallchief-ballet-star-who-was-inspiration-for-balanchine-dies-at-88/2013/04/12/5888f3de-c5dc-11df-94e1-c5afa35a9e59_story.html.

2 I learned about the concept of covering in Dolly Chugh's newsletter. Dolly Chugh, "What I Pray For," Dear Good People email newsletter, accessed November 2022, https://us19.campaign-archive.com/?u=f881146700e09f49303435ca1&id=6818685cdf

3 Bruce Markusen, "Clemente Overcame Societal Barriers en route to Superstardom," Baseball Hall of Fame, accessed on March 21, 2022, https://baseballhall.org/discover/baseball-history/clemente-overcame-societal-barriers-en-route-to-superstardom.

4 Horst W. J. Rittel and Melvin M. Webber, "Dilemmas in a General Theory of Planning," *Policy Sciences* 4, no. 2 (1973): 155–169.

5 Much research has been done on these three qualities. Personal power reflects being in control, having the freedom and autonomy to act independently of other people. Authenticity is about walking the talk. Integrity is simply doing

what you say and saying what you mean. Formally defined, integrity is "the consistency of an acting entity's words and actions" based on a virtue-ethics framework.

6 Ruolei Gu, Jing Yang, Yuanyuan Shi, Yi Luo, Yu LL Luo, and Huajian Cai, "Be Strong Enough to Say No: Self-Affirmation Increases Rejection to Unfair Offers," *Frontiers in Psychology* 7 (2016): 1824.

7 David K. Sherman and Geoffrey L. Cohen, "The Psychology of Self-Defense: Self-Affirmation Theory," *Advances in Experimental Social Psychology* 38 (2006): 183–242.

8 Adam D. Galinsky, Joe C. Magee, Deborah H. Gruenfeld, Jennifer A. Whitson, and Katie A. Liljenquist, "Power Reduces the Press of the Situation: Implications for Creativity, Conformity, and Dissonance," *Journal of Personality and Social Psychology* 95, no. 6 (2008): 1450.

9 Jennifer R. Overbeck, Larissa Z. Tiedens, and Sebastien Brion, "The Powerful Want to, the Powerless Have to: Perceived Constraint Moderates Causal Attributions," *European Journal of Social Psychology* 36, no. 4 (2006): 479–496.

10 Joe C. Magee, Adam D. Galinsky, and Deborah H. Gruenfeld, "Power, Propensity to Negotiate, and Moving First in Competitive Interactions," *Personality and Social Psychology Bulletin* 33, no. 2 (2007): 200–212.

11 M. Weber, *The Theory of Social and Economic Organization*, trans. A. M. Henderson and Talcott Parsons (New York: Oxford University Press, 1947).

12 Marianne Schmid Mast, Klaus Jonas, and Judith A. Hall, "Give a Person Power and He or She Will Show Interpersonal Sensitivity: The Phenomenon and Its Why and When," *Journal of Personality and Social Psychology* 97, no. 5 (2009): 835.

13 Vanessa M. Patrick and Henrik Hagtvedt, "I 'Don't' Versus "I Can't': When Empowered Refusal Motivates Goal-Directed Behavior," *Journal of Consumer Research* 39, no. 2 (2012): 371–381.

14 John Langshaw Austin, *How to Do Things with Words* (Oxford, UK: Oxford University Press, 1975); John R. Searle, and John Rogers Searle. *Speech Acts: An Essay in the Philosophy of Language*, Vol. 626 (Cambridge, UK: Cambridge University Press, 1969).

15 Vanessa M. Patrick and Henrik Hagtvedt, "How to Say "No": Conviction and Identity Attributions in Persuasive Refusal," *International Journal of Research in Marketing* 29, no. 4 (2012): 390–394.

16 Holly Weeks, "Taking the Stress Out of Stressful Conversations," *Harvard Business Review*, July 2001, https://hbr.org/2001/07/taking-the-stress-out-of-stressful-conversations.

17 Charles R. Snyder and Raymond L. Higgins, "Excuses: Their Effective Role in the Negotiation of Reality," *Psychological Bulletin* 104, no. 1 (1988): 23.

18 Vanessa M. Patrick and Henrik Hagtvedt, "I 'Don't' Versus "I Can't': When Empowered Refusal Motivates Goal-Directed Behavior," *Journal of Consumer Research* 39, no. 2 (2012): 371–381.

19 Lee Ross and Richard E. Nisbett, *The Person and the Situation: Perspectives of Social Psychology* (London: Pinter & Martin Publishers, 2011).

20 Christopher J. Bryan, Gregory M. Walton, Todd Rogers, and Carol S. Dweck, "Motivating Voter Turnout by Invoking the Self," *Proceedings of the National Academy of Sciences* 108, no. 31 (2011): 12,653–12,656.

21 James J. Bradac and Anthony Mulac, "A Molecular View of Powerful and Powerless Speech Styles: Attributional Consequences of Specific Language Features and Communicator Intentions," *Communications Monographs* 51, no. 4 (1984): 307–319.

22 Karen M. Douglas and Robbie M. Sutton, "When What You Say About Others Says Something About You: Language Abstraction and Inferences About Describers' Attitudes and Goals," *Journal of Experimental Social Psychology* 42, no. 4 (2006): 500–508.

23 Grant Packard and Jonah Berger, "How Concrete Language Shapes Customer Satisfaction," *Journal of Consumer Research* 47, no. 5 (2021): 787–806.

Chapter 4: Looking Inward to Develop Self-Awareness

1 George Herbert Mead, *Mind, Self and Society*, Vol. 111 (Chicago: University of Chicago Press, 1934); Shelley Duval and Robert A. Wicklund, *A Theory of Objective Self Awareness* (New York: Academic Press, 1972).

2 Charles S. Carver, "Self-awareness," in *Handbook of Self and Identity*, ed. M. R. Leary and J. P. Tangney (New York: The Guilford Press, 2012): 50–68.

3 Charles Horton Cooley, "Looking-glass self," *The Production of Reality: Essays and Readings on Social Interaction* 6 (1902): 126–128.

4 Paul J. Silvia and Maureen O'Brien, "Self-Awareness and Constructive Functioning: Revisiting 'the Human Dilemma,'" *Journal of Social and Clinical Psychology* 23, no. 4 (August 2004): 475–489.

5 Kenneth N. Wexley, Ralph A. Alexander, James Greenawalt, and Michael A. Couch, "Attitudinal Congruence and Similarity as Related to Inter-personal Evaluations in Manager-Subordinate Dyads," *Academy of Management Journal* 23, no. 2 (June 1980): 320–330.

6 Vanessa M. Patrick and Henrik Hagtvedt, "I 'Don't' Versus "I Can't': When Empowered Refusal Motivates Goal-Directed Behavior," *Journal of Consumer Research* 39, no. 2 (2012): 371–381.

7 Jennifer Porter, "Why You Should Make Time for Self-Reflection (Even if You Hate Doing It)," *Harvard Business Review* 21 (2017).

8 Jon M. Jachimowicz et al., "Commuting as Role Transitions: How Trait Self-Control and Work-Related Prospection Offset Negative Effects of Lengthy Commutes," working paper, Harvard Business School, 2016.

9 Laura Morgan Roberts, Jane E. Dutton, Gretchen M. Spreitzer, Emily D. Heaphy, and Robert E. Quinn, "Composing the Reflected Best-Self Portrait: Building Pathways for Becoming Extraordinary in Work Organizations," *Academy of Management Review* 30, no. 4 (2005): 712–736.

10 Ron Ashkenas, "How to Overcome Executive Isolation," *Harvard Business Review*, February 2, 2017, https://hbr.org/2017/02/how-to-overcome-executive-isolation.

11 Doris Kearns Goodwin, *Team of Rivals: The Political Genius of Abraham Lincoln* (London: Penguin, 2009).

12 William Damon, *The Path to Purpose: Helping Our Children Find Their Calling in Life* (New York: Simon and Schuster, 2008).

13 Simon Sinek, "How Great Leaders Inspire Action," TED, published on September 2009, TED video, 17:48, https://www.ted.com/talks/simon_sinek_how_great_leaders_inspire_action.

14 Howard Gardner, Mihaly Csikszentmihalyi, and William Damon, *Good Work: When Excellence and Ethics Meet* (New York: Basic Books, 2001).

15 Eleanor Roosevelt, *You Learn by Living: Eleven Keys for a More Fulfilling Life* (New York: Harper and Row, 1960).

16 Greg McKeown, *Essentialism: The Disciplined Pursuit of Less* (New York: Currency, 2020).

17 James M. Buchanan, "Opportunity Cost," *The New Palgrave Dictionary of Economics Online* (2008).

18 Richard P. Larrick, James N. Morgan, and Richard E. Nisbett, "Teaching the

Use of Cost-Benefit Reasoning in Everyday Life," *Psychological Science* 1, no. 6 (1990): 362–370.

19 Stephen A. Spiller, "Opportunity Cost Consideration," *Journal of Consumer Research* 38, no. 4 (2011): 595–610.

20 In every positive psychology lecture or workshop Bob Peterson gave, he left people with one key bumper sticker–like phrase: "Other people matter." When one thinks of what a good human life is about, it involves other people. Remember the Maori chant: "It's the people. It's the people. It's the people."

21 Niklas Göke, "Why You Really Should Say 'No' More Often," Nik.art, February, 2, 2019, https://nik.art/why-you-really-should-say-no-more-often/.

22 William Duggan, *Napoleon's Glance: The Secret of Strategy* (New York: Nation Books, 2002).

23 David Graeber, *Bullshit Jobs: A Theory* (New York: Simon & Schuster, 2018).

24 Roy F. Baumeister, Kathleen D. Vohs, Jennifer L. Aaker, and Emily N. Garbinsky, "Some Key Differences Between a Happy Life and a Meaningful Life," *The Journal of Positive Psychology* 8, no. 6 (2013): 505–516.

25 Linda Babcock, Maria P. Recalde, and Lise Vesterlund, "Why Women Volunteer for Tasks That Don't Lead To Promotions," *Harvard Business Review*, June 16, 2018, https://hbr.org/2018/07/why-women-volunteer-for-tasks-that-dont-lead-to-promotions.

26 Linda Babcock, Maria P. Recalde, Lise Vesterlund, and Laurie Weingart, "Gender Differences in Accepting and Receiving Requests for Tasks with Low Promotability," *American Economic Review* 107, no. 3 (2017): 714–747.

Chapter 5: Make Rules, Not Decisions

1 Alison Beard, "Life's Work: An Interview with Isabel Allende," *Harvard Business Review*, May 2016, https://hbr.org/2016/05/isabel-allende.

2 Gretchen Rubin, "A Little Happier: For Writer Isabel Allende, January 8 Is the Right Day to Begin," *Gretchen Rubin* (blog), August 30, 2021, https://gretchenrubin.com/podcast-episode/little-happier-isabel-allende-right-day-to-begin/.

3 Vanessa Patrick, "Getting to Gutsy: Using Personal Policies to Enhance (and Reclaim) Agency in The Workplace," *Rutgers Business Review* 6, no. 2 (2021).

4 Jennifer Wallace and Vanessa Patrick, "Life in Lockdown Is Testing Parents'

Bandwidth, but There Are Ways to Protect Your Mental Energy," *Washington Post*, April 27, 2020.

5 Tasha Eurich, *Insight: The Surprising Truth About How Others See Us, How We See Ourselves, and Why the Answers Matter More Than We Think* (New York: Currency, 2017).

6 Ruchika Tulshyan, "The 'I Just Can't Say No' Club Women Need to Advance in Their Careers," *Forbes*, June 30, 2016, https://www.forbes.com/sites/ruchikatulshyan/2016/06/28/the-i-just-cant-say-no-club-women-need-to-advance-in-their-careers/?sh=7303ea454917.

7 Peter Karoff and Jane Maddox, *The World We Want: New Dimensions in Philanthropy and Social Change* (Lanham, MD: AltaMira, 2007).

8 Stewart D. Friedman, *Leading the Life You Want: Skills for Integrating Work and Life* (Boston: Harvard Business Press, 2014).

9 Mario Mikulincer and Orif Marshand, "An Excuse Perspective of the Learned Helplessness Paradigm: The Self-Protective Role of Causal Attributions," *Journal of Social and Clinical Psychology* 10 (1991): 134–151.

10 Vanessa M. Patrick and Henrik Hagtvedt, "I 'Don't' Versus "I Can't': When Empowered Refusal Motivates Goal-Directed Behavior," *Journal of Consumer Research* 39, no. 2 (2012): 371–381.

11 Vanessa M. Patrick, "Own It: Identity-based Refusals are More Effective than Situational Constraints to Say No to Interpersonal Requests," (working paper, 2022).

Chapter 6: Bringing Your Whole Self to Your Empowered Refusal

1 "Madeleine Albright's Jewelry-Box Diplomacy," NPR, September 29, 2009, https://www.npr.org/templates/story/story.php?storyId=113278807.

2 Megan Gambino, "Madeleine Albright on Her Life in Pins," *Smithsonian Magazine*, June 2010, https://www.smithsonianmag.com/arts-culture/madeleine-albright-on-her-life-in-pins-149191/.

3 Brian Caulfield, "Steve Jobs Tried To Get Apple Employees To Wear Uniforms," *Forbes*, October 11, 2011, https://www.forbes.com/sites/briancaulfield/2011/10/11/steve-jobs-tried-to-get-apple-employees-to-wear-uniforms/?sh=24397ecb7d6c.

4 Jonathan Glancey, "'I Don't Do Nice,'" *The Guardian*, October 9, 2006,

https://www.theguardian.com/artanddesign/2006/oct/09/architecture.communities.

5 Gavin Meikle, "Six Elements of Vocal Variety and How to Master Them Part 1," inter-activ, July 18, 2017, https://www.inter-activ.co.uk/presentation-skills/six-elements-of-vocal-variety-and-how-to-master-them-part-1-volume/.

6 Stephanie C. Lin, Rebecca L. Schaumberg, and Taly Reich, "Sidestepping the Rock and the Hard Place: The Private Avoidance of Prosocial Requests," *Journal of Experimental Social Psychology* 64 (2016): 35–40.

7 John R. Sparks, Charles S. Areni, and K. Chris Cox, "An Investigation of the Effects of Language Style and Communication Modality on Persuasion," *Communications Monographs* 65, no. 2 (1998): 108–125.

8 John Antonakis, Marika Fenley, and Sue Liechti, "Learning Charisma. Transform Yourself into the Person Others Want to Follow," *Harvard Business Review* 90, no. 6 (2012): 127–130.

9 Norah E. Dunbar, "Power and Dominance in Nonverbal Communication," *The International Encyclopedia of Interpersonal Communication* (2015): 1–5.

10 Myra Brooks Welch, "The Old Violin": or "The Touch of the Masters Hand," https://www.onlythebible.com/Poems/the-Touch-of-the-Masters-Hand--Old-Violin.html

11 Pierre Philippot, Gaëtane Chapelle, and Sylvie Blairy, "Respiratory Feedback in the Generation of Emotion," *Cognition and Emotion* 16, no. 5 (2002): 605–627.

12 Juan David Leongómez, Viktoria R. Mileva, Anthony C. Little, and S. Craig Roberts, "Perceived Differences in Social Status Between Speaker and Listener Affect the Speaker's Vocal Characteristics," *PloS One* 12, no. 6 (2017): e0179407.

13 Elisabeth André, Elisabetta Bevacqua, Dirk Heylen, Radoslaw Niewiadomski, Catherine Pelachaud, Christopher Peters, Isabella Poggi, and Matthias Rehm, "Non-Verbal Persuasion and Communication in an Affective Agent," in *Emotion-Oriented Systems* (Berlin, Heidelberg: Springer, 2011), 585–608.

14 Adrian F. Ward, Kristen Duke, Ayelet Gneezy, and Maarten W. Bos "Brain Drain: The Mere Presence of One's Own Smartphone Reduces Available Cognitive Capacity," *Journal of the Association for Consumer Research* 2, no. 2 (2017): 140–154.

15 Shiri Melumad, and Michel Tuan Pham. "The smartphone as a pacifying technology." *Journal of Consumer Research* 47, no. 2 (2020): 237-255.

16 Ze Wang, Huifang Mao, Yexin Jessica Li, and Fan Liu, "Smile Big or Not? Effects of Smile Intensity on Perceptions of Warmth and Competence," *Journal of Consumer Research* 43, no. 5 (2017): 787–805.

17 Marianne LaFrance and Andrea C. Vial, "Gender and Nonverbal Behavior," in *APA Handbook of Nonverbal Communication* (Washington DC: American Psychological Association, 2016): 139–161.

18 In discussing these gender differences, LaFrance and Vial point out the importance of adopting the lens of psychological gender rather than the biological gender to understand these effects. In other words, that a male or a female subscribes to the societal definition of masculinity and femininity is more relevant than whether they are biologically masculine or feminine.

19 Nancy M. Henley, *Body Politics: Power, Sex and Nonverbal Communication* (Englewood Cliffs, NJ: Prentice-Hall, 1986).

20 Kristen M. Shockley, Allison S. Gabriel, Daron Robertson, Christopher C. Rosen, Nitya Chawla, Mahira L. Ganster, and Maira E. Ezerins, "The Fatiguing Effects of Camera Use in Virtual Meetings: A Within-Person Field Experiment," *Journal of Applied Psychology* 106, no. 8 (2021): 1137 -1155.

21 Lara L. Jones, Lee H. Wurm, Gregory A. Norville, and Kate L. Mullins, "Sex Differences in Emoji Use, Familiarity, and Valence," *Computers in Human Behavior* 108 (2020): 106305.

22 Raquel Laneri, "In Pictures: Seven Common Body Language Mistakes," *Forbes*, June 23, 2009, https://www.forbes.com/2009/06/23/body-language-first-impression-forbes-woman-leadership-communication_slide.html?sh=408db1d53933.

23 Lane Strathearn, Jian Li, Peter Fonagy, and P. Read Montague, "What's in a Smile? Maternal Brain Responses to Infant Facial Cues," *Pediatrics* 122, no. 1 (2008): 40–51.

24 Barbara Wild, Michael Erb, Michael Eyb, Mathias Bartels, and Wolfgang Grodd, "Why are Smiles Contagious? An fMRI Study of the Interaction Between Perception of Facial Affect and Facial Movements," *Psychiatry Research: Neuroimaging* 123, no. 1 (2003): 17–36.

25 Robin Roberts, "Robin Roberts," Rock'n Robin, Accessed on February 12, 2022, https://www.rocknrobin.tv/robin-roberts.

26 Corky Siemaszko, "Michelle Obama Embraces George W. Bush: Why That Photo Was So Moving," NBC News, September 26, 2016,

https://www.nbcnews.com/news/us-news/michelle-obama-embraces-george-w-bush-why-photo-was-so-n654451.

27 Clint Rainey, "The Power Huggers," *New York Magazine*, September 27, 2013, https://nymag.com/news/intelligencer/topic/huggers-2013-10/.

28 "Barbara Jordan: A Voice For Democracy," Texas Women's Foundation, Accessed on February 21, 2022, https://txwf.org/barbara-jordan-a-voice-for-democracy/.

29 Alex Tawse, Vanessa M. Patrick, and Dusya Vera, "Crossing the Chasm: Leadership Nudges to Help Transition From Strategy Formulation to Strategy Implementation," *Business Horizons* 62, no. 2 (2019): 249–257.

Chapter 7: Managing Pushback from Difficult Askers

1 Suzanne Simard, *Finding the Mother Tree: Discovering the Wisdom and Intelligence of the Forest* (New York: Penguin Random House, 2021).

2 Nannette Richford, "The Best Marigold as a Vegetable Garden Companion," SFGATE, September 3, 2019, https://homeguides.sfgate.com/marigold-vegetable-garden-companion-35309.html. Adapted also from this blog post I read on the Marigold effect: Jennifer Gonzales, "Find Your Marigold: The One Essential Rule for New Teachers," *Cult of Pedagogy* (blog), August 29, 2013, https://www.cultofpedagogy.com/marigolds/.

3 Jessica Bennett, "Welcome to the 'No' Club," *New York Times*, August 6, 2019, https://www.nytimes.com/2019/08/06/us/welcome-to-the-no-club.html.

4 "Black Walnut Toxicity," The Morton Arboretum, accessed on March 26, 2022, https://mortonarb.org/plant-and-protect/tree-plant-care/plant-care-resources/black-walnut-toxicity/.

5 Moving forward, I will for the purposes of simplicity use the term "walnut trees" to refer specifically to the juglone-rich black walnut variety.

6 Many books and research studies have addressed the issue of toxic and pushy people in our personal and professional lives. For example, in *The No Asshole Rule: Building a Civilized Workplace and Surviving One that Isn't* (New York: Business Plus, 2007), Stanford professor Bob Sutton documents the characteristics of assholes. He concludes that some people are certified assholes (chronic jerks) whereas others are temporary assholes (single-episode jerks). He includes an Asshole Rating Self-Exam (ARSE) to determine if you are a

certified asshole or on the road to becoming one. New York University professor Tessa West's new book *Jerks At Work: Toxic Coworkers and What to Do About Them* (New York: Portfolio Press, 2022), identifies seven types of worst offenders—the Bulldozer, the Gaslighter, the Credit-Stealer, etc.—and provides ways to respond to and outwit them.

7 Richard Carpenter and John Baites, songwriters, "Top of the World," recorded 1972, A Song for You, A&M Studios, released September 17, 1973.

8 Carl R. Rogers, "Empathic: An Unappreciated Way of Being," *The Counseling Psychologist* 5, no. 2 (1975): 2–10.

9 Gerald R. Ferris, Fred R. Blass, Ceasar Douglas, Robert W. Kolodinsky, and Darren C. Treadway, "Personal Reputation in Organizations," in *Organizational Behavior: The State of the Science*, 2nd ed., ed. J. Greenburg (Mahwah, NJ: Lawrence Erlbaum, 2003): 211–246.

10 Peter Bregman, "Nine Practices to Help You Say No," *Harvard Business Review*, February 15, 2013, https://hbr.org/2013/02/nine-practices-to-help-you-say.html.

11 M. Mahdi Roghanizad and Vanessa K. Bohns, "Ask in Person: You're Less Persuasive Than You Think Over Email," *Journal of Experimental Social Psychology* 69 (2017): 223–226.

12 Preston Ni, "14 Signs of Psychological and Emotional Manipulation," *Psychology Today*, October 11, 2015, https://www.psychologytoday.com/us/blog/communication-success/201510/14-signs-psychological-and-emotional-manipulation.

13 Michael Schrage, "Is It OK to Yell at Your Employees?" *Harvard Business Review*, November 8, 2013, https://hbr.org/2013/11/is-it-ok-to-yell-at-your-employees.

14 Donald E. Gibson and Ronda Roberts Callister, "Anger in Organizations: Review and Integration," *Journal of Management* 36, no. 1 (2010): 66–93.

15 Jeffrey Z. Rubin and Bert R. Brown, *The Social Psychology of Bargaining and Negotiation* (New York: Elsevier, 2013).

16 Adam Grant, *Give and Take: A Revolutionary Approach to Success* (London: Penguin, 2013).

17 Robin M Kowalski, *Behaving Badly: Aversive Behaviors in Interpersonal Relationships* (Washington, DC: American Psychological Association, 2001).

18 Andrew K. Przybylski, Kou Murayama, Cody R. De Haan, and Valerie

Gladwell, "Motivational, Emotional, and Behavioral Correlates of Fear of Missing Out," *Computers in Human Behavior* 29, no. 4 (2013): 1841–1848.

19 Kipling D. Williams, Wendelyn J. Shore, and Jon E. Grahe, "The Silent Treatment: Perceptions of Its Behaviors and Associated Feelings," *Group Processes and Intergroup Relations* 1, no. 2 (1998): 117–141.

20 Deborah South Richardson, "Everyday Aggression Takes Many Forms," *Current Directions in Psychological Science* 23, no. 3 (2014): 220–224.

21 Leah E. LeFebvre and Xiaoti Fan, "Ghosted?: Navigating Strategies for Reducing Uncertainty and Implications Surrounding Ambiguous Loss." *Personal Relationships* 27, no. 2, (2020): 433–459.

22 Bill Knaus, "Protect Yourself From Pushy People," *Psychology Today*, March 30, 2012, https://www.psychologytoday.com/us/blog/science-and-sensibility/201203/protect-yourself-pushy-people.

23 I have arrived at these five main strategies based on research on workplace bullying, studies on handling difficult people, and dealing with workplace jerks. To corroborate these workplace findings with dealing with walnut trees in daily life, I ran a survey (N = 327) and analyzed the responses. This section is based on a synthesis of various sources.

24 Since this is a study that uses recall, it is not surprising that respondents recall active pushback more readily than passive pushback. My intuition is that pushback strategy a walnut tree might employ depends on the type of person they are trying to influence. The students, being generally younger, might tend to experience more active pushback whereas more passive pushback strategies are employed for older and more experienced individuals.

25 In the book *Teachings of Don Juan*, Carlos Castaneda describes a conversation in which the narrator arrives at this startling realization.

26 Bill Knaus. "Protect Yourself From Pushy People," *Psychology Today*, March 30, 2012, https://www.psychologytoday.com/us/blog/science-and-sensibility/201203/protect-yourself-pushy-people.

27 Grant E. Donnelly, Anne V Wilson, Ashley V Whillans, and Michael I Norton, "Communicating Resource Scarcity and Interpersonal Connection," *Journal of Consumer Psychology* 31, no. 4 (2021): 726–45. https://doi.org/10.1002/jcpy.1226.

28 Neal R. Norrick and Alice Spitz, "Humor as a Resource For Mitigating Conflict In Interaction," *Journal of Pragmatics* 40, no. 10 (2008): 1661–1686.

29 Marian Friestad and Peter Wright, "Everyday Persuasion Knowledge," *Psychology and Marketing* 16, no. 2 (1999): 185–194.

30 Melody Wilding, "How to Say 'No' After Saying 'Yes,'" *Harvard Business Review*, September 20, 2021, https://hbr.org/2021/09/how-to-say-no-after-saying-yes.

31 Daniel T. Gilbert, Elizabeth C. Pinel, Timothy D. Wilson, Stephen J. Blumberg, and Thalia P. Wheatley, "Immune Neglect: A Source of Durability Bias in Affective Forecasting," *Journal of Personality and Social Psychology* 75, no. 3 (1998): 617; Timothy D. Wilson and Daniel T. Gilbert, "Affective Forecasting," *Current Directions in Psychological Science* 14, no. 3 (2005): 131.

Chapter 8: Getting Out of Our Own Way

1 "The Electric Ben Franklin," UShistory.org, July 4, 1995, https://www.ushistory.org/franklin/autobiography/page40.htm. The wording is exactly how Franklin documented it in his autobiography.

2 "Visiting the Benjamin Franklin Museum," National Park Service, March 21, 2022, https://www.nps.gov/inde/planyourvisit/benjaminfranklinmuseum.htm.

3 John Adams autobiography, part 2, "Travels, and Negotiations," 1777-1778, sheet 26 of 37 [electronic edition]. *Adams Family Papers: An Electronic Archive*. Massachusetts Historical Society. http://www.masshist.org/digitaladams/

4 Mark Muraven, Dianne M. Tice, and Roy F. Baumeister, "Self-Control as a Limited Resource: Regulatory Depletion Patterns," *Journal of Personality and Social Psychology* 74 (1998): 774–89.

5 Amos Tversky and Daniel Kahneman, "Rational choice and the framing of decisions," *Journal of Business* 59, (1986): 251–28.

6 Janet Metcalfe and Walter Mischel, "A Hot/Cool-System Analysis of Delay of Gratification: Dynamics Of Willpower," *Psychological Review* 106, no. 1 (1999): 3.

7 Vanessa M. Patrick, Matthew Lancellotti and Henrik Hagtvedt, "Getting a Second Chance: The Role of Imagery in the Influence of Inaction Regret on Behavioral Intent," *Journal of the Academy of Marketing Science* 37, no. 2 (2009): 181–190.

8 I learned this version of the story from the writings of the great Buddhist meditation teacher Thich Nhat Hanh in his book *Being Peace*.

9 Ethan Kross, Emma Bruehlman-Senecal, Jiyoung Park, Aleah Burson,

Adrienne Dougherty, Holly Shablack, Ryan Bremner, Jason Moser, and Ozlem Ayduk, "Self-talk as a Regulatory Mechanism: How You Do It Matters," *Journal of Personality and Social Psychology* 106, no. 2 (2014): 304.

10 Christopher J. Bryan, Gregory M. Walton, Todd Rogers, and Carol S. Dweck, "Motivating Voter Turnout by Invoking the Self," *Proceedings of the National Academy of Sciences* 108, no. 31 (2011): 12653–12656.

11 Nicole Mead and Vanessa M. Patrick "The Taming of Desire: Unspecific Postponement Reduces Desire for and Consumption of Postponed Temptations," *Journal of Personality and Social Psychology* 2015 (2015): 1–59.

12 Yannis Theodorakis, Stiliani Chroni, Kostas Laparidis, Vagelis Bebetsos, and Irini Douma, "Self-Talk in a Basketball-Shooting Task," *Perceptual and Motor Skills* 92, no. 1 (2001): 309–315.

13 Ethan Kross, Emma Bruehlman-Senecal, Jiyoung Park, Aleah Burson, Adrienne Dougherty, Holly Shablack, Ryan Bremner, Jason Moser, and Ozlem Ayduk, "Self-Talk as a Regulatory Mechanism: How You Do it Matters," *Journal of Personality and Social Psychology* 106, no. 2 (2014): 304.

14 Lindsey Streamer, Mark D. Seery, Cheryl L. Kondrak, Veronica M. Lamarche, and Thomas L. Saltsman, "Not I, but She: The Beneficial Effects of Self-Distancing On Challenge/Threat Cardiovascular Responses," *Journal of Experimental Social Psychology* 70 (2017): 235–241.

15 Diana Nyad, "Never, Ever Give Up," TED, published on December 2013, TED video, 15:23, https://www.ted.com/talks/diana_nyad_never_ever_give_up?language=en.

16 Colin Powell, *It Worked For Me: In Life and Leadership* (New York: HarperCollins, 2012).

17 Ziva Kunda, "The Case For Motivated Reasoning," *Psychological Bulletin* 108, no. 3 (1990): 480.

18 Thomas Gilovich, *How We Know What Isn't So* (New York: Simon and Schuster, 2008).

19 Higgins E. Tory, "Self-Discrepancy: A Theory Relating Self and Affect," *Psychological Review* 94, no. 3 (1987): 319.

20 Theodore A. Powers, Richard Koestner, Nathalie Lacaille, Lisa Kwan, and David C. Zuroff, "Self-Criticism, Motivation, and Goal Progress of Athletes And Musicians: A Prospective Study," *Personality and Individual Differences* 47, no. 4 (2009): 279 –283.

21 Theodore A. Powers, Richard Koestner, and David C. Zuroff, "Self-Criticism, Goal Motivation, And Goal Progress," *Journal of Social and Clinical Psychology* 26, no. 7 (2007): 826–840.

22 Juliana G. Breines and Serena Chen, "Self-Compassion Increases Self-Improvement Motivation," *Personality and Social Psychology Bulletin* 38, no. 9 (2012): 1133–1143.

23 Christa Smith, "3 Ways to Outsmart Your Inner Critic," *Psychology Today*, April 30, 2015, https://www.psychologytoday.com/us/blog/shift/201504/3-ways-outsmart-your-inner-critic.

24 TEDx Talks, "Sport Psychology -Inside the Mind of Champion Athletes: Martin Hagger at TEDxPerth," TEDx Talks, published on January 23, 2013, YouTube video, 12:01, https://www.youtube.com/watch?v=yG7v4y_xwzQ.

25 Gordon Tredgold, "50 Inspirational Pieces of Wisdom From Muhammad Ali," *Inc.*, June 7, 2016, https://www.inc.com/gordon-tredgold/muhammad-ali-50-inspiring-thoughts-from-the-greatest-of-all-time.html.

26 Janet Metcalfe and Walter Mischel, "A Hot/Cool-System Analysis of Delay of Gratification: Dynamics of Willpower," Psychological Review 106, no. 1 (1999): 3–19.

Chapter 9: Harness Your Trailblazing Potential

1 Richard L. Maddens, "Mrs. Chisholm Gets Off House Farm Committee," *New York Times*, January 30, 1969

2 Shirley Chisholm, *Unbossed and Unbought* (Boston: Houghton Mifflin, 1970): 82–83. The quotes from this story come from this autobiography by Chisholm herself.

3 *Chisholm '72*, directed by Shola Lynch,PBS, 2005.

4 Gerhard Peters and John T. Woolley, "Remarks on Presenting the Presidential Medal of Freedom," The American Presidency Project, November 24, 2015, https://www.presidency.ucsb.edu/documents/remarks-presenting-the-presidential-medal-freedom-16.

5 Nanette Gartrell, *My Answer Is No...If That's Okay With You: How Women Can Say No With Confidence* (La Jolla, CA: Atria Publishing, 2009).

6 Caitlyn Collins, a professor of sociology at Washington University in St Louis who studies gender inequality at work and at home.

7 Katharine Ridgway O'Brien, "Just Saying 'No': An Examination of Gender Differences in the Ability to Decline Requests in the Workplace," (PhD thesis, Rice University, 2014), https://scholarship.rice.edu/bitstream/handle/1911/77421/OBRIEN-DOCUMENT-2014.pdf?isAllowed=y&sequence=1.

8 Jim Fultz, C. Daniel Batson, Victoria A. Fortenbach, Patricia M. McCarthy, and Laurel L. Varney, "Social Evaluation and the Empathy-Altruism Hypothesis," *Journal of Personality and Social Psychology* 50, no. 4 (1986): 761.

9 Madeline E. Heilman and Tyler G. Okimoto, "Why are Women Penalized For Success at Male Tasks?: The Implied Communality Deficit," *Journal of Applied Psychology* 92, no. 1 (2007): 81.

10 Madeline E. Heilman and Julie J. Chen, "Same Behavior, Different Consequences: Reactions to Men's and Women's Altruistic Citizenship Behavior," *Journal of Applied Psychology* 90, no. 3 (2005): 431.

11 Linda Babcock, Maria P. Recalde, Lise Vesterlund, and Laurie Weingart, "Gender Differences in Accepting and Receiving Requests for Tasks with Low Promotability," *American Economic Review* 107, no. 3 (2017): 714–47.

12 In the movie, Kevin Doyle, the writer of the wedding announcements column and future love interest, makes an astute observation. He says "You'd rather focus on other people's Kodak moments than make memories of your own!" https://www.quotes.net/mquote/107652

13 Herminia Ibarra, Nancy M. Carter, and Christine Silva, "Why Men Still Get More Promotions than Women," *Harvard Business Review* 88, no. 9 (2010): 80–85.

14 Priya Fielding-Singh, Devon Magliozzi, and Swethaa Ballakrishnen, "Why Women Stay Out of the Spotlight at Work," *Harvard Business Review* 28 (2018).

15 Elena Greguletz, Marjo-Riitta Diehl, and Karin Kreutzer, "Why Women Build Less Effective Networks Than Men: The Role of Structural Exclusion and Personal Hesitation," *Human Relations* 72, no. 7 (2019): 1234–1261.

16 Lindsay Dodgson, "Men Are Getting the Credit for Women's Work through Something Called 'Hepeating'—Here's What It Means," *Business Insider*, March 8, 2018, https://www.businessinsider.com/what-is-hepeating-2017-9.

17 Mahdi Ebrahimi, Maryam Kouchaki, and Vanessa M. Patrick, "Juggling Work and Home Selves: Low Identity Integration Feels Less Authentic and Increases Unethicality," *Organizational Behavior and Human Decision Processes* 158 (2020): 101–111.

18 Josie Cox, "Why Women are More Burned Out Than Men," BBC, October 3, 2021, https://www.bbc.com/worklife/article/20210928-why-women-are-more-burned-out-than-men.

19 Mary E. Wade, "Women and Salary Negotiation: The Costs of Self-Advocacy," *Psychology of Women Quarterly* 25, no. 1 (2001): 65–76.

20 Ashley V Whillans, Jaewon Yoon, Aurora Turek, and Grant E. Donnelly, "Extension Request Avoidance Predicts Greater Time Stress Among Women," *Proceedings of the National Academy of Sciences* 118, no. 45 (2021).

21 Barbara A Carlin, Betsy D. Gelb, Jaime K. Belinne, and Latha Ramchand, "Bridging the Gender Gap in Confidence," *Business Horizons* 61, no. 5 (2018): 765–774.

22 Claire Shipman and Katty Kay, *Womenomics: Write Your Own Rules for Success: How to Stop Juggling and Struggling and Finally Start Living and Working the Way You Really Want* (New York: HarperCollins, 2009).

23 Tara S. Mohr, "Why Women Don't Apply For Jobs Unless They're 100% Qualified," *Harvard Business Review* (2014): 8.

24 Moira Forbes, "PepsiCo CEO Indra Nooyi on Why Women Can't Have It All," *Forbes*, July 7, 2014, https://www.forbes.com/sites/moiraforbes/2014/07/03/power-woman-indra-nooyi-on-why-women-cant-have-it-all/?sh=812854036bc7.

25 Michelle C. Haynes and Madeline E. Heilman, "It Had to Be You (Not Me)!: Women's Attributional Rationalization of Their Contribution to Successful Joint Work Outcomes," *Personality and Social Psychology Bulletin* 39, no. 7 (2013): 956–969.

26 Pauline R. Clance and Suzanne A. Imes, "The Impostor Phenomenon in High Achieving Women: Dynamics and Therapeutic Intervention," *Psychotherapy: Theory, Research, and Practice* 15, no. 3 (1978): 241–247.

27 Tomas Chamorro-Premuzic, "Why Do So Many Incompetent Men Become Leaders," *Harvard Business Review* (2013): 22.

28 Erensto Reuben, Pedro Rey-Biel, Paola Sapienza, and Luigi Zingales, "The Emergence of Male Leadership in Competitive Environments," *Journal of Economic Behavior & Organization* 83, no.1 (2012): 111–117.

29 Laurie L Cohen and Janet K. Swim, "The Differential Impact of Gender Ratios on Women and Men: Tokenism, Self-Confidence, and Expectations," *Personality and Social Psychology Bulletin* 21, no. 9 (1995): 876–884.

30 Katty Kay and Claire Shipman, "The Confidence Gap," *The Atlantic*, May 2014, https://www.theatlantic.com/magazine/archive/2014/05/the-confidence-gap/359815/.

31 Linda Babcock and Sara Laschever, *Women Don't Ask* (Princeton, NJ: Princeton University Press, 2009).

32 "Salary and compensation statistics on the impact of COVID-19," Randstad, accessed November 2022, https://www.randstadusa.com/business/salary-insights/?utm_campaign=rusa_Salary+Guide+2020.

33 Andreas Leibbrandt and John A. List, "Do Women Avoid Salary Negotiations? Evidence From a Large-Scale Natural Field Experiment," *Management Science* 61, no. 9 (2015): 2016–2024.

34 Christine L. Exley and Judd B. Kessler, "The Gender Gap in Self-Promotion," National Bureau of Economic Research, No. w26345 (May 2021) https://www.nber.org/papers/w26345.

35 Mary E. Wade, "Women and Salary Negotiation: The Costs of Self-Advocacy," *Psychology of Women Quarterly* 25, no. 1 (2001): 65–76.

36 Peggy Klaus, *Brag! The Art of Tooting Your Own Horn Without Blowing It* (New York: Warner Business Books, 2004).).

37 Kenneth D. Locke, "Agentic and Communal Social Motives," in *Agency and Communion in Social Psychology* (New York: Routledge, 2018), 65–78.

38 Robert J. Hogan and Brent W. Roberts, "A Socioanalytic Perspective on *Person-Environment Interaction*," in *Person-Enviroment Psychology: New Directions and Perspectives*, 2nd ed. (Mahwah, NJ: Lawrence Erlbaum Associates, 2000), 1–24.

39 Erik L. Knight and Pranjal H. Mehta, "Hormones and Hierarchies," in *The Psychology of Social Status* (New York: Springer, 2014), 269–301.

40 Ruth Feldman, Aron Weller, Orna Zagoory-Sharon, and Ari Levine, "Evidence For a Neuroendocrinological Foundation of Human Affiliation: Plasma Oxytocin Levels Across Pregnancy and the Postpartum Period Predict Mother-Infant Bonding," *Psychological Science* 18, no. 11 (2007): 965–970.

41 Jochen E. Gebauer, Jenny Wagner, Constantine Sedikides, and Wiebke Neberich, "Agency-Communion and Self-Esteem Relations Are Moderated by Culture, Religiosity, Age, and Sex: Evidence for the "Self-Centrality Breeds Self-Enhancement" Principle," *Journal of Personality* 81, no. 3 (2013): 261–275.

42 Jon K. Maner, "Dominance and Prestige: A Tale of Two Hierarchies," *Current Directions in Psychological Science* 26, no. 6 (2017): 526–531.

43 Brittany Cohen-Brown, "From Top to Bottom, Chimpanzee Social Hierarchy is Amazing!," Jane Goodall's Good For All News, July 10, 2018. https://news.janegoodall.org/2018/07/10/top-bottom-chimpanzee-social-hierarchy-amazing/.

44 "Women in the Workplace 2021." McKinsey & Company, February 28, 2022, https://www.mckinsey.com/featured-insights/diversity-and-inclusion/women-in-the-workplace.

45 Jack Zenger and Joseph Folkman, "Women Score Higher Than Men in Most Leadership Skills," *Harvard Business Review* (2019): 1–8.

46 Sheryl Sandberg, *Lean In: Women, Work, and the Will to Lead* (New York: Random House, 2013).

47 Brené Brown, *Daring Greatly: How the Courage to Be Vulnerable Transforms the Way We Live, Love, Parent, and Lead* (New York: Penguin, 2015).

48 Aimee LaPointe Terosky, KerryAnn O'Meara, and Corbin M. Campbell, "Enabling Possibility: Women Associate Professors' Sense of Agency in Career Advancement," *Journal of Diversity in Higher Education* 7, no. 1 (2014): 58.

49 Vanessa M. Patrick, "Getting to Gutsy: Using Personal Policies to Enhance (and Reclaim) Agency in The Workplace," *Rutgers Business Review* 6, no. 2 (2021).

50 Max Baron Aitken Beaverbrook, *Success* vol. 4586. (Boston: Small, Maynard and Company, 1922).

51 "Oprah talks to Maya Angelou." Oprah.com. December 15, 2000, https://www.oprah.com/omagazine/oprah-interviews-maya-angelou/.

52 Brooke Baldwin, Huddle: *How Women Unlock Their Collective Power* (New York: Harper Business, 2021).

53 Brian Uzzi, "Research: Men and Women Need Different Kinds of Networks to Succeed," *Harvard Business Review*, February 25, 2019, https://hbr.org/2019/02/research-men-and-women-need-different-kinds-of-networks-to-succeed.

INDEX

Note: Page numbers in italic refer to illustrations.

A

C

F

O

P

R

ABOUT THE AUTHOR

Dr. Vanessa Patrick is a professor of marketing and the Associate Dean for Research at the Bauer College of Business at the University of Houston. She has a PhD in Business from the University of Southern California and an MBA in marketing and a BS degree in microbiology and biochemistry from Bombay University in India. Patrick has published dozens of research articles in top-tier academic journals in psychology, marketing, and management, and popular accounts of her work have appeared in the *New York Times, Wall Street Journal*, NPR, *Los Angeles Times, Business Week, Fast Company, Forbes, Huffington Post* and *Washington Post.* In her research, she investigates strategies to achieve personal mastery and inspire everyday excellence in oneself and others and is a pioneer in the study of everyday consumer aesthetics. Patrick lives with her family in Houston, Texas.